The Joy of Christmas

Chicken Soup for the Soul: The Joy of Christmas
101 Holiday Tales of Inspiration, Love and Wonder
Amy Newmark. Foreword by Mrs. Nicholas Claus

Published by Chicken Soup for the Soul, LLC www.chickensoup.com
Copyright ©2016 by Chicken Soup for the Soul, LLC. All Rights Reserved.

The publisher gratefully acknowledges the many publishers and individuals who
granted Chicken Soup for the Soul permission to reprint the cited material.

Front cover, back cover and interior illustrations courtesy of iStockphoto.com/nokee
(©nokee)
Back cover illustration of Mrs. Nicholas Claus courtesy of iStockphoto.com/
AnjaRabenstein (©Anja Rabenstein)
Photo of Amy Newmark courtesy of Susan Morrow at SwickPix

Cover and Interior by Daniel Zaccari

Distributed to the booktrade by Simon & Schuster. SAN: 200-2442

Publisher's Cataloging-In-Publication Data
(Prepared by The Donohue Group, Inc.)

Names: Newmark, Amy, compiler. | Claus, Nicholas, Mrs., writer of
   supplementary textual content.
Title: Chicken soup for the soul : the joy of Christmas : 101 holiday
   tales of inspiration, love and wonder / [compiled by] Amy Newmark ;
   foreword by Mrs. Nicholas Claus.
Other Titles: Joy of Christmas : 101 holiday tales of inspiration, love
   and wonder
Description: [Cos Cob, Connecticut] : Chicken Soup for the Soul, LLC
   [2016]
Identifiers: LCCN 2016949005 | ISBN 978-1-61159-963-3 (print) | ISBN 978-
   1-61159-262-7 (ebook)
Subjects: LCSH: Christmas--Literary collections. | Christmas--Anecdotes. |
   Hanukkah--Literary collections. | Hanukkah--Anecdotes. LCGFT: Anecdotes.
Classification: LCC GT4985 .C45 2016 | LCC GT4985 (ebook) | DDC
   394.2663/02--dc23

PRINTED IN THE UNITED STATES OF AMERICA
on acid∞free paper

25 24 23 22 21 20 19 18 17 16   01 02 03 04 05 06 07 08 09 10 11

The Joy of Christmas

101 Holiday Tales of Inspiration, Love, and Wonder

Amy Newmark

Foreword by Mrs. Nicholas Claus

Chicken Soup for the Soul, LLC
Cos Cob, CT

Changing the world one story at a time®
www.chickensoup.com

Table of Contents

❸
~Holiday Miracles~

❹
~Family Fun~

❺
~Holiday Memories~

❻
~Through the Eyes of a Child~

❼
~Holiday Decorating~

❽
~Taking Care of Each Other~

❾
~Holiday Traditions~

Foreword

I just had the loveliest week reading all these wonderful stories about the joy of Christmas. There's nothing like putting your feet up in July and pretending that December 24th is not just around the corner.

Because it is! Nick and I work hard all year, but things get crazy come Labor Day. That's when the elves are returning from their vacations, the reindeer are getting back to their flying practice, and the toy factory adds a second shift.

I don't know why, but there seem to be more *good* boys and girls every year, and while I know that's great for all of you parents and grandparents and aunts and uncles below the Arctic Circle, that's even more work for us.

But I'm not complaining. Nick and I love doing this and we wouldn't trade it for anything, not even that Florida vacation that someone keeps calling to tell us that we've won.

The stories in this book were such a treat for me, because I got to see what happens the rest of the Christmas season too, not just what Nick tells me about when he gets home Christmas morning. I loved reading about how you all get into the Christmas spirit, the acts of kindness you perform for strangers, the funny things your kids say, how you decorate your houses, and your family traditions.

Nick and I have our own traditions, too. On Christmas Eve, I make him a big pot of pasta with a tomato and veggie sauce (always watching his cholesterol for him), iron his lucky red boxers, and make sure that his cell phone is charged and is set for Roaming.

I make a special salad for the reindeer too — carrots and spinach and kale. Yes, kale has made it up to the North Pole. The reindeer, especially the younger ones, like it a lot better than Nick, but I sneak it into his veggie pasta sauce too.

Once Nick takes off — and he'll be gone almost twenty-four hours because of all the time zones around the world — I get busy preparing for Christmas morning. When Nick and the reindeer get back they expect a big breakfast and they want me to make a fuss over them. But then, Nick goes off to lie down, while I still have plenty of work to do.

He's off napping and getting all the glory, but I've still got elves to feed, reindeer stables to maintain, and then there are those Elf on the Shelf temps. They all come drifting back from their assignments, and they expect a big welcome and a place to stay and food and clean laundry, when all they really did was sit around and watch children behave all December.

I'm just saying.

So thank you, Chicken Soup for the Soul, for this relaxing interlude reading these stories. I really appreciated the break. And I hope that your readers will put their feet up, too, during their own busy holiday season, and spend a few minutes every day reading these entertaining and inspirational stories.

And look, I know that Nick has written his own forewords for Chicken Soup for the Soul and he has talked about the cookies. I don't give him cookies at home because I know how many he will eat on Christmas Eve. Can you leave him the cookies but try to make them a little *less bad* for him? Less sugar and less butter? You're not the one who has to live with a grouchy guy on a diet all January!

In closing, I want to wish you a very happy holiday season, whether you're celebrating Christmas or Hanukkah or just plain enjoying time with your families.

~Mrs. Nicholas Claus

August 3, 2016

CHAPTER 1

The Joy of Christmas

The True Spirit of Christmas

Christmas is not a time nor a season, but a state of mind.
To cherish peace and goodwill, to be plenteous in mercy,
is to have the real spirit of Christmas.
~Calvin Coolidge

The Angels' Angel

Be an angel to someone else whenever you can,
as a way of thanking God for the help your
angel has given you.
~Eileen Elias Freeman,
The Angels' Little Instruction Book

Walmart's automatic doors whooshed open, and my two sons and I hurried in from the cold as a light snow began to fall. I was glad our youth leader, Regina, had obtained permission to set up inside for the angel tree service project. Brian and Jeremy looked forward to helping solicit presents for underprivileged kids, but I doubted their zeal would have lasted long in the biting wind.

I hurried the boys along, wondering how eight-year-old Jeremy would hold up. In addition to a foot problem that caused pain if he stood or walked very much, he had attention deficit disorder. Keeping his mind on one thing for very long was difficult.

Even though it was only 9:00 a.m., Christmas shoppers packed the aisles. Carols played overhead as we scanned the brightly lit store for our fellow volunteers. We finally spotted a group of children of various ages near the jewelry counter. They stood next to an artificial tree covered with pink and blue paper angels.

"What a great spot," I said as we joined them. "So close to the front and right by the cash registers."

Regina gave me a rueful smile. "Yes, except that by the time customers come this way, they're finished shopping and are ready to check out. No one wants to go back and buy another gift, even though it's for a good cause."

I studied the angels more closely. Each one was imprinted with the first name and age of a child whose gift purchased that day might well be the only one he or she received. More than a hundred of these angels decorated the tree. The boys and I planned to buy gifts for two children, but we couldn't provide for them all.

After a few unsuccessful attempts at getting donations, Regina divided the kids into two groups. "Let's cover both entrances and catch customers as they come in. Try to steer them over here before they start their shopping. I'll stay by the tree."

Jeremy jammed a red Santa hat on his head. "Come on, Mom. Let's go!"

Catching his enthusiasm, Brian and I followed with another mom and her son. Our excitement soon waned as shoppers passed by with a brusque "No, thank you," sometimes not even looking at us.

Jeremy took a different tactic. When shoppers came in, he fell in step beside their carts and began explaining about the angel tree. "Their moms and dads don't have enough money for presents. If we don't help, they won't get anything for Christmas. All you have to do is go pick an angel off the tree and buy a toy. Just ten or fifteen dollars. If that's too much, you can give us some money, and we'll collect more until we have enough to buy a present."

My young son hardly drew breath between sentences. His words were sincere and heartfelt. His round, cherubic cheeks and beatific smile sealed the deal. Time after time, customers thrust money at him. Some were probably afraid if they didn't, they'd be stuck with this child for the rest of their shopping trip. But many smiled and altered their course to come by the tree and choose an angel themselves. One shopper pointed out Jeremy and told Regina, "How could anyone resist that angelic face?"

When Jeremy's pockets became stuffed with money, he would triumphantly run back to me and ask if we could go and shop. We'd grab a couple of paper angels and hunt for just the right gifts. After we checked out, we took the gifts to other volunteers in customer service who wrapped them with bright Christmas paper. Then we headed back to the entrance, Jeremy's cheeks flushed with excitement at doing it all over again.

Even though he was getting tired, Jeremy stuck to his mission without complaint. For three long hours, he beseeched people, collected money, and bought presents, repeating the cycle until all the angels were adopted. Many of the real-life children represented by pink and blue bits of paper on an artificial tree received gifts that Christmas through his efforts.

Jeremy beamed with pride when Regina praised him for working so hard for needy children in our county. But on the way home, all he could talk about was how glad he felt that no one was left out. All the kids would get presents.

My son was the angels' angel that day. He ignored his own pain and disability to help those less fortunate, but he didn't look at it that way. From his point of view, he received the greatest gift — a full heart from bringing joy to others.

~Tracy Crump

Someone Cared

*Christmas is doing a little something
extra for someone.*
~Charles Schulz

I was a "miracle baby," an only child, so my parents tended to spoil me, especially at Christmastime. They wanted to make certain my Christmases were special and memorable. And each one truly was. I still have vivid memories of my parents' proud smiles on Christmas morning as I opened one gift after another and squealed with delight.

As the years passed and I grew older, Christmas remained a much-anticipated event. My mother loved to shop, cook and decorate. She also was determined to make opening gifts on Christmas morning a bit of a marathon. She, my dad and I would take turns unwrapping one gift at a time, which usually took hours because my mother wrapped every little item separately. A desk set that came with a pen, box of paper clips, a stapler, etc., would become eight gifts rather than just one. That way, we could prolong and savor the unwrapping for as long as possible.

They say that opposites attract, and when I met my future husband, Joe, it proved to be true. I was sociable and outgoing. He was quiet and shy. I had a close, loving family. His relationship with his family was strained.

Joe and I began dating one January and after a whirlwind courtship, were married that October. As our first Christmas together approached, I looked forward to it with the same childlike anticipation I'd always felt. But when I rambled on excitedly about the gifts I was going to buy, the decorations I was going to hang and the foods I was going to cook, I noticed my husband wasn't sharing my enthusiasm. I finally asked him why he seemed so apathetic about the happiest time of the year.

"Because it never was happy for me," he said. As he spoke, I was surprised to see tears filling his eyes. "My dad had a problem with... well, keeping money. He and my mother argued about it all the time. We moved a lot, from one apartment building to another, always one step ahead of the bill collectors. Once, when I was about eight, I saved up some money by cashing in the five-cent deposit on pop bottles I found in the alley near our apartment building. Then I walked over to Woolworth and bought a small set of plastic toy soldiers. I wrapped them in notebook paper as a Christmas gift to myself. I cherished those soldiers and kept them until I grew up and actually became a soldier."

When I later related Joe's story to my mother, she couldn't hold back her tears.

"That's just terrible!" she said, sniffling and reaching for a tissue. "We're just going to have to make it our mission to give him the best Christmas ever — one that will make up for all of those he missed as a child!"

And we did exactly that. We splurged and bought him every gift he possibly could want. My mother planned a Christmas menu that contained all of his favorite foods. We even visited a Christmas tree farm, where we chopped down our own tree. We were determined to give Joe a Christmas spirit overload.

On Christmas Eve, Joe and I stayed at my parents' house so we could get up bright and early for the annual gift-opening marathon. Never had I seen so many gifts piled under the tree... and the majority of them were for Joe. I could barely wait to see how thrilled he was going to be with everything we'd selected for him.

As we sat and opened our gifts, my parents and I couldn't help but notice that Joe didn't seem as pleased or excited as we'd anticipated. In fact, when he opened an expensive toolset that he'd really been wanting, he actually looked uncomfortable.

Hours later, after all the gifts had been opened, and stacks of boxes and packages lay at our feet, my mother dared to ask Joe, "Didn't you like the things we bought for you?"

"Oh, they're all great," he said, "but a little overwhelming."

"We wanted to make your Christmas special," my mother explained. "We wanted to make up for all of the Christmases you missed as a child, and for all of the gifts you never received."

My husband looked directly into my mother's eyes and said, "But I didn't need all of these gifts to make my Christmas special. All I ever needed was to know that someone actually cared enough about me to remember me. That's the best gift of all."

So on that Christmas morning, back in 1971, we realized that Christmas gift-opening marathons weren't what made Christmas special or memorable — being with people who truly loved you was.

Joe passed away a week before Christmas in 2012.

I still put one special gift for him under the tree that year... a small set of plastic toy soldiers.

~Sally A. Breslin

Operation Christmas Thank You

There are no strangers on Christmas Eve.
~Adele Comandini and Edward Sutherland,
Beyond Tomorrow

It was October and we were attending the fire hall's open house with our five-year-old son Isaiah and three-year-old daughter Angeleaha. Isaiah stood in awe of the massive yellow trucks, with all of their shiny chrome and interesting gadgets. The firefighters were more than happy to answer his many questions about each piece of equipment. He fidgeted with his plastic firefighter's hat as he studied the collection of scale models in the large glass display case in the office. "When do you get to play with those?" he asked the accompanying firefighter.

The firefighter hid his amusement as he answered very solemnly. "We don't get to play with them. The chief keeps them locked away in that cabinet."

Isaiah was lost in thought as we walked home that evening.

Halloween came and went, as did Remembrance Day. With colder weather setting in, our thoughts turned to Christmas. It was important to us to keep the true spirit of Christmas at the forefront of our holiday activities. The last thing we wanted was our children seeing Christmas as a commercial event.

We sat the two children down and explained that there were many children that didn't have the same things they did. Some children didn't have a mommy or daddy, enough food to eat, or new toys to play with at Christmas. We explained that Santa Claus sometimes needed a bit of help from Christmas Ambassadors to provide gifts or food for those in need.

Both children listened very intently. Isaiah's eyes shone! "Can we take presents to the firefighters? Santa doesn't visit the fire station and they aren't allowed to play with all those fire trucks! We can take them

toys to play with on Christmas!"

At first we didn't know how to respond. We had long since forgotten about the model fire trucks in the display case at the fire hall! Apparently Isaiah had not. His dad cleared his throat. "Well, that is a good idea, but they don't really have time to play with toys because they are too busy keeping us safe from fires at Christmas."

Isaiah became very serious; he knew his dad was right. Being a firefighter was a very important job. Angeleaha had been sitting quietly playing with some blocks. "Candy… they want candy," she said quietly.

I looked at my husband. "Not quite what we had in mind," I said.

"It's not a bad idea though," he replied.

That first year we set out on Christmas Eve, led on foot by our two children to the fire hall, police station and paramedic stations to deliver boxes of chocolates. The kids were given a warm welcome at each stop and a tour of the units and their trucks.

As the children grew, the operation matured. We added coffee, lunch, dessert trays, and candies. We began deliveries to the Ontario

Provincial Police and the hospital emergency room, too — six emergency response locations in total. We began taking photographs and posting to a Facebook page in hopes that others would start the campaign in their own cities.

We have five children now, and the fourth was born with a serious medical problem. For the first time we fully understood and appreciated the role of emergency services in a very personal way. During one medical emergency, which occurred during a blizzard, we had to call an ambulance to take Nathaniel to the hospital as he screamed in pain. The roads were too dangerous to navigate, but the paramedics still came, and they got us to the hospital safely.

Then on December 18th, 2014, while crossing the street, a car hit my husband and me. The car had slammed into me first, sending me scraping across the pavement several feet before coming to a stop. My husband had been picked up and thrown onto the hood by impact. A fire truck was first on scene, and I was helped onto the truck step, shaking and crying. Firefighters kept me talking, making sure I was coherent until paramedics arrived on scene.

I was helped onto a stretcher and rolled into the ambulance, where one soft-spoken paramedic assessed my vitals and provided me with ice packs for my bruises. The other paramedic climbed in the driver's seat and called back, "These are the parents of the kids who bring us goodies on Christmas Eve!"

I was shocked. I'm not sure why, but I didn't think we were recognizable, and I really didn't view what our children were doing as anything out of the ordinary. We were saying thank you, showing our appreciation.

Our first little Christmas elves, Isaiah and Angeleaha, are now teenagers. They raise money each year to pay for the treats that they and their siblings deliver to all our first responders.

This year will be our twelfth Operation Christmas Thank You. It's the highlight of our family's Christmas.

~Danielle Kuhn

The Best Luxury of All

Blessed is the season which engages the
whole world in a conspiracy of love!
~Hamilton Wright Mabie

My friend Nell was feeling guilty one year during the holiday season. She was throwing away the solicitations for donations that arrived in the mail from various good causes because she was saving her money to spend on gifts.

Then she remembered a piece of advice she had read somewhere: "If you want to give away money, go to the bank, take out as much cash as you can afford, and distribute it to people on the street."

This appealed to Nell. Nearly every day, she saw homeless people and others in need. But she never paid much attention as she whizzed by in her car, and she even crossed the street to avoid the scary-looking ones when she was walking.

Nell thought about her "Fiver Envelope." Whenever she received a five-dollar bill as change in a transaction, she saved it. After gathering a bunch, she would treat herself to a massage or some other luxury. She decided to take the one hundred dollars she'd accumulated and give it away.

Nell found her first beneficiary one early cold morning at the post office. A dented maroon car, the back bumper tied on with a rope and stuffed with clothing, pulled into a parking space. A weary woman struggled to get out of the vehicle and up the post office steps.

Nell pulled a five from her wallet and folded it in half. When the woman entered the building, Nell asked, "May I give you something?"

The woman looked wary as Nell held out the money. "Why?"

"Because it's Christmas."

The woman took the money. "That's it? For no other reason?"

Nell said, "Yes," and wished her a Merry Christmas.

"Thank you so much."

Nell felt very happy.

Next was a young wispy woman wrapped in layers of clothing to stave off the cold rain. She was walking with a black Pit Bull that wore a padded doggie jacket. Nell pulled to the curb and got out of her car. "May I give you something?"

Again a wary look.

Nell held out a five.

The woman grinned, and then looked close to tears. "I'm so glad I turned around and started walking this way. Otherwise, I wouldn't have met you." She gave Nell a hug.

A few days later, Nell was walking to her car in the grocery store parking lot. She noticed a woman putting her baby in a car seat in a dented pickup truck.

As Nell held out her offering, the woman backed away. "I shouldn't take it."

Nell reached her hand out further. "Please, I want to give it to you."

"Thank you. I really do need gas money." She invited Nell to the live nativity scene produced by one of the local churches on Christmas Eve. She said her baby would be playing the role of Jesus. She blessed Nell as she walked away.

A few days later, Nell saw a middle-aged woman fishing through a public trashcan. When she gave her five dollars, the woman beamed. "Thank you. It's my birthday."

Nell's heart soared. "Happy birthday, my dear!"

Every time Nell gave away money, she felt immense joy. Most of the interactions took less than a minute, but during that time she was able to look a person in the eyes, touch his or her hand and, in a few instances, receive a hug. This was so much better than using all those saved five-dollar bills for a massage.

She gave away her last five to someone she saw frequently — a tall, lean man who appeared to be homeless. He wore a camouflage jacket and walked a dog with a matching brindle coat.

It was shortly after the New Year and raining when Nell spotted him. He was walking so fast that she pulled a block ahead so that she could intercept him.

She wasn't sure how he would react because he seemed so self-contained, as if he preferred to be alone.

"Hi," she said.

He returned the greeting with a surprising twinkle in his eyes.

"May I give you something?" She held out the folded bill.

"Are you serious?" he asked.

"Yes, please, I want to give it to you."

He grinned. "Thank you."

She had never been close to him. She looked at his face — really looked at it — and saw a kind man in his forties with warm, dark brown eyes. She reached down and petted his dog, grateful that he had a companion. Why he was alone was a mystery, but she was glad to make a connection with this nice man.

"Happy New Year." As the words left her mouth, she regretted them. They sounded hollow and trite given his situation.

"Happy New Year to you," he said, leaving her with the gift of his smile.

~Kate Erickson

Gratitude Gave Grief a Holiday

Only by giving are you able to receive more than you already have.

~Jim Rohn

S teve passed away in September, and I wondered how I would survive the holidays without him. The Christmas décor that showed up in the stores after Halloween was a harsh reminder that Christmas would be very different this year.

Steve and I had always practiced year-round philanthropy, and even more so around the holidays. Donating to charity, "adopting" those in need, and participating in various fundraisers was a longtime family tradition, but that year, I didn't feel like celebrating, much less shopping. I was lost without my soul mate and repeatedly asked our two adult sons, "What are we going to do?"

Soon the charitable solicitations began to arrive and I dreaded what would follow — the announcements of the fundraisers in which we had always taken part. Writing a check would be easy, but contributing anything that required my involvement seemed impossible.

Friends and family offered their support and kindness as the holidays approached, and I was able to focus a little more on my own blessings. We had always been the givers, not the receivers, at Christmastime.

And then I finally realized something. The best way I could get through the holidays was to continue Steve's legacy and do what he would have done if he were still here.

The first thing I did was continue our tradition of "adopting" someone from our local senior services organization. It only took a brief call to get the wish list of a local senior citizen who had no family or financial resources. Shopping anonymously for someone I didn't know brought a bit of joy back into my life. It was fun to anticipate how surprised my adoptee would be when she received all the items on her wish list instead of just one. I felt a little like my old self — I was shopping again and enjoying it!

The second opportunity to participate in helping others was more  difficult. For years, Steve and I had made gingerbread creations for the Big Brothers/Big Sisters annual fundraiser. This was an important tradition to us, and as soon as we entered the competition each year we would lay out the plans for the next year. Steve had decided that we would make Noah's Ark this year. My eyes moistened as I held the invitation to the fundraiser, thinking that the Ark would never be made now.

I was about to toss the invitation in the trash, but then I changed my mind. Our older son liked to make his own gingerbread creations for the event, so I saved it for him.

Later, when I handed Chris the invitation, he immediately said, "Mom, we need to do Dad's idea for the whimsical Noah's Ark." And thus began our collaboration. It was so much fun creating the animal characters Steve had envisioned. I laughed at Chris's suggestion to "put the skunks at the very back of the ark away from all the rest." It was just what Steve would have done!

In the end, I was so grateful to my son for insisting that we make Steve's Ark a reality, especially when it won third place and sold for the highest bid of the night to help the organization. And, we were also both surprised and humbled when the gingerbread festival that year was dedicated to Steve.

There was then another unexpected, wonderful and generous surprise for us. Steve's company created an annual "Steve Julian Award" for employees who demonstrated his same outstanding service to their clients and coworkers. My family was invited to the annual luncheon at which this coveted award is now presented each year. How grateful we were that others wanted to honor Steve's memory too!

I learned much that year, especially that generosity is always reciprocated, whether by another person's kindness or by the simple feeling it creates for the giver. But my most important lesson was that being grateful for one's blessings, and sharing them with others is sometimes the best way to regain a little happiness.

~Vicki L. Julian

The First Gifts of Christmas

How beautiful a day can be when kindness touches it!
~George Elliston

For the last two months, Duke Medical Center in Chapel Hill, North Carolina had been our home while my husband Randy received treatment for an inoperable brain tumor. In early December Randy underwent his final radiation treatment and we received clearance from his doctors to return home to Kentucky. I knew this would be our last Christmas together.

There wasn't much joy or Christmas spirit in my heart as our long journey ended and we entered our neighborhood that cold and snowy December night. But then I glimpsed a bit of yellow ribbon tied to a tree, fluttering in the wind, and then I saw another yellow ribbon tied to a tree in the next yard, and then another and another... an avenue of yellow ribbons welcomed us as we slowly drove down our street.

As we pulled into our driveway we saw a "Welcome Home" sign adorning the garage door. Fresh pine garland and ribbon trimmed the mailbox and the outdoor lights. Christmas candles glowed warmly in every window of our home.

Dazed, we opened the front door, stepped inside and found Christmas waiting for us. The tree, beautifully lit, stood in its place by the window. The ornaments, waiting to be hung, filled a basket under its limbs. Ribbon and pine graced the mantel and all of our Christmas decorations were lovingly and perfectly placed throughout our home. As Randy and I walked, virtually speechless from room to room, we discovered small Christmas gifts, bearing our names, tucked here and there throughout the house and the refrigerator and freezer filled with casseroles and fruit.

Rather than coming home and frantically pulling the Christmas boxes and bins out of the attic and simultaneously unpacking our suitcases, Randy and I spent our first morning at home leisurely watching it snow, drinking hot cocoa and hanging ornaments on our tree. We wrapped Christmas gifts, made soup, and sat by the fire holding hands reminiscing about Christmases long ago. The selfless love of our friends who gathered together and readied our home for our return served as a loving reminder of the true spirit of Christmas. These friends gave the best of themselves — their most precious gifts of time and talent and love — and there are no sweeter gifts than those.

~Shannon Erickson

Table for Eight

Friends are family you choose for yourself.
~Author Unknown

What do you do on Christmas when your family is far away? My husband and I didn't have any family nearby, so the holidays always made me feel a little lonely.

Then one year, I had a thought: "Let's throw a party!" We had friends who weren't going to see their families either. So why not fix a meal and create a new tradition? I could already picture the meal. A traditional menu of turkey filled with cornbread stuffing, mashed potatoes, green bean casserole and all the fixings. Just like my aunt used to make. It probably wouldn't be as delicious as my aunt's cooking, but I sure could give it a try.

My husband loved the idea. We got excited. We made a list: turkey, potatoes, yams, pumpkin pie, and appetizers, too. Nothing was too good for our adopted holiday family. It would be a night of good food, old and new friends, and most important... new traditions.

Hesitantly, we invited friends. We knew the holidays brought out mixed emotions in people. Our list grew larger. Two, three — eventually we had a party of eight people. We wondered if we'd be able to fit everyone in our tiny dining room. Did we even have enough plates? In our enthusiasm we hadn't thought of that.

"Who cares?" my husband proclaimed. "That'll be part of the memory."

Christmas quickly arrived. We got busy cooking, decorating and before long we were no longer *pretending* to be happy about the holidays. We actually *were* happy. In our excitement we had prepared a virtual feast compared to our normal dinner of Top Ramen or tuna melts. The smell of turkey wafted from the oven as we nibbled on deviled eggs and waited for our guests to arrive. "Let's hope they all come hungry. Actually let's hope they come at all!" It was already ten minutes after their scheduled arrival time and no one had shown up.

As the first guest arrived, we let out a huge sigh of relief. She wasn't even expected, as she had planned to fly home. "Is it still okay if I come? I thought I'd be at my parents." We welcomed her in.

Soon our cramped apartment became cozy with people. Friends introduced themselves to each other, former strangers united for a day. Laughter and love filled our home. Thankfully everyone showed up. The only one dissatisfied with the arrangement was our cat. A noted loner, he made a beeline to his favorite spot in the bedroom and wanted no part of anything. Even a smidgeon of turkey didn't lure him out. We joked that we needed a Scrooge for Christmas and this year it was him. We'd make sure to give him extra attention once everyone went home. And catnip! After all, it *was* Christmas and he deserved a treat too.

After a prayer was said and plates were filled, we went around the table. Sharing our favorite Christmas memories and something we felt was a blessing in our lives. A Christmas that I had been dreading had become a day to bond, break bread and share experiences.

Throughout the years, my Christmas guest list has changed, but the one thing that hasn't changed is the magic of Christmas. I'm glad I listened to that unexpected voice and that I reached out to friends that December. I'm even more thankful that they responded and took the time to share the day with us. It was a Christmas blessing indeed.

~Joanna Dylan

Mom's Secret Mission

When I was young, I admired clever people.
Now that I am old, I admire kind people.
~Abraham Joshua Heschel

My mother grabbed her car keys and said, "Be back in a few hours."

"Where are you going?" I asked, puzzled that she'd be leaving on the busiest day of the year—Christmas Eve.

"There's an errand or two that I forgot to do. Be back soon," she said as she scurried out the back door.

Since we had company coming for Christmas dinner the next day, there were still things to do. I asked my dad if Mom had left us a to-do list, and he said no. We both knew that something was up.

"Maybe she forgot to get someone a gift," he said.

"You know how she despises going out on Christmas Eve," I reminded him. Mom never failed to start her shopping in August and was finished with her list by Thanksgiving.

Her temporary absence was indeed a mystery.

She was back at the house a few hours later, just as she had promised, and I asked if she got her errands done.

"Yes," was all that she would say, and I didn't feel like pressing. Maybe she had gone out to get that telescope that I wanted.

The next year, my mother disappeared again during the day on Christmas Eve. She continued to do so every year for the rest of her life. We didn't question it anymore.

The year she passed away I got a sweet letter from a man named Robert, who wanted me to know what my mother had done for him and his family for the last seven years.

Dear Johnny,

I just wanted you to know how much my family and I appreciate what your mother has done for us for all these years. Every year on Christmas Eve day your mom comes to my house dressed like Mrs. Claus and gives my kids a Christmas that we can't afford to give them. She has given them shoes, shirts, jeans, toys, and candy. I know your heart is heavy and that you are missing Miss Sue. We do, too. We loved her and just wanted you to know what she has done for us.

Love,
Robert and Nellie and the kids

That short note was the best gift that I ever received from anyone, better even than that silly old telescope.

~John Dorroh

The Year Elmo Saved Our Christmas

In about the same degree as you are
helpful, you will be happy.
~Karl Reiland

Bridget was a shining light in our lives and it was a shock when she died at age six a few days before Christmas in 1993. She was born with spina bifida and despite her grim prognosis, she was a courageous, funny and loving little girl. She taught everyone who met her that life can be happy no matter what kinds of challenges it hands you.

Every year after that I faced the holidays with some dread. But I didn't want to disappoint my other children despite the emptiness in my heart. So I started shopping nice and early, and one August day in 1996 I came across an adorable Elmo doll that laughed when it was tickled. Tickle Me Elmo hadn't become the phenomenon yet that it would turn out to be — that Christmas's "must-have" gift. There were plenty of them in the store. So I bought it, paying about $20. I wasn't even sure which kid it was for.

Months later, I was watching the news with my teenage son Matt when a story came on about Tickle Me Elmo and the lengths people were going to get one. I commented to my son, "I have one of those." He was quite surprised and excited, explaining he could get $500 or more for it on the street. I said, "No, it's Christmas… that's not right." He thought I was crazy, and then we both forgot all about it.

On the morning of December 21st, the third anniversary of Bridget's death, I wasn't sure how I was going to get through the day. I knew I would replay the horrible night in my mind: her struggle to breathe, the ambulance, the hospital and telling her brothers and sisters she was gone. The other children were the only reason I got out of bed that day.

As I sat drinking my coffee, my son Matt came home from the repair shop where he had taken a TV to be fixed. He said, "Hey, Mom, do you still have that Tickle Me Elmo doll?"

He explained that the woman who owned the repair shop was asking everyone if they knew where she could get one. It was the only thing her four-year-old granddaughter wanted for Christmas and she was certain that Santa would bring her one. The woman had been trying everything to find one for Santa to deliver — from checking newspaper ads to entering raffles — with no success.

I turned to Matt and said, "Let's go for a ride."

I walked into the repair shop with Elmo in my arms and tears in my eyes. When the woman saw me, she jumped up and down, crying, and saying. "How much do I owe you? What do you want for it? Thank you so much!"

I told her I didn't want anything but to make a little girl happy. I explained about Bridget and what joy it gave me to make a Christmas dream come true for another little girl. Although the rest of the day was a struggle, I kept thinking about the joy on that grandmother's face. Santa was going to come through for her granddaughter, and it was a joy for me to be the reason that happened.

~Maggie Whelan

Chicken Soup for the Soul

Make a Difference

*It's easy to make a buck. It's a lot
tougher to make a difference.*

~Tom Brokaw

W e were eating dinner in a restaurant shortly before Christmas. It was packed but we had finally been seated in a booth by the bar. I was watching a man with a backpack who was sitting on a bar stool and sipping a glass of water.

It was cold and raining outside and this man's clothes did not look right for the weather. I kept watching to see if he would order any food, but he just kept sipping that free glass of water.

When the waitress brought our food I couldn't eat. It didn't seem fair that I was going to have a hot meal and this man was only going to have a glass of water. I walked up to the bar and spoke to him. He confessed that he didn't have the money to buy anything to eat. He had just come in to warm up and get out of the rain for a while. In fact, he hadn't had anything to eat that day.

I called the bartender over and arranged for the man to order a complete dinner. He was reluctant to ask for what he really wanted, but I got him to order a steak and a brownie with ice cream for dessert. When I saw him glance at the beers, I ordered him a beer, too.

The gentleman's eyes got misty, which almost made me cry. He asked if he could come by and rake our yard or do something to pay me back, but I told him to help someone else when he could. Then we would be even. He gave me a hug and I left him to his dinner.

I am in no way rich, but that day I felt like I was the richest person on earth. I've never forgotten that feeling and I've made it a habit to continue doing whatever little things I can for other people.

~Donna Faulkner Schulte

The Joy of Christmas

The Perfect Gift

*It isn't the size of the gift that matters, but
the size of the heart that gives it.*
~Eileen Elias Freeman,
The Angels' Little Instruction Book

The Scheme

Sometimes the smallest things take
the most room in your heart.
~Winnie the Pooh

"Look what I found!" I exclaimed as I held up a stuffed animal for my sister, Jenny, to see.

She smiled and showed me what was cradled in her hands. It was the exact same Winnie the Pooh that I was clutching. While we were exploring the local Disney Store, we had both selected the same Christmas-themed Winnie the Pooh.

"This is what I want for Christmas," I declared.

Jenny looked at me. "But that's what *I* want for Christmas."

My eyes narrowed, and my smile disappeared. I hated anything that made us seem like twins. I refused to be seen wearing the same colors, sporting the same jewelry, or playing with the same toys. This was a problem.

I thought about it for a minute. "We could both put it on our Christmas lists and see who gets it." We both realized this was not the solution. If our parents knew we wanted the same thing, neither of us would get it. Asking Santa seemed to be a long shot because you couldn't be sure what he would leave under the tree.

"There might be another way," Jenny suggested.

"What?"

"I get it for you, and you get it for me."

I thought about it. This would mean not telling our parents that we knew what the other sister was purchasing for our Christmas gift. I was a stickler for the rules, and I wasn't sure I was ready for such a big scheme. "What if they find out?"

"I won't tell if you won't."

This was it. I had to choose. The bond between a little girl and a stuffed animal is passionate and unbreakable, and I could not be parted from my beloved Winnie the Pooh. His red felt nightshirt and nightcap were too adorable, the green stocking he held was too soft, and the cup of milk in his other paw was too amazingly lifelike. I was enchanted.

"Let's do it."

We returned the bears to their display and left the mall with our mother. Our letters to Santa would contain nothing about the bear. We wouldn't mention our desire to our parents either. Then, on the day we were taken out separately to purchase a Christmas gift for the other sister, we would head to the Disney Store. After wandering around for a bit to make it seem as if we were really considering everything, we would pick out the Winnie the Pooh and declare it was the perfect gift.

After both shopping trips were completed, my parents discussed our purchases. "Did you know that Jenny bought the same thing for Kristine?" Mom asked after Dad told her what I had chosen for Jenny.

"Really? They bought the same thing?" Dad was surprised.

"Yeah. Jenny said it was exactly what Kristine would want."

"Guess they'll be in for a surprise on Christmas morning!"

Little did they know what we had been plotting.

"Did you get it?" Jenny asked me when we were alone.

"Yeah. You?"

"Yup, just like we planned."

"Wow." I could not believe that we had pulled off the first part of the plan.

"Now all we have to do is wait."

I shook my head. "I don't want to wait. Christmas is so far away. I wish we could at least open them on Christmas Eve." We had always envied the families that opened gifts after church that night instead of waiting until Christmas morning.

"They might let us." Jenny seemed hopeful.

"Maybe."

"Let's both ask."

Our parents relented and said we could choose one gift to open after we returned from church that night. We had done it. We had successfully kept the secret without looking guilty or suspicious, and we would finally be reunited with our bears.

Of course, Jenny and I knew exactly which gift to choose when the time came. Tearing off the paper, we were delighted to behold the gift we wanted most.

Our parents could not hold back their laughter as they waited for us to realize what had happened.

Cuddling my new bear I said, "Thank you, Jenny."

"Thank you, Kristine," Jenny replied.

However, this is when everything fell apart. We were too happy and proud of our scheme to be appropriately shocked that we held the same bear.

"Did you know that you bought each other the same thing?" our dad wanted to know.

Jenny and I looked at each other and giggled. "Yes." We admitted we had planned the entire thing for months.

Our mother was still suspicious about all the other presents that were under the tree. We often helped our parents wrap gifts and could easily have one more trick up our sleeves. "Did you tell each other everything that you got?"

"No!" Jenny responded.

"We didn't," I promised.

"Yeah, okay." Our mother didn't quite believe us.

Though the other presents we opened that year were wonderful, nothing was quite as magnificent as our Christmas Winnie the Poohs.

Of course, our big plan was not devious enough to get us into any trouble, though it did take several years before our parents would trust us to know what the other sister would receive without telling her. Gifts were hidden in our house and remained secret until the moment they were opened. To this day, my mother is still nervous about telling me what she's bought for my sister even though we've never done anything like that since.

My sister and I are adults now, and we still have those bears. We've always treasured the memory of that Christmas and have told the story many times. To me those bears represent more than a childhood prank; they represent my unbreakable bond with my sister.

~Kristine Eckart

Christmas Time

Gifts of time and love are surely the basic ingredients
of a truly merry Christmas.
~Peg Bracken

I remember looking forward to Christmas with great joy when I was a child — the presents, decorations, special foods, the story of Jesus's birth, Christmas carols. In my early adulthood I remember Christmas as a fun time spent with my parents and brothers. And when I got married at twenty-six, my husband, Owen, and I set about making Christmas a great holiday for the two of us. Even though there were challenges adjusting to the expectations of each other's families, we enjoyed the season.

Then, after seven years of marriage, our daughter Rosemary was born, and with her came the fun of Christmastime with a new baby. Three years later, Ryan joined our family and Christmas was even more fun. Together we picked out and decorated our Christmas tree. We hung stockings by the chimney, we read Christmas stories and spent Christmas Eve at my parents' house with my family.

Then, something changed. Maybe it was because I felt that I was the person in charge of making Christmas happy for everyone else. Maybe I started dreading the season because of a relative we felt obligated to invite at Christmastime who brought with him criticism, arguments and bad cheer. Maybe it was because gift giving with some family members felt meaningless, especially since we mailed presents all across the country to relatives who seldom spoke to each other during the year. Maybe the culmination of many long Minnesota winters was weighing me down. Whatever the case, instead of being a season of happiness and joy, Christmas loomed ahead of me not as a wonderful holiday but as an event that threatened to overwhelm me.

When Owen and the kids asked me what I wanted for Christmas eleven years ago, I had reached my tipping point. "I don't want things," I said in despair. "What I want is to get things done."

I could see the looks of confusion on my kids' faces. At ages five and two, I'm sure they could tell that I was sad but likely didn't understand why. I wish I could have simply given them a list of things to buy me, but what I wanted didn't come from a store. What I wanted was help getting things checked off my never-ending to-do list.

On Christmas morning, Owen handed me a carefully wrapped box. "This one is for you," he said. I did my best to smile as I started to unwrap the package. Inside, I found one of our household clocks wrapped in tissue paper. "Our clock?" I asked, puzzled.

"Open the card," was Owen's reply. The kids leaned in close as I opened the envelope. Inside I found a card that Owen had made on our computer. There was a Christmas tree on the front and inside was a poem written by Owen in which he wrote that he was giving me a gift of time — a whole day of his time to paint our bedroom and help make our new house feel more like a home.

I started to cry, but these were tears of happiness. "Thank you," I said, wiping away my tears as Owen and the kids hugged me. By some miracle, Owen knew exactly what I needed for Christmas that year — the gift of his time.

Come January, when the decorations had been put away, we bought the green paint I had picked out months before. Then Owen took a day off from work and arranged for my parents to watch Rose and Ryan. The two of us set to work painting our bedroom. Weeks later, with the snow melting and green grass starting to appear in the yard, I looked at my freshly painted room and realized the color we'd painted our walls was not just the spruce-green of Christmas trees but also a color that reminded me of the freshness of spring.

That gift of time was a turning point for my family and me. It's not as if Christmas was magically easy and stress-free from then on, but each year I have found more joy in it, and as a family, we've made some changes to the way we approach the season and the way we give gifts. We still make our favorite Christmas foods and decorate, but I am much less concerned about things being just so. We still celebrate with my family but we decided that it was okay to tell that one grumpy relative to visit at a less stressful time of the year.

And somehow, without much fuss, each year we stand in awe as we light the tree and declare that it is absolutely perfect. The best tree ever! I feel less stressed about finding perfect gifts now and more joy in listening to Christmas music and spending time with family. Instead of shipping gifts across the country, we donate funds in honor of family members through our church's alternative giving fair. We still buy gifts for our close family, but we also make a point of giving gifts that involve time — like taking my brothers out to lunch at our favorite restaurant or going to a Christmas concert together.

The gift of time is something we can all give. Maybe it's setting aside an hour or two one evening to play a board game with family or taking a friend out for coffee. Maybe it's helping someone do errands or watching a young couple's children so they can go on a date. Best of all is the fact that the gift of Christmas Time can be given and received all year long.

~Myrna CG Mibus

The Christmas Surprise

You know you're in love when you can't fall asleep
because reality is finally better than your dreams.
~Dr. Seuss

"**M**erry Christmas, darling. I love you, and I promise this will be over soon and we'll be together again." My voice was quivering ever so slightly that night, despite my attempts to hide it. I tried so hard to protect her from the things going on around me, and like all good soldiers, I had to put up a brave front for loved ones back home.

But this time, I had a much different reason for hiding my emotions. It was not fear, but rather an overwhelming excitement that threatened my calm demeanor. For as I hung up that phone half a world away from my sweet Southern belle, the single most expensive call of my life ended, and what would become my greatest adventure began. And if my plan came to fruition, this Christmas would be like no other before or since.

At the time, I was a twenty-year-old staff sergeant stationed in Southeast Asia, compelled by duty to the field of war, far away from my loving bride of three years. Our communications during that year consisted of infrequent handwritten letters and even more infrequently traded cassette tapes.

Words cannot even begin to describe how much I craved hearing her sweet voice in person. We had already missed so much time together during that very difficult year; our wedding anniversary had come and gone, celebrated only with those same letters and tapes.

And now this was to be our first Christmas apart in the six years since we first met. While the military made an admirable attempt to provide us with a Christmas experience, I had determined that neither distance, nor oceans, nor even war would prevent us from experiencing the joy of this holiday together.

As I hung up that phone in the USO, I walked out of the dilapidated building to a waiting bus for Bangkok, carrying the money I had put aside each month for the trip. As the bus bumped along the twisting jungle road, I had ample time to dwell on the adventure I had been planning almost from the beginning of my June arrival in Southeast Asia. Everything leading up to that day was scripted, down to the tiniest detail — the bus, the flight, even that last-minute phone call.

I boarded my flight in the enormous Bangkok airport only four days prior to Christmas. The first leg of that almost twenty-four-hour journey would take me high above the lush, bombed-out hills of Cambodia, barely skirting the war zones of Vietnam. Our brand-new Boeing 747 would skim over the high, chiseled mountains of Asia and glide carefully down between the tall apartment towers built into the side of the mountains surrounding Hong Kong's Kai Tak Airport, our first stop. I experienced more than a few uneasy moments during that landing, as our aircraft bounced down the runway, wings dangling precariously on either side over the waters of Victoria Harbor. After a short layover to take on passengers, we returned to the air, headed for an uneventful flight to Tokyo, and then eastward across the Pacific to Honolulu. During what seemed to be an unending journey, the amber sphere of the sun seemed to set multiple times in the sky as we traversed the deep blue expanse below. And the closer the plane came to delivering me into the arms of my love, the more excited I became.

After leaving Honolulu, the sun set one last time, revealing before us in the darkness a large, low dome of light glowing dimly at first in the black, distant east. At once equally amazed and confused by this phenomenon, and knowing that it was far too early for the sun to be rising ahead of us, I slowly began to recognize that the glow in the darkness ahead was actually the mainland of Southern California, still hours away. With each passing moment, the light grew closer and more pronounced, drawing us ever so slowly into its beauty. The closer we got, the more nervous I became, and the more my resolve began to waver. I couldn't wait for the surprise. By the time we reached Los Angeles International Airport, I had to hear her voice.

"Hi hon, how are you?" I asked.

"Wow, our connection is so good. Why are you calling again?"

"Hon, there's a reason the connection is good; I'm in Los Angeles." Dead silence greeted me on the other end of the line. "Did you understand me?"

"No…" she said.

Slowly, I repeated, "I'm in Los Angeles."

The words no sooner left my mouth than I heard "Mama, HE'S IN LA!" I don't remember much more of the conversation, nor do I recall very much about that last hour before landing in Phoenix. I do remember running into her waiting arms. We kissed, I lifted her off her feet, and as we clung to each other there in the airport terminal, it felt as if I had never left her side.

We did not sleep that night; in those early morning hours, as we lay in each other's arms, oblivious to all around us, talk seemed to flow much easier than any time before or since. It was as if we were meeting for the very first time, getting acquainted once again. And for the next thirty days it was Christmas. That was the most wonderful present I ever gave her, and I don't think the glow from the surprise ever wore off.

~Rus Franklin

14

Chicken Soup
for the Soul

Built with Love

He didn't tell me how to live; he lived,
and let me watch him do it.
~Clarence Budington Kelland

He had the typical lifestyle of a district manager for a busy grocery chain. He was always on call and there were always problems to be solved. He traveled too much, too. Due to this hectic and stressful schedule there wasn't much opportunity for his young family to see him. And when he was home, he was much too exhausted to enjoy it.

As a child I didn't understand why my father was gone so much. In my simple, innocent mind his absence meant that there were other places he'd rather be and other people who were more important.

But on Christmas Day, when I was ten years old, I was given a dollhouse. It was an unusual gift for a rough and tumble girl who preferred climbing trees to playing dress-up. I was perplexed but also completely enamored of it at the same time. It was so large I could have almost lived in it myself. I studied the dollhouse, all the details and finishes. It was a beautiful, two-story farmhouse with a wraparound porch. The house was mounted on a mobile platform that had been covered with artificial grass turf to look like a yard. Inside it had a kitchen, den, bathroom and two bedrooms that were begging for decorations and doll furniture. Despite my tomboy tendencies, my mind started to run wild

with ideas to make this magnificent farmhouse come to life.

What I didn't know then, but would later understand, was that the greatest gift was not actually the dollhouse but the fact that my busy father built it himself. He managed to turn his office into a workshop and squeeze in hanging shingles, attaching siding and painting the foundation between meetings and travel. He would stay late into the night and go in earlier in the mornings to do a little more each day. This was not a small task for a man not known for his handiness. However, my dad lovingly put that remarkable dollhouse together for his precious little girl and he did it completely on his own.

On Christmas Day he proudly showed me all the features of the dollhouse he had labored over for months: the doors that opened and closed; the foundation he'd painted half a dozen times to give it the perfect texture and color; and even the first pieces of furniture he'd picked out to get me started on the decorating. All in all he had spent well over forty hours making sure this house would be fit for his tomboy.

And he even recognized that despite my tomboy interests, I would still love that dollhouse. The gift started me realizing that his absence wasn't at all about him finding other things more important than his family. In fact, he was working hard at his job to painstakingly create a life for all of us, with the same care and attention and devotion that he had put into that dollhouse for me. All in all, that dollhouse was the greatest gift he could have ever given me.

~Jennifer R. Land

15

Chicken Soup for the Soul

Artie

Sometimes being a brother is even better than
being a superhero.
~Marc Brown

I rushed through the big glass doors of Lehman's Pharmacy. I was there to buy my grandmother's hearing aid batteries while my mother waited outside in the car. She would notice if I took too long, but this was my chance to visit the love of my life — Artie.

I rushed to his aisle, and there he was, right where I last saw him: a brown, fuzzy little guy with a large tan nose that fit perfectly over my shoulder as I squeezed him tightly. I adored that aardvark stuffed animal.

But my mother noticed, saying, "You took a *long* time in Lehman's — and I looked — there weren't huge lines. Next time, your brother is going in with you."

Oh, great! My brother, Rich, was going to accompany me into the pharmacy. He would watch me like a hawk and report everything to our mother.

I wasn't going to give up seeing my precious Artie. So, as we walked into the store together, I suggested to Rich that he get the batteries, since he was older. He agreed, but said I shouldn't be going off to look at the cosmetics, as I wasn't allowed to wear them yet.

He needn't have worried about that; I was already heading toward

Artie. There he was, awaiting me. I grabbed him and hugged him tightly, his tan nose fitting perfectly on my shoulder. Just then, I heard him: "What in the world are you doing?"

My cover was blown. "This is Artie," I said. "His nose rests perfectly on my shoulder, and I hug him every single time I come here. Don't tell Mom. I know we can't afford him, and I hope he doesn't get sold, because I just love this little guy."

The look on Rich's face was unreadable, but I knew deep down that he wasn't going to make fun of me. In fact, a few times when he accompanied me to the pharmacy, he said, "Go on and hug your ugly animal, if it's still there, and I'll get Gram's batteries."

One day, Rich was working with Dad somewhere, so Mom took me to Lehman's alone and said, "You get to go in by yourself, again. Just don't take forever, okay?"

I rushed into the pharmacy and went straight to Artie's shelf. But he was gone. I searched high and low. I wanted to cry, but I kept holding out hope that Artie would be on one of the shelves that I hadn't checked.

Suddenly, a voice from the counter interrupted my search. It was Mrs. Lehman herself. "Are you looking for that stuffed animal you hug every single time you're here?"

"How did you…?"

"Know? We do have mirrors in the store, dear. See them? We can see almost everything. Honey, I'm sorry to tell you but someone came in here the other week and bought the aardvark."

I was crestfallen.

"Dear, I am truly sorry. I know how much you loved him, but we carry stuffed animals to sell — not to hug and put back on the shelf."

She was right — I knew she was right. So why did I feel so empty and upset? I weakly thanked her as I paid for Gram's hearing aid batteries. Then I slowly walked out to my mom's car with my head hanging low, trying to hide my tears. I prayed that Artie had found good home.

A month went by, and it was Christmas Eve. We were allowed to open one present that night and save the rest for Christmas morning.

Rich walked up to me and said nonchalantly, "Here, you may

want to open this one, or you may not — it's up to you."

My interest was piqued. I shook it. It was soft. But it didn't feel like clothing. My heart was thumping as I ripped open a section of wrapping paper and revealed a tan piece of cloth — a piece that resembled an aardvark's nose! It was Artie!

I squealed with delight, my mother looked confused, and my brother smiled proudly as I hugged him. Then I hugged Artie close to me, his little tan nose resting perfectly on my shoulder.

~Rebecca L. Jones

Hidden Blessings

Any man can be a father. It takes someone
special to be a dad.
~Author Unknown

Christmas carols and organ music filled our tiny church as I dutifully sat by my family for our annual Christmas Eve service. The excitement and expectation of the Christmas season hung in the air as I sang. My mouth was moving but my mind was racing with excitement of another kind. Until this night I thought of myself as a good church girl who respected her parents, but that was before they forbid me to have anything to do with an older boy who worked at the bowling alley.

In a secret phone conversation, I agreed to meet him that night at 10:00 p.m. at a park near my house. As the music ended and the prayers began, I was planning how I would sneak out of the house. I justified my behavior by convincing myself that my parents, especially my father, could never understand me.

I snuck out and then I snuck back in. And then I almost got caught. In the blackness of the December night the lights of our Christmas tree glittered. Through the shadows I could see the bent figure of my father kneeling beneath the tree. I was barely breathing as I pushed my back tight against the wall, hoping he would return to his bedroom so I could sneak back upstairs to my room.

My entire body trembled. I was chilled from being outside. But then all of a sudden I felt hot with shame and guilt as I watched my father lovingly put out his gifts for us. I had betrayed his trust and the boy never even showed up!

Suddenly the house went black; my father switched off the tree lights and was coming toward me in the dark. I quickly ducked into the bathroom and sat down on the toilet.

"Oh, sorry," he said as he pushed open the door squinting at me in order to focus in the dim light.

"Get back to bed," he said forcefully. "I still have some things to tend to before morning." With a surge of relief, I ran up the stairs being careful not to wake anyone else in the family. As I got into my flannel nightgown and snuggled beneath the covers I began to cry. I cried for my own disappointment and for the boy who never came, I cried for not listening to my parents, I cried to God and asked him to forgive me. I cried knowing that I must face up to my parents and talk honestly with them.

I tossed and turned but sleep did not come. My mind wandered back to Christmas mornings of the past. This year I didn't expect much in the way of presents; I knew money was a problem. The year had been full of unexpected changes for our family. My mother returned to her teaching job, my grandparents moved in with us, my father was struggling to build up his new business, and there was a pile of unpaid hospital bills.

My older brother had suffered a ruptured appendix, which required him to have several surgeries. Just as he was recovering, my middle brother broke his leg playing football and was sent to the same hospital to have his shattered leg pieced back together. After he returned home on crutches, I had an appendicitis attack that sent me to that same hospital. As my eyes fluttered shut, I smiled at the memory of my father telling the nurse that he needed to sit in the wheelchair after he was handed the hospital bill for all three of us. He sat down and put me on his lap as the nurse guided us toward the car. He had a gift for finding humor even in difficult moments!

The smell of Grandma's cinnamon rolls roused me from my sleep and I heard my mother's voice calling out, "Merry Christmas, everyone.

Come on down for breakfast." The world outside my window looked fresh, clean and pure white. Snow was falling. The earth was getting a fresh start, that's what I needed, too — a fresh start.

As we gathered for breakfast I watched my father pour his coffee. He lifted his cup to his lips, smiled directly at me, and put his big hand over mine. "I wasn't the only one wandering around in the dark last night." He looked away and continued speaking to all of us, saying, "I realize I've not been home much, I'm working hard to get this business going to provide for our family, you have all had to make sacrifices and for that I am grateful. There isn't much under the tree this year, but let's see what there is."

Bags of whole walnuts and boxes of Cracker Jacks were piled in a heap under the tree. We all looked at each other thinking, "Is he crazy?" He grinned while tossing everyone a bag of walnuts and a pair of nutcrackers. "Well," he said, "get going, start cracking." One by one we discovered that some of the nuts had been opened, cleaned out, filled with a surprise and glued back together again. Inside were coins, folded dollar bills, movie tickets, and assorted trinkets. Soon the room exploded in gleeful expressions of surprise, joy, and laughter. We found more prizes hidden in the Cracker Jack boxes like watches, rings, bracelets, small toys, money and IOUs for trips to the zoo, circus, camping at the lake, and going to the movie theater in Detroit.

Gratitude filled my heart. Only my father could have come up with such a creative idea to help us give thanks and laugh in spite of our circumstances. That evening we gathered in the kitchen for hot cocoa and warm walnut cookies that Grandma made from all the cracked walnuts. My father took me aside and said, "We're long overdue for a talk." My heart was ready to forgive and be forgiven and my rebellious attitude melted as he held me in his arms.

Even though he passed away a long time ago, I can still hear his voice: "Start cracking and see what hidden blessings can be found even in the difficult moments of life." Thank you, Dad.

~Norma Heffron

Darren's Christmas Video

When you look at your life, the greatest happinesses
are family happinesses.
~Dr. Joyce Brothers

I hesitantly place the old videotape in the VCR. It's Christmas 2015, and it's been a long time since we've watched this video. My thoughts drift back to the day I found it in our mailbox shortly before Christmas 1990.

I remember holding the slightly marred manila envelope in my trembling hands, clutching it to my chest, for fear it would bear bad news.

Although I didn't recognize the name on the return address, I knew it was someone who was serving in the Army's 82nd Airborne Division with my son Darren. It concerned me that Darren wasn't the sender.

Darren had been deployed to Saudi Arabia for Desert Shield that August; but we knew from his letters that the 82nd was preparing to go into Iraq at any time. The thought was frightening!

My husband and kids were there when I returned from picking up the mail. We opened the package and discovered, to our delight, that it contained a Christmas video recorded by Darren as part of the USO's "Better than a Letter" project.

Attached to the video, was this beautiful handwritten letter dated December 4th:

Dear Mrs. Pullen,

Greetings from Saudi Arabia. This is John, Darren's squad leader, with a gift for you. Inside is a VHS tape that Darren made last night. The reason I am sending it is because Darren is getting some eyeglasses made. You will understand why when you see the tape. I don't know when he will be back so I'm making sure that it is sent out with the rest of the tapes.

This also gives me the opportunity to say thanks for all you have done. People like you and your family make all of us service personnel proud to be Americans. You have done a fantastic job raising Darren and I count him as one of my best troops and a friend.

If it does come to war over here you can rest assured that I will take care of him. Heck, without him we wouldn't get those great cookies. As a squad leader I know how to take care of valuable assets like that.

Well, Mrs. Pullen, it's time for some Army training. Enjoy the tape and have a Merry Christmas.

Sincerely,
John F.

Our hearts were full before we even began to watch the tape. What a blessing to have our son serving with such awesome fellow soldiers. I knew I'd never forget John's comforting words.

As my husband placed the tape in the VCR, we gathered close to the TV to see Darren for the first time in nearly a year.

I didn't make it much past "Hi, Mom," before the tears were flowing. I never knew that a video could be so heartwarming and so heartbreaking at the same time.

Not many people owned video cameras back then, so having the opportunity to actually see and hear our son was extraordinary. Today it is commonplace for families to see their soldiers no matter where they are in the world.

We immediately noticed why Darren needed new glasses; his thick, black-horned-rimmed BCGs, or Birth Control Glasses (as the soldiers called them), were held together with duct tape, making them even more unattractive. But, to our eyes, he still looked extremely handsome in his combat fatigues, heavy boots, and desert tan.

Darren began by wishing us a Merry Christmas, and then addressed each member of the family with a special message:

"Mom, your poem was great, but it really made me sad. Please keep sending cookies; they are a hit with all the guys.

"Your letter was hilarious, Dad. Your spelling was pretty good, too.

"Timmy and Elijah, thank you for the drawings, they make me so happy; and be good for your mommy." That was for his three- and five-year-old nephews.

"Sis, the guys love the pictures you send; but I'll have to talk to you when I get home about showing too much leg." He chuckled.

"I've been working out, Tim; I'm catching up with you." He smiled, showing off his biceps for his older brother.

"I miss you so much, Granny!"

He went on to mention each of his siblings and asked us to pass on his wishes for a Merry Christmas to extended family and friends.

Our twenty-one-year old son had grown up out there in the desert. He spoke purposefully, choosing his words carefully, and taking time to organize his thoughts prior to changing topics.

He said it was difficult to believe they'd been there four months already, and that he had no idea when they'd be coming home. He was happy that new tents had arrived that day, and said they'd be spending both Christmas Eve and Christmas Day on guard duty.

"We've been training hard, but in our limited free time, we play basketball in the sand with our makeshift hoops, and write lots of letters back home. I love you all; it's real sad talking to you like this." Ironically, the thirty-minute tape ran out just as he finished his sentence.

I think everyone agreed that Darren's video was the very best Christmas present we received that year.

In February 1991 the 82nd Airborne Division paratroopers went into Iraq. Thankfully, the war was over quickly; and after the liberation of Kuwait, the 82nd began its redeployment back to Fort Bragg.

Now it's twenty-five years later, and we sit down to watch the video once again on Christmas, blessed to be joined by Darren's sons Nathan and Andrew, who are home on leave from the U.S. Army.

Both boys were born after Darren was honorably discharged from the military, and this will be their first time seeing the video. Although I'm pretty sure they've heard all about their dad's army adventures, it should be fun for them to watch.

John's letter is still with the tape, so I pass it over to the boys and Darren to read as I turn on the VCR player.

"He was such a great guy," Darren says, as he recalls his squad leader John. "He really did love your cookies, Mom."

The thirty-minute tape seems to go by quickly as everyone laughs at Darren's glasses and talks about how much the military has changed over the years. But, the boys look so much like their dad in their fatigues that the resemblance is almost uncanny. They thoroughly enjoy watching the video, and my heart is warmed by the sight of the three of them sitting on the couch together.

I look around the room at all the kids and grandkids and I'm reminded that we have so much for which to be grateful, not the least of which is Darren's Christmas video.

~Connie Kaseweter Pullen

Labor of Love

If the relationship of father to son could really be
reduced to biology, the whole earth would blaze with
the glory of fathers and sons.
~James Baldwin

Farm chores were as predictable as the sun rising and setting each day. The cows were cared for and milked by my husband and his brother seven days a week, regardless of holiday festivities. There was no sleeping in for them, even on holidays.

Then our fourteen-year-old twins came up with a stellar idea. They decided to surprise their dad and uncle with the gift of sleeping in on Christmas Day. Bruce and Blaine recruited their little brother Steve and their cousin Jon to become members of this loving conspiracy. Nearly every day since they were little, they had helped with both morning and evening chores — feeding calves from a suckle bucket, separating the hay bales into chunks, washing udders, and scraping down the walkway; therefore, they knew what needed to be done.

After finishing Christmas Eve supper, the boys feigned sleepiness, changed into their pajamas and brushed their teeth with no prodding. Without the usual protests, they disappeared upstairs for bed.

"I'm surprised the boys are ready for bed so early," my husband remarked.

"Oh, they played hard in the snow today, up and down the hills on the toboggan," I replied, fluffing up the sofa pillows to avoid looking into his eyes. "Let's enjoy the peace and quiet for a change."

After cleaning up the kitchen, we cuddled on the sofa with our Siamese cat curled up by my side, his purr motor on high volume. While we gazed at the glittering Christmas tree, Bing Crosby crooned "White Christmas" from a record on the stereo.

Upstairs, the boys set the alarm clocks in their bedrooms for an early rising, closing their doors to muffle the sound.

Sworn to secrecy, my sister-in-law and I made certain we did not set the alarm clocks for our husbands.

Long before daylight, the boys tiptoed down the stairs, donned heavy outerwear and sneaked out of the house. The icy slap of Minnesota wind greeted them as they raced on the crunchy snow to the warmth of the barn.

They found forty cows lowing for their breakfast, calves out-bawling one another for attention, the heavy scent of bovine breath and overnight manure — inspiration for the boys to shift into high gear, determined to finish the milking, feeding, and barn cleaning before their dad and uncle awakened. Jon and little Steve did their part by feeding calves, running errands, and taking direction from Bruce and Blaine, who assumed the role of elders.

"Jon, you climb up in the haymow and toss down the bales for later," ordered Blaine. "I'll get going with the silage."

Bruce called to Steve, "Come with me and we'll start washing udders. Bring the balm with you."

Trying not to show his fear, Steve crouched by the first cow and did as he was told. They soon had the milkers attached to the first cows, and the pipeline throbbed with warm milk streaming into the bulk tank.

"Jon, it's time to put a scoop of ground feed on top of the silage," said Blaine.

Back in the warm, quiet house, I quietly sneaked out of bed without disturbing my snoring husband. Wrapping my robe around me, I groped my way out of the bedroom in the dark and headed to the kitchen to begin breakfast preparations for the boys. As I stirred the pancake batter and started the bacon sizzling in the fry pan, a sense of pride and joy washed over me as dawn crept over the eastern horizon, bathing the sky in glorious hues. I breathed a prayer that the new heifer, Trudy, wouldn't cause any trouble.

Suddenly Bruce was back in the house, changing into his dad's jacket and cap. "No time to talk now, Mom," he whispered. "I'll explain later."

Back in the barn, he sidled up to high-strung Trudy, lowered his voice and stroked her flank.

"Easy now, Bossie, take it easy, take it easy," he murmured. Fooled by the disguise, Trudy settled down and stood still to have her udder washed and the milker apparatus attached.

In record time, they finished up — sweet-smelling straw fluffed under the forty cows and in the calf pens for fresh bedding; the milking equipment washed, disinfected, and hung to dry in the milk house.

By 8:00 a.m. the boys raucously bounded into the house, shouting and laughing. Startled awake by the commotion, their dad stumbled over the cat as he emerged from the bedroom.

"What's going on? What time is it?" he moaned. "I must have overslept!"

"Merry Christmas, Dad! Surprise!" they yelled, smiling ear to ear, as they threw their arms around their dad. "Yes, you did oversleep, but the chores are all done! We love you, Dad! Merry Christmas!"

A similar exchange was taking place at the house next door between their uncle and cousin.

Our sons and nephew continued this Christmas morning labor of love throughout their high school and college years. We no longer farm, my husband has passed away, and the boys are now middle-aged with sons of their own. They often reminisce about the special gift they gave for so many years and of the joy their kind deed brought to their dad and to them. Given with love and paid for with effort, this gift meant more to my husband than anything money could buy.

~Margaret M. Marty

19

My Crazy Dad

*I believe that what we become depends on what our
fathers teach us at odd moments, when they aren't
trying to teach us. We are formed by little
scraps of wisdom.*
~Umberto Eco

I thought my dad had lost his mind. Night after night he asked
me to look at the angel on the top of our Christmas tree. She
wore a little gold net skirt and she was pretty, but we had
bought her a long time ago. She was old news.

"Isn't she pretty, Donna?"

"Sure, Daddy, it's the same angel we've had for years."

I was an eighteen-year-old college freshman and I knew my dad
was ancient, being in his mid-forties. He was definitely losing it.

There were still two weeks until Christmas, and he was pointing
out the angel to me almost every day.

The Sunday before Christmas I found my dad sitting on the couch
looking up at that angel again. He smiled at me and pointed toward
the angel again. What in the world was going on with this man?

Finally, it was Christmas morning. Dad was still talking about
our beautiful Christmas angel. We opened our gifts and then Daddy
brought out the camera and a chair.

"Donna, come over and stand on this chair," he said. "I want to take
your picture next to the angel." Now I knew he was out of his mind.

"Go ahead, Donna," my mother whispered. Did I have to worry about her state of mind, too?

I stood on the chair and turned toward the cheap little angel made in China — obeying my "aging" parents.

And then I saw them — diamond studs inserted into the angel's skirt. My dad had wanted me to find them early because he was so excited. I felt like such a brat to have doubted him.

I miss my dad. He's been gone thirteen years now and one of the earrings has gone missing, too, but that warm feeling of being loved will never go away. I'll never forget how cute he was that Christmas when he was so excited and proud to give me those diamond earrings.

~Donna Van Cleve Schleif

Gifts of Hope

The wings of hope carry us, soaring high above the driving winds of life.

~Ana Jacob

The doctor stared into my eyes, "I'm sorry," he said. "Your condition is permanent." I should have felt shock, disbelief or even sadness. But I felt nothing. I was already numb; he had only confirmed what I suspected to be true. Pain and disfigurement would be my constant companions for the rest of my life. An unexpected illness had taken its toll, leaving in its wake a broken, insecure person who just wanted to be herself again.

"If you need anything, just let me know," dozens of kind people offered. My answer was always the same — a small smile and a thank you, but I would never ask them for help. Somehow that would have been admitting I was weak and that I couldn't handle life.

With each passing month, I felt myself sinking a little deeper. No one knew the dark place I was in. I put on a good face, never letting on how much this illness had cost me. I had lost hope, and a life without those four small letters became very bleak indeed.

One morning, a couple weeks before Christmas, I opened my front door to a bright colored bag sitting on my porch. "How sweet," I thought. "One of my neighbors must have left some holiday goodies for my kids."

I picked up the bag and was shocked to see that it was addressed to me.

I'll admit, I felt a small thrill that someone had left me a gift. My kids received presents and trinkets all the time. A trip to the dentist meant balloons and digging in the treasure box; birthday parties yielded bags of goodies. But as an adult, I had learned not to expect happy surprises. Magic was for the children.

That gift tag even had a poem on it:

On the first day of Christmas,
We've often heard it said,
It's nice to give your friends
A box of candy with a bow of red.

The bag contained a box of chocolates tied with a red bow. I stood there staring in disbelief. Someone had done this for me. I wondered: if this was the first day of Christmas, would there be a second? The next morning I woke feeling a bit lighter as I raced to the front door to find another package waiting.

On the second day of Christmas
Some stickers and sticky tape,
To help you wrap the presents
To be opened Christmas Day.

And on it went for twelve days. Candles, tissue paper, candy, soda, fancy pens, gum... each wrapped present with a tag containing a poem. So many wonderful things that brightened each day, reminding me that someone cared enough about me to make the effort to shop for gifts, wrap them up, write gift tags, and place them on my front steps in the middle of the night for two weeks.

I asked every one I knew about this mysterious gift-giver. I would tell them the story about the lovely packages arriving on my porch. "Is it you?" I would ask, hopeful that I could discover the identity of this secret angel. As much as they wished it had been their idea, it never was.

As I opened each gift, I found something in those bags that the sender never knew he or she had left at my front door. They were gifts of hope. Hope that there was still goodness in this world. Belief that people still cared. And the realization that I was wrong to have given up on myself.

One of the clues mentioned there would be twelve days, so it was bittersweet to open the last. It had given me something to look forward to each morning. With a grateful heart, I silently thanked this elusive person who had brought me so much joy. I didn't even think to check the porch the next morning. To my surprise, later that day I found yet another gift waiting.

Yesterday was the last day of surprises,
But here is a little hint.
Can you guess who's responsible
For this stuff being sent?

I would finally know the identity of my secret Santa! Slowly unwrapping the tissue paper, I savored the last gift from this kind friend. I pulled out a sparkly ornament in the shape of a red bicycle.

But that didn't help. I searched to the farthest recesses of my mind for someone relating to this red bicycle, but came up completely empty. I tried a play on words, rhyming, analogies... nothing. I had absolutely no idea. Years later, I am no closer to learning its origins than I was on that first day when I held that red bicycle in my hands for hours.

Perhaps never finding out the giver's identity made it all the more special. It taught me the meaning of true kindness. It was the people that didn't ask, but just did, who touched me the most. A card to let me know a friend was thinking about me. A meal that unexpectedly showed up at my door. A gift basket after a surgery that I told no one about. Like the gifts on my porch, those acts of kindness stayed with me and showed me how to be a blessing to others.

I decided to banish these words from my vocabulary: "If you need anything, just let me know." Instead, I would give my friends who were facing a rough situation a small pick-me-up. A book, a candle, a card, a sweet treat, a handwritten note — the options were endless.

Even though I pick out something I think they might enjoy, I've discovered that what's inside the bag doesn't really matter. It's the hope that I offer that makes a difference. I want my friends to know that despite their troubles, life can still be good.

As I wrap these little presents every now and then, I remember the magical twelve days of Christmas gifts that made their way to my door during my darkest hour. Now I get to say thank you over and over again to my mysterious benefactor for the hope I received when I wasn't sure I could ever believe again.

~Katie Bangert

The Cookie Plate Christmas

When someone you love becomes a memory, the
memory becomes a treasure.
~Author Unknown

One Christmas, two years after my mother died, my sister gave my husband and me two place settings of Christmas china. Over the years, I added more pieces to my collection.

One year, when it was close to Christmas, I went shopping for more pieces of our Christmas china. What I really wanted was the cookie plate. I knew it was one piece I would really use. But when I saw that the price of that one plate was three hundred dollars I knew it would never be a possibility!

Arriving home, I had a message from my father to call him. He said that he had been going through a cedar chest and found something of my mother's that I might like.

The next day, I went to my father's to see what he had found. When I pulled my present out of the gift bag, I was speechless. It was the cookie plate that went with my Christmas china.

My father had not known I was collecting the Christmas china. He didn't know I had been shopping for that piece the day before.

The cookie plate was the only piece of Christmas china my mother ever owned. Everyone in the family had forgotten about it.

So, even though my mother had been gone for a decade, I still received a wonderful gift from both of my parents. We always call this special Christmas the "Cookie Plate Christmas."

~Katie Martin

A Giant Box of Love

If the whole world were put into one scale, and my
mother in the other, the whole world
would kick the beam.
~Lord Langdale

It couldn't have been easy for my mom — a single mother with three energetic kids ages ten to sixteen, who worked long hours to provide us with clothing and food. Somehow she did it, keeping us busy and out of trouble. Sometimes she had to be really creative.

One Christmas, Mom came home from work with three boxes... three refrigerator boxes. Seriously. Refrigerator boxes. That weekend, she sent us out to the garage with those boxes and several cans of paint. Our only instructions were to paint them however we wanted. We had no idea what those boxes would be used for and I painted mine my favorite color: bright purple. To add a touch of whimsy, I added huge yellow and orange flowers. It was the 1970's, after all. I can still picture that box; it was awful, really quite hideous, but my ten-year-old self was so proud!

After our day of painting, my siblings and I put those boxes out of our minds and began to look forward to Christmas Day. We knew Mom didn't have a lot of extra money; we shopped at the thrift store for school clothes, gathered supplies at Pic-N-Save, and bought day-old bread at a local bakery. But that certainly didn't keep me from wanting something very special that year. A just-for-me gift that wasn't a hand-me-down from my older brother or sister.

I knew, though, it was unlikely. We didn't have the money for the one gift I wanted and I was okay with that.

Christmas Eve came, and we followed our tradition of going to Christmas Eve service at church. We sang all the standard Christmas songs. Our pastor spoke of the birth of Jesus, the choir sang, the nativity scene was played out. Afterward, we sipped apple cider and munched on sugar cookies. My friends and I talked about what we hoped would be under the tree. I didn't even mention the special gift I wanted.

I kept telling myself that it wasn't going to happen. I would be happy with whatever my mom gave me.

We headed for home and followed another tradition of opening our stockings and one gift. Just one. As always, our stockings were full of candy, small toys, and a pair of socks. Finally, we opened that one gift — matching pajamas. We drank hot cocoa and sang a few more carols. Then it was off to bed.

On Christmas morning, we were not allowed to even peek in the living room before breakfast. This Christmas was no exception. After inhaling eggs, bacon, and toast, we ran to the living room… and stopped dead in our tracks.

Those refrigerator boxes were in front of the tree. But we still weren't allowed to open them. We had to sit quietly in our matching pajamas and read the story of Christ's birth from the book of Luke.

After prayer, we were finally allowed to open the giant boxes.

My sixteen-year-old sister's box was hiding a bright red beanbag chair, a very cool thing for a teenaged girl. She immediately settled in to what would be her favorite seat. My fourteen-year-old brother found a refurbished drum set in his box.

And in mine?

My very first, all-for-me bicycle! Exactly what I wanted! It too was refurbished, but that didn't matter. It was sparkly and purple with pink and white tassels! The basket was white with purple flowers! It was perfect. Just perfect. I could ride all I wanted without having to wait for my brother or sister to let me use theirs, which was never as often as I would have liked. I don't know how she did it, but my mom had once again made a Christmas wish come true.

Yes, it couldn't have been easy, but somehow, my mom made that Christmas one of the best I'd ever had... and few since have topped it. No other refrigerator boxes have appeared before my tree. And no other gift has illustrated a mother's love in quite the same way.

~Sauni Rinehart

The Joy of Christmas

Holiday Miracles

Christmas… that magic blanket that wraps itself about us, that something so intangible that it is like a fragrance. It may weave a spell of nostalgia. Christmas may be a day of feasting, or of prayer, but always it will be a day of remembrance—a day in which we think of everything we have ever loved.
~Augusta E. Rundel

23

Chicken Soup for the Soul

Relative Strangers

Miracles come in moments. Be ready and willing.
~Dr. Wayne Dyer

It was Christmas morning, and I was the first one up at my parents' house in Vancouver. It was only seven, but I knew my best friend Rita would be awake because she had young children.

I dialed the number and heard someone say "Hello" in a weak, "crackly" voice.

"Rita, are you all right?" I asked in shock.

"Who is this?" said someone who was not Rita.

Oh no. Apparently, I had reached a wrong number and bothered an elderly woman on Christmas morning. I apologized for waking her, but she said, "Not to worry. It is nice to have someone to talk to, as I don't have anything to do today, nor anyone to talk to." My heart went out to her, and we began chatting.

I had phoned Rita on the Island, which is a long distance number, so I was curious as to where this woman lived. "Burnaby," she said.

"Wow!" I thought. That was local and not even in the same area code as Rita's number. How could my call to a long distance number have been directed to this woman nearby?

The woman said that her name was Faith, she was eighty years old, and a widow. She had no children and nothing to do on Christmas so she was glad that I had called. I talked to Faith for an hour, and she was so sweet that I asked my mother if we could invite her over for Christmas dinner. She said yes and Faith accepted our invitation and hurried off to get ready.

The mood in our rather somber household was transformed. My stepfather was dying of cancer, so we had been planning a low-key Christmas Day. Now our home's atmosphere was transformed from "doom and gloom" into joy as we awaited our mystery guest.

We had a wonderful time with Faith, and then, as she was saying her goodbyes, my mother realized that we had not exchanged last names.

"What is your last name?" my mother asked, to which Faith replied, "Holden."

"No!" my mother said. "That's MY last name. What is your last name?"

Faith, looking confused, repeated, "That is OUR last name. Holden. H-o-l-d-e-n."

What are the odds?

We sat down on the living room couch and Faith revealed even more surprising coincidences. Her late husband was from England, as was my stepfather Jim Holden, and both families had immigrated to Winnipeg, Canada. Faith's husband and Jim were the second of four children, with the same combination of brothers and sisters in the same birth order, and all of the siblings remained childless after marriage. Faith and my mother had attended the same high school.

How was it possible to dial a long distance number on Christmas morning, but end up connecting with a local number and a person who needed us as much as we needed her, and was possibly a family member, too?

We remained friends with Faith until her passing a few years later.

~Mary Ellen Angelscribe

24

Pages of the Past

*I think miracles exist in part as gifts and in part as
clues that there is something beyond the
flat world we see.*
~Peggy Noonan

"Y ou are not going to believe this!" said my friend
Susy. "We were opening gifts on Christmas morning and I handed Bill that book that you found.
He unwrapped it, gasped, and burst into tears!"
Susy and Bill were celebrating their second Christmas together
after a number of lonely years. Bill had been widowed after a happy
fifty-year marriage to his first wife, Maggie, and Susy had been divorced
for a long time.

When I spotted a book that I thought Susy might like to give
Bill for Christmas, I had texted her. We were selling it in the Book
Nook at Northland Public Library in Pittsburgh, Pennsylvania where
I volunteered. The book was called *Consider the Lilies*, and it was in
beautiful shape for a secondhand book. It checked all the right boxes
for Bill: a retired minister, avid gardener and nature lover.

Susy had texted back that it sounded just right, so I had picked it
up for her. When she leafed through it and saw the pretty watercolor
prints and lovely Biblical quotes, she declared it the perfect gift for Bill.

Neither of us had noticed the inscription at the front of the book:

To Bill and Maggie
Love, Meta

This book had been given to Bill and Maggie more than thirty years ago — in Michigan! He and Maggie had given the book away when they left Michigan for Pennsylvania many years ago.

Seeing that book again on Christmas morning was a shock and a surprise to Bill — maybe even a message. I choose to think it's Maggie's way of telling Bill "Merry Christmas. Be Happy." And I cannot think of a better Christmas present or love story than that!

~Rosemary McLaughlin

A Random Gift of Sweetness

There is no greater loan than a sympathetic ear.
~Frank Tyger

ennis glanced at his watch and smiled. He was tired and there were only forty-five minutes to go until closing time at the Rite-Aid where he worked. The store was nearly empty anyway, even though Christmas was right around the corner. It was probably because it was raining.

The automated doors opened and a middle-aged couple entered purposefully, wet from the persistent precipitation. The man was carrying a portfolio under his trench coat to protect it from the rain. The woman was wearing a stylish red raincoat, very appropriate for the holidays, but looked sad and stressed. Dennis offered his assistance.

"You print photos, right?" the man inquired with an accent that tipped Dennis off that the gentleman wasn't local.

"Yes sir, machine's right over there," Dennis said, pointing past colorful, holiday displays featuring an assortment of gift ideas. "Let me assist you, please."

As the trio walked over to the kiosk that housed the photographic equipment and supplies, Dennis noticed that the couple looked tired and sad.

Dennis positioned himself behind the equipment, and briefly

reacquainted himself with its functionality. "Okay, how can I help you good people?"

The man started to speak, but the words did not come. So his wife, her graying blond hair covered with a rain bonnet, explained: "We have some photos from our wedding nearly thirty years ago we'd like to get copies of," she said. "Please make them pretty. They're for John's mother, my mother-in-law, Joyce."

Dennis smiled warmly at the couple. "That's very nice. A Christmas gift, huh?"

"Well… no, not exactly. We've promised her these photos for years, but always put it off. Maybe we were just lazy, or forgot, I don't know. She always wanted a set from our wedding day, but it just never happened. It's funny how things get away from you in life."

"Well, better late than never, right?" said Dennis.

The woman pursed her lips together tightly and gave a slight nod in agreement.

Dennis went to work reproducing the stack of about fifty photographs, but halfway through the process the machine began to overheat. Somewhat embarrassed, Dennis called another employee, Sandy, to the section to assist. They needed to make this holiday gift for this nice couple before the store closed.

For nearly fifteen minutes, Dennis and Sandy tinkered with the equipment, disassembled and then reassembled components, until finally, they got it working properly again. The couple never complained and patiently stood there throughout the ordeal, in dripping attire.

With only five photos left to copy, Dennis, with a note of excitement, exclaimed, "I just know your mom's going to be overjoyed to finally get these photos from you guys! I almost wish I could see her face when she opens them up."

There was a long, awkward silence from the couple. Dennis immediately sensed he had said something that initiated the uncomfortable moment, and quickly apologized. "Sorry, I'm being chatty tonight; we're almost done. Thank you for your patience, folks."

"No, you're fine, Dennis," John answered, reading the employee nametag. "These photos are indeed for my mom but she won't be able to see them. You see, she died this week and the funeral is tomorrow. We'll put the photos in her casket, cradled in her arms."

The man sighed heavily, and his wife wiped away a tear. "You were right, Dennis, 'better late than never', huh?"

Dennis asked Sandy to finish the job and he stepped away. The couple had been so patient, so kind, despite the equipment malfunctions and circumstances, all the while dealing with the pain of losing a loved one and right before the Christmas holidays. Dennis wanted to offer some token, some small gift, to recognize their goodness and positive spirit. He wandered down one of the aisles and randomly grabbed a seasonally decorated bag of red, green and gold foil–wrapped candied mints, and discreetly purchased them with his own cash. Then he bagged the item and pushed it aside.

The couple approached the register to pay for their completed photos. Dennis smiled and rang up the purchase, and thanked the couple again for their patience, then offered his condolences. They nodded and began to leave.

"Oh wait, sorry, I nearly forgot," Dennis announced. "It's nothing, really, but I wanted to get you two something for your incredible patience tonight with our stubborn equipment, and with it being so close to Christmas and all." Then he handed them the plastic bag with the candy. The couple shyly accepted the gift and pulled out its contents. They both started crying.

Dennis began to apologize.

"No, no, you're fine," the lady stammered with a smile. "You see, you just made our night, Dennis. The only way I can say it is you are an angel… our Christmas angel."

Dennis was dumbfounded. It was only a simple bag of chocolate mints.

The man explained, "You would've never known it, but every Christmas when we would visit my mother in New York for the holidays she would give us three things: a gift card to our favorite restaurant chain, something she quilted that year, and…" He couldn't finish the sentence.

"A bag of Andes chocolate mints," his wife concluded. Then she repeated, "A Christmas bag of Andes... the exact same thing you just gave us." Dennis could not speak. Out of hundreds of items he could have selected from the shelves for this couple, he had selected the one item that offered them hope and peace and joy and love.

"Thank you Dennis; we'll never forget you," John managed as they began to leave the store. "You have no idea how much this means to us!"

Then the couple departed into the rainy chill of night while Dennis silently locked up the store, turned off the lights and set the alarm system. But not before purchasing a second bag of Andes chocolate mints, an early Christmas gift to take home to his wife.

~David Michael Smith

26

The Apron Angel

This is the message of Christmas: We are never alone.
~Taylor Caldwell

When I asked my five-year-old granddaughter what she wanted to give her kindergarten teacher for Christmas, she said, "Grandma, I want to give my teacher a special Christmas present, because I love her." She didn't want to give her teacher an apple ornament, a piece of costume jewelry, or a gift card. She wanted "something that no one has ever given her before!" I told her we'd sleep on it and talk about it more the next morning.

Usually, I don't remember much, if anything, about my dreams, but when I awoke the next day, I recalled every single detail about the most vivid dream I'd ever had. My Grandma Blanche visited me. That in itself was surprising because she had died when I was only five, so I didn't really know her. Grandma Blanche said she would show me a unique gift that my granddaughter could give her teacher — one that no one would have ever given her before.

And then she showed me the most beautiful red lace apron I'd ever seen. At first I laughed, telling her it was see-through and too fancy for the kitchen. She explained, though, that it was a hostess apron. The hostess put it on *after* she finished cooking.

Grandma then showed me how to make the apron. I paid close attention to the design, the bric-a-brac, as she called it, along the hem and the pocket, and the rhinestones formed into a diamond shape in the center of the sash. Grandma assured me that the teacher would love it.

For a long time after I woke that morning, I sat on the side of the bed thinking about that dream. It was so vivid. How could I have been visited by a grandmother I hardly knew, with a gift idea for her great-great-granddaughter's teacher?

I called my mom. As I described everything in detail, she remained quiet. And, when I finally paused what she said blew me away. She told me her mom was a seamstress and would often make "hostess aprons"

 to earn extra cash. She always gave them to her children's teachers as Christmas gifts, and those teachers always loved them.

My mom also told me that she had kept one of her mom's aprons all these years, and that even though she never wore it, she kept it tucked away in a special place and pulled it out from time to time. She said that as I was telling her about my dream, she pulled it out and was holding it in her hands.

I was speechless. Not only did I not remember my grandmother, I certainly never knew about her having made aprons. But, I remained open to the possibility that something unexplainable was happening, and told my mom that I was going to purchase the materials and attempt to make what I saw in my dream. Then I would compare it to what she had.

Several hours later, I was confident I'd recreated, with the help of my granddaughter, what I saw in my dream — in red, like in the dream, and in black. The bric-a-brac was placed just as I saw it along the hem. The rhinestones formed a diamond in the center of the waistband. The sash was long enough to make a nice bow in the back.

It was time to compare what I had to what my mother had, so

off we went to her house.

As I unwrapped what I made and Mom walked into her living room with what her mother had made, we all gasped — they were identical! I had made an exact replica of what my mother held in her hands. We both knew that something special had happened, and for the longest time we just looked at them, in silence, and tried to make sense of it all.

After the Christmas break, I received the most beautiful note from my granddaughter's teacher, thanking me for the "most unique gift" she'd received during her teaching career. She promised that she would wear this apron every time she entertained, and would always be reminded of my granddaughter. While I cannot explain how I remembered every single detail of that dream, or how my grandmother seemed to know the intended recipient of the apron, what I do know is that something special happened that I will never forget.

My granddaughter is now grown, with children of her own, but every year our family still talks about the angel of a grandmother neither of us knew, but who visited in a dream and gave us a gift we'll always treasure.

~Victoria Jones

27

On the Wings of Faith

Faith and prayer are the vitamins of the soul; man
cannot live in health without them.
~Mahalia Jackson

On a crisp, autumn afternoon in October 2008 I was standing in the kitchen with my wife, Karen, while she cooked dinner. I was describing the day's events when I heard the sound of a horn repeatedly honking at my mother's house next door.

My heart skipped a couple of beats and a sickening wave of terror came over me, as the car horn kept going off. Something was wrong! I had recently taught my elderly mother that if she was in distress she should press the alarm button on her car's key fob.

"Mother must be in trouble!" I said, as I dashed out the door.

I could see my mother seated behind the steering wheel of her white Mercury in the driveway. I was running as hard as I could to get to her, watching in horror and disbelief as she drove away from me. She sped off between the two live oak trees and down the hill toward the lake behind the house.

"Hit the brake!" I yelled.

I watched in horror as her vehicle got closer to the water. All of a sudden, the vehicle took a hard left, narrowly missing the small wooden deck and staying on dry ground. Mother then kept driving along the side of the lake.

I finally reached the car and banged my hand on the trunk. Mother hit the brake and I motioned for her to lower the window.

"Mother, what are you doing?" I blurted out.

"What's wrong with you, Jim?" she calmly replied.

"Where are you going and why are you honking your horn?"

Mother gave me a warm, sweet smile and stated, "I'm chasing those geese back to the lake where they belong. They're pooping on my driveway!"

I stood there stunned, totally out of breath. My heart was pounding. I slowly turned and began the walk back to the house to tell Karen that Mother had just been on a wild goose chase!

Later that evening, I spoke on the phone with my sister Debbie, and she laughed so hard she cried when I told her what Mother had done. Then, a few days later, when I talked with Debbie again she shared with me that she and her husband, Clay, had decided that a large ornamental goose would be the perfect Christmas present for Mother, in honor of her goose antics.

Tragically, in November, my fifty-two-year-old sister broke her ankle when she stepped off a curb the wrong way. She developed a blood clot and she passed away on Sunday, November 23rd. It all happened so suddenly, and it changed our family forever.

When Clay went to pick up Debbie's personal items from her office he found that she had asked her co-worker, Tamara, to be on the lookout for the biggest ornamental goose she could find. Tamara had bought a goose on the same day Debbie died. She had intended to surprise Debbie with it when she came back to work on Monday morning, but that was never to be.

At Christmastime, Clay and his sons Andy and Ben presented Mother with the goose as a gift from Debbie, Clay, and the boys. It started out as a gift with one meaning, but it ended up having a deeper purpose — reminding us of all the beautiful memories we had shared over the years.

"I hope you keep the goose and every time you look at it you think of Debbie," Clay said.

Clay reminded Mother that geese share the same attribute as he and Debbie's marriage had — they mate for life unless one of them is killed or dies.

Mother and I have gotten in the habit of walking down to the lake and looking for the geese every autumn. This year, as we walked down to the lake and watched for the geese to swoop down again, we could feel fall in the air. The migrating geese would be coming soon.

We stood at the lake, each of us thinking of Debbie. I was wishing there was a way for her to still be with us — some kind of sign that she was here and watching over us.

"Look, Jim!" Mother said.

I looked up to see a flock of geese flying above us in V- formation. I was speechless as they descended and glided effortlessly across the lake. My prayers had been answered.

Today that Canada Goose stands in Mother's den to remind us of Debbie's love for each of us, and the day the geese came to visit when we needed them most.

~Jim Luke

28

Chicken Soup for the Soul

Mom's Wish

Let perseverance be your engine and hope your fuel.
~H. Jackson Brown, Jr.

Mom came to live near us in Ohio after learning she had breast cancer. At eighty-eight, her memory was also failing. One evening, as we discussed the approaching holidays, I asked the question that had been on my mind for weeks.

"What's your Christmas wish?"

Thoughtfully, she gazed out at the tall pine trees lining her yard. John and I found her a place only five minutes from us, and she'd settled in nicely, already enjoying the wildlife appearing in her yard every day.

"I want a nativity scene just like the one we had on the Christmas tree farm years ago," she quietly confessed. "How about you? What's your wish?"

"To see you smile…" I murmured, fighting back tears.

"Sounds like we both could use that manger scene…"

I remembered that nativity well. Families arriving at our sixty-two-acre tree farm enjoyed visiting Mary, Joseph and Jesus, the three wise men, the shepherd and animals.

John and I got busy that night searching for large plastic molded figures like the ones Mom and Dad owned years ago. We couldn't find them anywhere, not even on the Internet.

Finally, we found a three-piece set consisting of Mary, Joseph and Baby Jesus at Kmart. We were still holding out for the eleven-piece set like the one Mom and Dad had years ago. Still, we ventured across town to purchase the three-piece set before they sold out, placing it in the corner of the garage.

John and his son made sketches of the stable they would build. Relatives made frequent calls, trying their best to locate the "rest" of the holy family.

"It seems like everyone is getting excited about my manger scene," Mom thoughtfully commented one evening, a big smile on her face.

Days passed, and we still hadn't gotten any closer to finding the remainder of the nativity scene. John and I had tons of errands to run and chores to do at our own home.

Then, Mom spent three days in the hospital. The nativity scene was all but forgotten… until one evening as we sat in front of a cozy fire watching a football game. I noticed John slowly rubbing his chin, a sure sign he was deep in thought.

"You know, my parents had a nativity scene when I was a little boy. I wonder if it's possible that those plastic figures are still stored away in the empty garage they once owned."

We drove across town to the garage, and started rummaging through hundreds of items that were still there. Suddenly John found it. I watched in amazement as he uncovered a tall shepherd holding a lamb, three wise men who'd seen better days, an angel, a camel, and a cow. There was a Mary figure too, but no Joseph or Baby Jesus.

"Let's get these guys home to our warm garage. I can get them in shape in no time!"

That evening, John powerwashed each figure. I set to work with brushes and paints.

When the paint dried, I called John out to the garage.

"They are even more beautiful than the original ones," he said. "But will they still light up?"

John slowly plugged each figure in one by one while I held my breath. Every single figure lit up as if fifty years had not passed.

"And remember, we have Mary, Joseph and Jesus. I'm so thankful we bought that threesome when we did!"

Hurriedly, we opened the box, placing the most important "part" of the scene in the center of the room. Since we now owned two "Mary's," I got busy transforming one of them into an angel with glistening wings.

The next day, John and his son erected the stable under the tall pines in Mom's front yard. We arranged the figures on top of mounds of straw and mounted a gold tree in the top branches of a nearby tree.

That night, as the lights twinkled and the figures beckoned the cars slowly making their way up the street, Mom's eyes filled with happy tears.

"Thank you for making my Christmas wish a reality."

The holidays were soon just happy memories. Winter snows melted, ushering in springtime's gentle rains. Tiny buds appeared on the trees… even the bird's cheerful song seemed different.

Mom had insisted we leave the nativity scene in the pine grove even though I thought it looked out of place.

One morning as I prepared Mom's bacon and eggs, I brought up the subject again.

"Mom, don't you think it's time to put the nativity scene in your barn until next year? We'll be putting your fountain out soon. It might look a bit cluttered having both out there."

Mom thoughtfully stirred her coffee before speaking.

"That scene bears a message. I want it to remain right where it is."

I swallowed the urge to argue, silently praying. An inner voice immediately answered.

"What difference does it make to you if your Mom wants to share her faith with others in this way?"

"Forgive me, Lord…"

The rest of the day flew by. Soon John and I were making our way back to Mom's with her evening meal and medicine.

Together, we shared dinner seated in front of her picture window. As the sun lowered in the sky, brushstrokes of purple, gold and orange painted God's awesome tapestry.

"Isn't the scenery beautiful here in the country?"

Suddenly Mom gasped.

"Look!"

John and I stared out across the acres of green. A ray of dappled evening light beamed across the lawn and directly onto the nativity scene. There, in the very center of it, knelt a young man. His head was reverently bowed, his hands clasped together. The three of us watched in silent awe.

"I wonder who he is…"

Before any of us could move, the young man disappeared.

I glanced over at Mom, unable to utter a sound. Her face was as radiant as the remaining beam of light.

"The manger scene remains," she quietly stated.

"You betcha!" I replied.

The heavenly angels had made that decision perfectly clear.

~Mary Z. Whitney

The Warning

*The tie which links mother and child is of such pure
and immaculate strength as to be never violated.*
~Washington Irving

I had felt that something was wrong ever since my seventeen-year-old daughter went out earlier that evening. Even after she came home and went to bed, I still felt a sense of foreboding. I kept telling myself, "She's safe. You just checked on her."

But that feeling of imminent doom continued to haunt me for the next hour. Then it stopped. I checked my daughter again and she was sleeping quietly.

The next morning we learned that a friend of my daughter's had died in an accident. It happened in those early morning hours when I lay awake, staring terrified into the blackness. My daughter's friend looked a lot like her and their birth dates were only weeks apart. And, most important, although they were unrelated to each other, their first and last names were identical in spelling.

From my earliest childhood, I had had this sixth sense that would alert me to significant happenings before they occurred. My family moved to Southern California when I was eight and for the next couple of years, I would always know when friends or relatives from Northern California were about to drop in to visit. Mom had learned to act on my feelings. She'd give the house a quick cleaning and make sure we were having a nice dinner. Late that afternoon, the very friends or relatives I had told her about would arrive to surprise us and find a sparkling clean house and the special dinner we "just happened" to be eating that night.

Several years later, on Christmas Eve, my daughters and I were supposed to drive up to visit my brother and his family about fifty miles from us in Washington State. We planned to get there in time for Midnight Mass.

But that afternoon, as I bustled about my house, wrapping presents and getting ready to leave, my happy thoughts about the coming evening suddenly turned dark. I felt that familiar heaviness settle in my stomach. I tried to ignore it. Everyone was expecting us. My mother was already there from California. This was Christmas, and bad things don't happen at Christmas. What could possibly be bothering me?

And then it came to me. Part of the drive to my brother's house was around a lake — on a curving stretch of two-lane road with high rocky bluffs on one side and a straight drop-off into deep water on the other. It was a beautiful drive on a sunny summer day, but a hazardous one on an icy winter night. Through the years, that deep lake had claimed many lives. Something was warning me not to take the drive that evening.

We couldn't go. But everyone was expecting us. My mother was already there. Reluctantly I called my brother's house. As Mom answered, my stomach continued to roil. When I explained, she didn't hesitate. "If something's not right, don't even think about coming out. Just take care of yourselves."

"We might be able to come tomorrow," I offered tentatively. "It's just tonight that's wrong."

"Only if you're sure. Don't take any chances."

I promised and hung up the phone. As I knelt again beside the wrapping paper and gifts, the feeling of foreboding left me.

The next morning was fine, and we drove to my brother's home. I didn't feel the slightest panic or uncertainty on any part of that ride, not even as we wound around the lakeshore and I stared into those freezing depths. I didn't hesitate either, when later that afternoon, my older daughter asked if she could take my car and drive home with my younger daughter and my niece. Mom and I planned to spend the night and drive back the next day in Mom's car. My sister-in-law and I gave permission, and the girls left for home.

When Mom and I got home the next afternoon, my older daughter, wide-eyed, greeted us. "Remember you were scared about driving on Christmas Eve?" I nodded.

She gestured to her younger sister. "Well, we didn't tell you, but we planned to ask if we could drive out in my car that night, instead of with you." She grinned sheepishly. "I know you would've agreed because I would've pestered you until you gave in. After we got home yesterday, we went for a ride in my car. We were in town, so I wasn't going fast. I pulled up to a stop sign and my brakes failed. I steered over to the side of the road and stopped, so we were all right."

Her next words came out in a rush. "I checked the odometer. The distance I drove yesterday afternoon, if I'd been driving on Christmas Eve night like I planned, we would have been at the lake when my brakes went out. I would have been going faster and wouldn't have been able to stop. Mom, we would have gone into the water."

I looked at my mother. She looked at me. Simultaneously, we lifted our eyes heavenward and fervently whispered, "Thank you."

~Louise Lenahan Wallace

Our Guardian Angels

*The guardian angels of life fly so high as to be beyond
our sight, but they are always looking down upon us.*
~Jean Paul Richter

I t had been a year of heartache. My father and my aunt died, and then I got laid off, followed soon thereafter by the hospitalization of my elderly mother. And then there was my divorce, too, and the sale of my house in a bad market.

And yet, the strange thing is, each day I felt like I was being helped.

Rentals were scarce in my neighborhood but one became available just when I needed it, and it was right around the corner from my sons' school.

The day the three of us moved into that rather dilapidated house, I realized the stove was not working, and while I was wondering what to do, there was a knock on the front door. A truck was parked on the road and its driver now stood in front of me. He was at the wrong address, but he was in the refurbished appliance business. I recall with clarity what I said to him: "You've got to be kidding me." I had a stove the next day.

My old car needed some work. My new neighbor turned out to be a mechanic who helped me very much, yet asked for very little.

With uncanny regularity, spaces in the crammed parking lots of the hospital, the lawyer's office and the stores became available exactly when and where I needed them.

And so it went, day after day, occurrences that singularly could be dispelled as coincidence, but collectively made me awestruck with wonder.

Christmas was coming, and my sons and I had decorated a tree, but there was no money for gifts. And even though I had recently turned forty and was indisputably an adult, I longed for the guidance of my mother, my father and my aunt.

As I was thinking about them, I prepared lunch for my boys, who would be home at any moment. Suddenly, a simple envelope with a law firm's name inscribed on the upper left corner flew through the mail slot and floated like a paper airplane over the scratched wooden floorboards of the tiny foyer. I didn't open it right away; I wasn't ready for negative news. I had had enough.

Later that day, the letter was still sitting on the counter. I stared it down for a moment as if I were accepting a challenge. I held it up to the light of the kitchen window to try to see inside it without actually opening it. Finally, I got up my nerve and sliced open the envelope with a knife from the kitchen drawer. A thick piece of paper came out — a letter. And a check!

The letter said it was a distribution from my aunt's estate, and that there would be more after this. I sat down on a kitchen chair and I cried. I cried for all the losses and I cried for all the undeniable wins.

I was quite aware that this check had come just in time to save our Christmas. The letter was dated December 17th. I can see that date whenever I want because it is hanging on my wall. I had the letter framed to honor my aunt and always remind me to never take for granted the help I received.

After I got that check, I was off to the mall, where the carols blaring from loudspeakers and the noise of shoppers in long lines were all music to my ears. Everything felt magical.

My older son wanted nothing but a puppy. That was it. No other toys or gifts; I had worried over how I would explain that we could not afford a dog, but now that problem was behind us. My son's one wish could come true.

He named her Merry, for Merry Christmas, and that Jack Russell

Terrier was his companion for the next fifteen years.

Ever since that magical time, when everything and everyone seemed to conspire to help us through a difficult time, I have believed in guardian angels. I have felt them all around me.

~Nancy Thorne

31

Chicken Soup for the Soul

The Reminder

Dreams are illustrations... from the book your soul
is writing about you.
~Marsha Norman

It was just before sunrise. I shuffled into the family room, which was aglow from the lights on the Christmas tree. The faint smell of pine drifted about. All was silent save for the old clock on the mantel ticking away.

At first I didn't notice him sitting on the couch.

When I did, I wasn't startled or surprised, even though it had been almost six years since I had seen him. For some reason I didn't find it strange, even though part of me said I should have.

He wore the old tattered yellow robe I remembered him wearing from my childhood. He didn't look like he did at the end of his life — taut, hallow and frail, just before God stopped his heart and called him home. No, he looked like he did when he was full of life. During that time when I was a boy and he mowed an acre of lawn on a hot summer day fueled only by a glass of sweet tea.

Now he was staring at the lights on the tree and gently petting the dog whose head rested on his lap. It was as if they'd been friends forever.

I sat on the floor in front of the couch near him, just as I did when I was little. I caught a hint of the Old Spice aftershave he always used.

"Hello, Dad," I said quietly.

He smiled, glanced at me, and then looked back at the tree. There was a soft glow on his face from the lights.

"You know something, son," he said. "This was always my favorite day of the year."

His voice was so familiar. That was the voice that used to chide me for not finishing my homework, or boom when he told me how proud he was of me. That voice would tell a story that brought laughter from everyone, or gently tell me that everything would be okay.

"I used to love Christmas Day," he said. "I loved the fact that for at least one day we were all together, all happy. That we were all a family."

He looked over at me. His gentle smile made me feel a warmth I had not felt in years.

"It didn't matter what happened the other 364 days of the year," he said. "For that one day…"

He chuckled, "You know your mom and I had our little disagreements through the years."

He looked back at the tree still smiling.

"We used to fight like cats and dogs," he sighed. "But that woman loved me unconditionally. And Lord knows I loved her. No matter what crazy scheme I had — buying that failing trucking company, moving halfway across the country — she stood by me. Didn't matter what it was; she kept me in clean underwear, kept our house clean, and kept you kids fed and healthy."

He was silent for a moment, stroking the dog's head.

"And you kids," he laughed quietly again. "Man, you kids used to argue, yell at each other."

"But you know something?" he said. "On Christmas Day, we were always together, happy. We were a family. Opening presents, smiling laughing. Eating way too much. Never arguing, just loving each other."

"God how I treasured that," his voice trailed off. He sighed before continuing. "It's a shame we could never carry that feeling over the rest of the year. It didn't seem long before we were back to the routine."

"Just a shame," he whispered.

He looked back at me. I remembered the same look from the times when he told me, "If you're going to do something, do it right, or don't do it at all."

"I hope you can understand it," he said. "Understand how lucky you are. You have people who love you unconditionally, a wife who keeps you in clean underwear, keeps your house clean and your kids fed.

"And those kids," he paused and smiled. "They are happy, healthy and thriving.

"Try to keep this feeling," he said. "The feeling on Christmas Day when you have your family all here, happy, healthy, smiling, laughing, loving one another. Try to keep that feeling every single day of the year.

"Never, ever lose that. That feeling of being grateful for what you have." He sighed again.

"There are richer men, bigger houses, people who have more 'things,'" he paused for a moment. "But there are many who will never know the love of a family.

"I was richer than any billionaire. Blessed beyond belief. Had more than I ever needed. I had you kids and your mom… and at the end of the day that's all I ever needed.

"And son, that's all you'll ever need, too."

He looked back at the tree.

"I had such a good life." A single tear rolled down his cheek. His voice was near a whisper. "A very good life. And every Christmas Day I was reminded of just how good a life I had."

I looked over at the tree, trying to soak in the words he had spoken. The lights blurred and merged as tears filled my eyes. As always, he was right.

But I wanted to hear more. Hear the voice that brought me so much comfort as a child. The voice that taught me so much. The voice that shaped the man — the father — that I have become.

As I turned, however, he was gone. My cheeks were damp. I wiped my face and then reached out and touched the spot where he had been sitting, hoping, praying he would return. The dog softly whimpered, but the spot remained empty. I imagined I could still detect the scent of Old Spice in the air, melting away and replaced with the scent of pine. The old clock on the mantel continued ticking.

I didn't want to wake up. I wanted to remain in the dream just a little longer.

Soon, I sat by the Christmas tree for real, looked at the glowing lights and smiled. Because I am grateful: for family, friends, and life.

I have a very good life, and every Christmas Day I am reminded just how good it is.

It's something we all need to remember. A feeling we should carry with us every single day of every single year. Whether we have a vivid dream to remind us or not.

~Greg Engle

32

Chicken Soup for the Soul

A Divine Mistake

Act as if what you do makes a difference. It does.
~William James

We were flying home after spending the Thanksgiving holiday with our children in California. We spotted a red scooter in the in-flight catalog, and even though it was for children and teens, we thought it might be fun to use on the bike path behind our house. When we got home, I ordered two scooters from the catalog.

The next day, I was surprised to see the identical scooter at our local discount store. It was ten dollars less than in the catalog, so I bought the scooters at the store, saving twenty dollars plus shipping. And now we had our scooters right away.

I called the catalog company and canceled the order. It was no problem.

We rode those scooters all December.

On Christmas Eve, which was a Saturday, I was making French toast when the doorbell rang. My husband answered the door and a deliveryman handed him a very large package that he signed for. Jokingly he asked me, "Hey, is it close enough to Christmas that we can open a gift?"

"Sounds good to me," I replied with a laugh.

I handed him the scissors and he carefully cut across the top of the brown wrapper and pulled out two boxes, each containing a red scooter. We were shocked. Looking at the return address label, my husband remarked, "I thought you canceled the catalog order."

"I did. I'll call again to make sure the scooters are deducted off my credit card and arrange to have them picked up."

I called and patiently explained to the customer service representative that I had canceled my order on November 29th, but it had been delivered anyway. She put me on hold for several minutes and then came back on the line and assured me that my order had been canceled on November 29th. In addition, she said there were no charges to my credit card and they had no record of shipping two red scooters to my address.

She told me to keep the scooters.

Since it was Christmas Eve I suggested to my husband that we call our pastor and ask if he knew of a family that needed presents for their kids. When Pastor Kim answered, my husband explained, "Pastor, we have ended up with two new red scooters for free. We were wondering if you knew of any kids that might need a present."

"Well this is certainly the right day for a miracle," said the pastor. "You see, I don't go to the church office on Saturdays because I am here all day on Sunday. But early this morning I had a feeling that I should go to my office. As soon as I walked in the door I received a phone call from a young mother of two elementary school children. She was crying and desperate because she had no gifts for them and their electricity and heat will be shut off on Monday. She was hoping someone from our church would help her. I told her I would call some members and see what I could do. I just hung up the phone from talking to her. And now you are calling with the very gifts she needs for her children."

I was excited. "Will you please call her right back? Tell her we will bring the red scooters to you."

"And the money to pay her utility bill too," added my husband.

"This is indeed a morning to remember," exclaimed Pastor Kim. "I'll call her back and wait here for you."

As I quickly wrapped each scooter in beautiful red and silver foil paper, I marveled at how this sequence of improbable events would help a young mother and her two children on Christmas Eve. My husband and I felt blessed to be part of this small Christmas miracle.

~Brenda Cathcart-Kloke

33

Our Christmas Angel

Unselfish and noble actions are the most radiant pages
in the biography of souls.
~David Thomas

In December 2000, I landed a contract programming mainframe computers for an investment company in Tacoma, Washington. My wife was seven months pregnant with our fifth child, and my other four children ranged in age from fifteen to seven. Suddenly, I was earning almost $100,000 a year, and we moved into a huge five-bedroom home two days before Christmas.

We had a great Christmas that year, and after our baby was born I was convinced that we had finally made it. I could provide my children with the lifestyle that they deserved. We ate out almost every night and we splurged on lots of silly things.

In August of 2001, I signed a three-year extension to this lucrative contract. I felt very secure in this job — definitely blind to reality. We spent money as if it grew on trees, and I hadn't even thought about saving for the proverbial rainy day.

Then, on September 11, 2001, when those towers fell in New York City, they brought my world down with them. The investment company that I was working for terminated all its programming contracts. My plans and dreams were gone in the blink of an eye.

As September gave way to October that year, we found ourselves living in a travel trailer at a state park campground. We had three dogs and five kids, the youngest just starting to walk. My income had gone from upper middle class to the poverty level overnight. I was reduced to surviving on a weekly unemployment check while I looked for work.

Needless to say I was feeling very bitter and depressed.

We were still in that trailer, moving from campground to campground throughout the fall. Thanksgiving came and went, and Christmas was approaching. By scrimping wherever we could, my wife and I had managed to set aside about $100 for gifts for the kids. It was sure to be a thin Christmas, but we would still make it as happy as possible for our family.

My youngest son made a friend that November, as only a seven-year-old can, and the two boys spent many days together. This other young fellow was at the campground visiting his grandmother, who had retired from a lifetime of teaching elementary school and was traveling in her RV. She took the boys on many a nature walk and even helped them make homemade Christmas presents for their families, using pinecones, bark, string, construction paper, and used candles.

About a week before Christmas, my son was gloomy. His friend's grandma was going to be moving on, and they would probably never see each other again. His newfound friend stopped by our campsite on the morning that they left, and his grandmother stopped by as well, for a cup of campfire coffee. We thanked her for the time she spent with the boys, and the help she gave them with their gifts.

As she was leaving, she turned to my wife and said, "Oh, I almost forgot. This is for your family." She handed my wife an envelope, and then with a smile and a wave, she was gone. My wife opened the envelope. Inside was a card, and as my wife read it, her eyes filled with tears. I asked her what it said, and she just handed it to me, unable to speak.

It was just a simple Christmas card, but when I opened it up, I was rocked to my core.

Inside was a handwritten message that said, "I am only one, but still I am one. I cannot do everything, but still I can do something; and because I cannot do everything, I will not refuse to do something that I can do. May your family be blessed this Christmas." Inside were ten crisp twenty-dollar bills.

To this day, I am moved to tears by that wonderful woman's spirit of love and compassion. I wish I could have thanked her in person. She'll never know that in one single moment she not only tripled our Christmas budget but also showed us the true meaning of Christmas. Her gift was more than just generous; it touched all of our lives in a huge way.

The following year was a better one, and one of the ways that we attempted to pay it forward was by taking Christmas dinner to a few people who were in that campground for the holiday. Giving away those food bags felt as good as getting any present I ever remember.

Sometimes the special angels in your life appear from nowhere, and they touch you before moving on. I wish that I had known our Christmas angel better, for the day she gave us her gift, I became her student, and I hope that someday I too can change a family's life like she did ours that day.

~Dusty Grein

The Joy of Christmas

Family Fun

We didn't realize we were making memories, we just knew we were having fun.
~Author Unknown

34

Turnabout Is Fair Play

Adulthood is when the ghosts of childhood appear.
~Terri Guillemets

When my daughter Jennie was old enough to know that Christmas morning meant colorfully wrapped surprises, she began creeping down the stairs at about 3:00 a.m. Because I'm a mother (or maybe just because we lived in a creaking, ancient farmhouse), I'd hear her footsteps no matter how quietly she descended.

"Go back to bed," I'd whisper from our bedroom door at the foot of the steps. "It's too early to get up." Eventually we made it a rule that she could not leave her room until 5:00 a.m.

Just before five, I'd hear her cross the hall to her older brother's room. "Chris, it's almost time." And as the clock struck the hour, her insistent "Chris, we can go down now, wake up!"

When he was young, Chris would leap up at her call, as eager as she was to open gifts. When he became older, he reluctantly obeyed. As an adolescent, he ignored her badgering as long as possible. He eventually relented — Jennie was difficult to ignore. Her wakeful vigil didn't wane until she reached her teens.

As annoying as those pre-dawn dramas were, when they ceased, I missed them. The delight of Christmas morning was diminished when there were no stage whispers or urgency to open gifts. With the onset of the teen years, the children stayed up watching movies at night, so

Christmas morning arrived later and later.

Eventually, I became the one to yell up the stairway. "It's nine. Let's open presents!" They'd come downstairs in robes and slippers, rubbing their eyes. Christmas became a subdued event. No squeals of delight, just a simple thank you and "I think I'll go back to bed for a while."

One Christmas Eve I had not yet wrapped any of the presents piled in my closet. When the kids had finished watching their movie, my husband Jim and I commandeered the television. (This was in the day when households had only one set.) It was after one by the time Chris and Jennie were asleep. Although exhausted, I still had a job to do.

I pulled out the presents I had squirreled away, along with paper, tape, scissors, and a bed sheet to cover everything if a child came downstairs before I was finished. I wrapped gifts until three while Jim watched and we reminisced about other Christmases. We laughed as we recalled Jennie's impatience for Christmas to arrive and the many times we had sent her back to bed.

Jim said, "I'm tired. I plan on sleeping until noon."

"We can't sleep in. We need to get up at a decent hour to open presents. Then go to my folks for dinner."

"Let's wake the kids and open presents right now," he suggested. "They've awakened us enough in their lifetimes. It's our turn."

I laughed at the idea, but when Jim persisted, I finally agreed that it was "poetic justice." We went to the bottom of the stairway and between bursts of laughter, called to them, "Wake up, it's time to open presents." When there was no response, we yelled louder. Jim thumped on the walls until two sleepy faces appeared from opposite doorways.

"What's going on?"

"It's time to open presents!"

"What time is it anyway?"

"Present opening time. The same time you used to wake us up."

They shuffled down the stairs in their pajamas and bare feet, shaking their heads at our antics. "I can't believe you woke us up this early," Chris groused, then chuckled. Jennie seconded the complaint with, "This is stupid," but giggled.

We took turns tearing open our presents, then drank cups of

hot chocolate. When we were ready to call it a night (or a morning,) one of the children said, "Let's not make a habit of this." The other repeated with a shake of the head, "I can't believe this. Don't you know kids need their sleep?" I wondered if the next day would bring further recriminations.

The next afternoon, however, when we gathered with extended family, Jennie and Chris boasted to their cousins, "You won't believe what our parents did. They got us up in the middle of the night to open presents!"

Years later, when the gifts were long forgotten, the memory of this early awakening lived on. In the re-telling of the tale it became even funnier and now it's our favorite family Christmas story.

~Diana L. Walters

35

Chicken Soup for the Soul

The Christmas Breeze Box

If you carry your childhood with you, you
never become older.
~Abraham Sutzkever

My brother and I were examining the cardboard shoebox in the back of the hall closet. He took the top of the box off as he explained, "We can use this box to catch a cold Christmas breeze."

"A Christmas breeze?"

My brother and I lived in a small, desert town where the only breezes that blew were hot Santa Ana winds. I didn't understand what my brother was talking about, but he was eight years older, so I trusted him.

"Santa left this last Christmas. I asked him for a breeze from the North Pole." He shrugged his shoulders. "You know. To prove that he's real."

My eyes widened. "Santa gave you a breeze from the North Pole?"

"Oh, yeah. When I opened it, a cold wind blew out and brushed against my face. It had snowflakes and everything."

I was speechless as I envisioned my brother surrounded by a frosty magical swirl of snowflakes and Christmas glitter.

He nodded. "And, next weekend, Mama and Daddy are taking us to the mountains for the day. Surely there will be snow there. I'll use this box to capture a breeze. Then, I'll have it in case I need it."

"Why would you need it?"

"For a day in July when it's hot and sweaty and the air conditioner is broken. I'll pull out my captured breeze and use it to cool down. But, don't tell anyone else."

"Why not?"

He leaned in my direction. "They'll want to steal it from us."

I immediately became my brother's accomplice in this breeze capturing endeavor. I searched the house over for another cardboard box.

The next weekend our family went to the mountains and my brother and I ran back and forth with our boxes, attempting to trap the wind. After our boxes were full, we quickly closed the lids. When we arrived home, my brother stored our boxes in the garage refrigerator.

"We don't want the cold breeze to spoil," he winked.

"Mikey, could we save mine for Christmas?" I asked

"Christmas? Don't you want it to cool off on a hot day?"

He went on to paint the scene for me: He and I on the front porch, waving our snowy breezes, the envy of the neighborhood.

"But, I would love a snowy breeze Christmas morning. We never get snow here on Christmas. This way we could."

"Well, okay." It was agreed.

From that moment on, I kept an eye on our breeze boxes. My greatest worry was that they would be thrown out accidentally.

Sure enough, we had a sizzling day in July when the temperature soared past 100 degrees. My brother and I sat on the front porch, attempting to cool off.

"I think it's time for a snowy breeze," I said.

My brother slowly nodded his head and then led me to the garage. He opened the refrigerator and dug out one of the breeze boxes.

"Now," he warned, "once it is released, there's no getting it back in the box. We'll have to wait until next winter to get another one."

I eyed him seriously. "Do you think we should save it?"

"Maybe. There might be a day even hotter than this. And, our AC might break."

"Better put it back just in case."

And, there it stayed for I don't know how long.

But, one summer day, years later, when it was warmer than expected, I told my own two young daughters the story of Uncle Mike's breeze box.

When I was finished my older daughter had an idea. "Maybe we should have a warm breeze box." She shrugged. "You know. To help keep warm on a cold, snowy day. We do live in snow country, after all. A warm breeze box makes more sense."

She found an old shoebox, laid it out on the grass to trap sunbeams, I suppose, and went off to dance in a sprinkler.

That next December, the first item on my girls' Christmas list was a wish for a captured North Pole breeze. Uncle Mike explained that due to the population increase since the 1970's, Santa isn't able to send out snowy breezes to every family. There's only so much snow up there.

But, that Christmas, a certain little girl decided that she should give a gift to Santa instead — a warm breeze box. She left it under the tree for him, with "To: Santa" carefully written on the lid. She hoped he would notice it and take it with him.

And, by all accounts, he did.

~Michele Boom

36

Best House Ever

*There are no seven wonders of the world in the eyes of
a child. There are seven million.*

~Walt Streightiff

Even though I was a single parent on a limited budget, my
son Ryan and I always had a special Christmas. I bought
decorations for our tree at yard sales and purchased our
Christmas gifts throughout the year when I saw a good
deal. We put up our tree in late November and took our time decorating it. We always made some decorations ourselves, as our little
fake tree needed all the help it could get.

The year Ryan turned six years old I decided we would make our
own gingerbread house. While I am a good cook, I am a notoriously
bad baker. However, I convinced myself that making gingerbread from
scratch would be even easier than making cake from a box.

Although I was always on a budget, I dropped my inhibitions for
our fantasy gingerbread house. Ryan and I had a grand time selecting
lots of candies to decorate our edible house.

The plan was to bake the gingerbread one evening and assemble
the house, then decorate it the following evening. Ryan was so excited
that he told his friends, teachers and anyone else who would listen.

I picked Ryan up early from daycare on that first Monday in
December. We measured and mixed and rolled out our gingerbread.
Then, with ruler in hand, I carefully cut the four walls and two roof

parts that we needed. I had a picture from a magazine that I used as my guide. We ate dinner while the gingerbread baked, and while it cooled we prepared our work area on the dining room table. Ryan sorted the candies onto separate plates while I mixed up a bowl of stiff icing to use as the glue for the walls and roof.

My first indication that we had a problem was when I realized that my gingerbread pieces were as heavy as bricks. There was no way our icing would hold the pieces in place. We tried everything from thickening the icing to using books to hold the four walls together, but nothing worked.

Our fun project had turned into an exercise in frustration as the four walls of the house imploded over and over again. Ryan was relieved when I told him we were going to stop working on our house for the evening. After his bath and bedtime story he quickly fell into a deep sleep.

I went back to the dining room table and studied my poor excuse for a gingerbread house. I realized that no one would ever be able to eat these rock pieces of gingerbread so there was no sense continuing the process with edible icing. Out came the real glue.

And then I had a great idea. I found cardboard and some duct tape, and I made a model of our gingerbread house. When that was as sturdy as possible, I glued the gingerbread pieces to the cardboard interior. Done! By 1:00 a.m. I had a gingerbread house that was ready to be decorated.

Ryan was so excited when he found our sturdy gingerbread house the next morning.

That evening I sat back, listened to Christmas songs on the radio and watched my six-year-old have a great time gluing candy to his house and its cardboard base. The next day we put it out for display on the coffee table beside our tree. A few days later one of his friends came for a visit and, as they looked at the oddly decorated house, I heard Ryan proudly explain that NOTHING on his gingerbread house could be eaten because it was held together with REAL GLUE.

I loved Ryan's view of our world as a child, especially during Christmas. Through his eyes I could see that we did indeed own the most special Christmas tree in the world and that standing beside it was the best gingerbread house ever to grace a table.

The best Christmas gift Ryan ever gave me was when, as an adult, he told me that he never knew we didn't have a lot of money. In his mind we'd been wealthy because we so frequently had the most special things in the entire world — like our Christmas tree and that little, glued-together gingerbread house.

~Laura Snell

Home

*Christmas is, of course, the time to be home — in
heart as well as body.*
~Garry Moore

I t was my first year away at college, and I had not planned on
going home for the holidays. I wasn't alone — I was actually
staying with different friends on the East Coast. Home for me
was Indiana, but instead I was jumping between New York,
Connecticut, and Vermont.

Traveling over the holidays was actually quite nice. My friends
were all warm and comforting. Their families also were immensely
gracious, offering me kind hugs and genuine smiles as though I were
of their own blood. However, the warmth I saw in these households
made me miss my own mother even more. She was back in Indiana
with my three younger brothers spending her first Christmas and New
Year's without her only daughter.

It was Christmas Day when I decided I would go back.

I purchased a round-trip ticket to Indianapolis, with a return to
New York before my classes would start up again. My friend Casey and
her father drove me to Westchester Airport a few days after Christmas.

On the way, Casey turned to look at me in the back seat and
asked, "So, is your mom excited?"

"She doesn't know I'm coming," I said, feeling a tinge of excitement at the prospect of surprising her. I had missed my opportunity

to do so on Christmas, but at least I would be able to surprise her for New Year's.

Casey's grin widened, clearly thrilled at the idea of my surprising my mother as well. "Oh my gosh, she's going to love that!"

The flight to Indianapolis was fairly short, and I arrived in the evening. I collected my bag and went outside to wait for my ride. I had called a family friend, Sabrina, to pick me up. After explaining my intent to surprise everyone, she had been more than happy to help me by sneaking me into my house. Sabrina had spoken with my family earlier that day, so she knew my mother and brothers were out at the moment.

As we drove back, I answered Sabrina's daughter Abby's questions about what my life in New York was like. I stopped suddenly as I noticed a car driving behind us. We were about to pull into the driveway of my family's house, and on impulse I ducked down. Sabrina looked at me confused.

"What are you doing?" she asked.

"I'm pretty sure it's my mom and brothers driving behind us."

"Oh dang," she said, before turning back to Abby. "Abby, sweetie. When we get out we can't say Layla's here. Layla needs to be invisible."

Abby nodded, eager to be a part of our "game."

Before getting out, Sabrina glanced at me. "Wait here. I'll text you when I'm inside and you can come in and surprise her."

I remained hidden as Sabrina and Abby got out of the car. Outside, I could hear my mother and brothers greet them. It was only a moment before the voices faded and I knew they had all gone inside.

Five minutes later, Sabrina texted me that it was time. I felt a rush of adrenaline as I got out of the car and made my way to the front door. Quietly, I opened it, sneaking in and shutting the door as quietly as possible. I could hear voices in the kitchen as I crept to the doorway.

"Hello!" I exclaimed, my voice light and an octave higher than normal.

My mother gasped. As soon as she realized I was really there, her blue eyes got watery. She gave me a tight hug.

"Oh, Mom, don't cry," I said, not expecting the reaction I got.

But as my mom parted from me, I could hear the crack in her voice as she tried to speak. "I didn't know you were coming home."

I smiled, feeling a strange and almost overwhelming sense of emotion myself. "I wanted to surprise you."

My mom, still almost sobbing, asked how I got there, and if anyone knew. Sabrina chimed in that no one else knew as she filmed the whole interaction with her phone. I had almost forgotten she was there.

The truth was, it hadn't felt like the holidays until I went home. Now that I was there, I felt like I was starting Christmas all over again — my real Christmas.

~Layla Tavassoli

Pajama Joyride

*In childhood, we press our nose to the pane, looking
out. In memories of childhood, we press our nose
to the pane, looking in.*
~Robert Brault

"Wake up, Sweet Pea!" Momma leaned over my bed. Confused, I sat up and looked around. The moon still glowed high in the sky through my curtains. It couldn't be time to get up. My eight-year-old eyes were still clouded with sleep. I walked over to my closet to get dressed, but Momma stepped in my way.

"We're going on an adventure!" She grabbed my hand and picked up my slippers from the floor of my closet. I reached behind me to get my Christmas angel doll from my bed and smoothed her pink silk dress as we descended the staircase hand in hand.

Momma's eyes danced with excitement, and she looked up at my daddy, who led the twins down the staircase behind us. Each of them clutched a stuffed toy soldier in his arms. We walked single-file past our twinkling Christmas tree and out the front door into the cold Chicago wind.

Our trusty red station wagon waited for us in the driveway. Ruby had traveled many miles with us, and another adventure was in the making. Jonathan and Benjamin curled up on either side of me in the back seat. The soft wool blanket surrounded our legs, and we sat wide-eyed, hugging our Christmas dolls.

"We're going on a pajama joyride!" Momma exclaimed. Handing me a stack of Christmas books on tapes, she said, "Pick one!"

Ruby took us all around the western Chicago suburbs that night. We saw Christmas lights of all colors: classy white, neon, and colored. There were decorations in all shapes and sizes: light-up reindeer, blow-up Santa Clauses, and nativity scenes.

The warmth from Ruby's heater could not compare to the warmth in my little heart.

Giggles of joy quickly turned into squeals of excitement as our joyride ended in the parking lot of Krispy Kreme Doughnuts. The "hot n' ready" sign glowed like a beacon in the night. We scrambled out of the car and into the shop.

Our noses left tiny prints on the glass. We gaped in amazement at the machinery that made the glorious glazed doughnuts. Our three little bodies squeezed into one side of a small booth.

We devoured doughnuts as the five of us critiqued the lit-up houses we had seen on our joyride. We walked out of the store, sticky hand in sticky hand, and cuddled up in Ruby's back seat for the ride home. We went back to bed that night with smiles on our doughnut-glazed faces.

We're in our early twenties now. Beloved Ruby has been replaced more than once. Our legs are longer and our pajamas no longer have attached feet. The books on tape have been replaced by iPods blasting Christmas songs. We moved five times, too. Yet, every year, we're still surprised when Mom announces we're going on a pajama joyride.

~Emily Morgan

All Grown Up

*Grandmas don't just say "that's nice" — they reel back
and roll their eyes and throw up their hands and smile.
You get your money's worth out
of grandmas.
~Author Unknown*

Christmas shopping with my fourteen-year-old grandson was a new experience for me. He had a long list of family and friends for whom he wanted to buy gifts, and he had jotted down some ideas. He brought money he had earned himself.

My role was to drive him to the requested stores and occasionally (when asked) give my opinion on an item. It was a sharp contrast from previous years when he seemed to disappear down the toy aisle, scribbling a list of the things *he* wanted.

I enjoyed the adult camaraderie and marveled at how much he had grown up as we started toward the door of our third store. He stopped suddenly at a display of wallets, and admired a black leather trifold one. After thoroughly examining it he set it back down and courteously held the door for me as we continued out of the store.

I wondered if he wanted the wallet for himself. I needed a gift idea. I didn't even have to ask.

"Gramama, I really need a new wallet," he said as he pulled a shabby billfold from his pocket.

"Score," I thought to myself. I would go back and get the new wallet for him later. But I wanted to make sure I got the right one, so I casually asked, "So what features do you look for in a wallet?"

"MONEY," he replied.

I guess he really *had* grown up!

~Kathie Slief

40

Eli Has Left the Building

*Being a family means you are a part of something very
wonderful. It means you will love and be loved for
the rest of your life.*
~Lisa Weedn

"I don't want Eli to go," whispered six-year-old Madi,
the youngest of our three girls. It was December 23rd,
almost time for Eli, our house elf, to return to the
North Pole.

Madi looked up at Eli perched on the fireplace mantel, his lips
frozen in a joyous smile that reached right up his rosy cheeks. She
crawled onto the couch with me, squirming her way under my quilt
and resting in my lap. I stroked her hair. "Eli will always be part of our
family. Enjoy the time we have with him now so it's special," I said.
She still looked worried.

"I'll miss him," she said.

"I bet he'll miss you too."

Eli was named after Madi's kindergarten crush, and we were now
stuck with the name even after she decided that the human Eli was
icky. He arrived every year on the first of December to observe our
three girls and report back to Santa on their behavior.

Eli takes an interest in our family activities. When we painted
acrylic Christmas trees and Santa Claus's boots, we left out a brush
and canvas for Eli. While snug in our beds, Eli painted us a picture

Family Fun | 123Family Fun | 123

of a wrapped present and signed his name. We hung his canvas on the wall with ours.

We dug out our big book of short Christmas stories to read a few each night leading up to Christmas. One morning we caught Eli sitting with the book in his lap turned to the first page of the next story. Eli likes to hear holiday stories just like us.

When we baked chocolate chip cookies to prepare for Santa's arrival, we awoke in the morning to find Eli had decorated them with red and green sprinkles.

Madi looked forward to getting up every morning to see what Eli had done overnight.

On Christmas Eve morning, Madi woke me with urgent news. Her little face was almost touching mine and her eyes were wide as saucers. "Mommmm," she whispered breathlessly.

"What, honey? You hungry? What time is it?"

"There's a big present in the living room. Can I open it?"

"Um, really?" I swung my legs to the floor. Madi grabbed my hand and led me to the living room. Sure enough, there sat a large box wrapped in shiny red and white striped paper and topped with a big red bow. I sent Madi to wake up everyone else.

Then, with everyone gathered around the mystery present, I lifted the tag and read aloud, "To my family. From Eli, your house elf. Thank you for welcoming me into your home and for letting me join your family activities. I've never had a family before. Now I can say I do. I will miss you all so much this year. I can't wait until next December. I hope we paint again. That was my favorite. I cannot wait to report all the good things about your family to Santa. Love, Eli."

"We'll miss you too, Eli!" Madi said. The three sisters went to work tearing off the paper and opening the top of the box.

The girls shrieked as they pulled out the gifts inside. There were Christmas-themed pajamas for each member of our family, popcorn, cocoa and a Christmas movie. They ran off to try on their pajamas.

I looked up at Eli's favorite perch on the Christmas tree, now empty.

"Thanks, Eli," I said. I looked forward to sharing our traditions again with him the next year. I would miss him, too.

~Mary Anglin-Coulter

Home Sweet Home

*The light is what guides you home, the warmth is
what keeps you there.*
~Ellie Rodriguez

Sitting through Sunday morning church in a crowded hotel room wasn't my two-year-old daughter's idea of a good time. I scooped her onto my lap. She squirmed in protest and scolded me in Cantonese. Fortunately, Hannah wasn't the only antsy little girl. Several other couples from our adoption group entertained their own fidgety daughters.

I grabbed the Christmas book I'd brought from home. Home. After twenty hours on a plane and two weeks of traveling on buses and boats to various areas of China, I was exhausted and so ready to go home. We just needed to get our visas and final paperwork, and then we could take our daughter home.

Hannah flipped open the book to a picture of baby Jesus. I knew she didn't understand, but I wanted to at least introduce her to Christmas. It seemed strange. Christmas was only a few days away, yet nothing around us looked like it.

"Are there any prayer requests?" The pastor interrupted my thoughts.

My husband lifted his hand. "Hannah."

Since the day we first met her, Hannah had been fighting a raspy cough and itchy rash. The orphanage gave us a tube of white cream. So far, it hadn't helped.

She wiggled on my lap and scratched her tummy. Poor little girl, I thought. Not sick enough to go to a hospital, but sick enough to feel miserable. Doug and I planned to take her to our family doctor as soon as we returned home.

We ended the service with a few Christmas carols. My mind drifted back home. By now, family members would be almost finished with last-minute holiday details. Gifts would be wrapped. Cookies baked. I could almost smell the delicious aroma of my mom's homemade potato soup. Every Christmas Eve my siblings and I gathered at Mom's for soup and presents after church. I longed to share those simple family traditions with our new daughter.

I touched Hannah's forehead. Still warm. Sadly, Christmas Eve at Grandma's house would have to wait until next year.

Two nights later we arrived in Guangzhou. As we drove to the hotel I stared out the window, mesmerized. I couldn't believe it. The entire city was decorated for Christmas. Garland and ribbon covered festive trees. Streets sparkled with colorful lights. The beauty took my breath away. Now more than ever, I longed to celebrate Hannah's first Christmas with our families.

Then we heard wonderful news: our visas came early! My mind started spinning. Maybe we could change our flights. Hannah could see the doctor sooner and get started on the proper medicine. She might even feel better by Christmas. Leaving early could make a huge difference.

All morning I called the airline. Each time I spoke with a different person, yet always heard the same disappointing news. "Sorry Ma'am, we can't change your ticket. It's too close to Christmas."

My hope of spending a traditional Christmas at home was crushed right along with my spirits. I decided to get some fresh air. I'd spotted a gift shop within walking distance of the hotel. Maybe I could find something to keep Hannah occupied in the hotel room.

I stood in the gift shop and gazed at a shelf full of toys. Sweet, little baby dolls. Brightly-colored stacking blocks. I picked up a package of rattles and shook them in my hand.

Suddenly, my eyes filled with tears. For years my husband and I had prayed for a child of our own. Now here we were with our own precious little girl. What more did we need? It really didn't matter if we were home, in China or sitting in the waiting room at the doctor's office. We could celebrate our first Christmas as a family anywhere!

Now that I was reconciled to spending Christmas in China, what did I hear on the way back to my room but that two other couples from our group had been allowed to change their airline tickets? Doug and I looked at one another. What did we have to lose? I called the airline one more time.

"Listen," I said, taking a deep breath. "I have a sick little girl that needs to get to the States and see a doctor. Now I know you can do this. You did it for my friends, and you can do it for us."

I plopped onto a chair as annoying music blared into my ear while I waited on hold. Doug gave me a questioning look.

Within a minute, the lady returned to the line. "I think I can help you."

I jumped to my feet. "Yes!" I'd reached the right person. We were finally going home.

That Christmas Eve we attended church with our family. I gazed down at my beautiful little girl in her red velvet dress and black, shiny shoes. After two days of antibiotics, Hannah felt much better even though she still didn't sit quietly.

Later, at Mom's house, I changed Hannah into comfortable clothes, including a brand-new sweatshirt from my grandmother displaying a little house and the words "Home Sweet Home." The words on the front seemed so appropriate, and Hannah, now twenty-three, still treasures it.

I slipped the sweatshirt over Hannah's head. "Home Sweet Home," my mom said, reading it aloud. She patted Hannah's head. "Are you glad to be home, Hannah?" Hannah didn't respond. She just smiled, grabbed her spoon and shoveled in some more of Grandma's delicious potato soup.

~Stacie Chambers

St. Lucia Surprise

Grandchildren are the dots that connect the lines from
generation to generation.
~Lois Wyse

Ffft. The match flares orange, creating a pinpoint of light in the December darkness. It is 6:30 a.m. and my ten-year-old twin daughters and I stand in my mother-in-law's driveway, shivering. Underneath their white dresses, the girls wear long johns and winter boots, but still, without coats, hats, and mittens, they're uncomfortable. We'd better get moving.

I light the candle and hand it to Chloe.

"What about my crown?" Leah whispers.

From the car, I get her headpiece — a crown of plastic candles topped with battery-operated bulbs — and set it on her head. Then I grab the boom box. "Let's go."

The crown and candle glow as we creep, giggling conspiratorially, up the steps to Sylvia's front door.

"Do you think she's awake?" Chloe asks.

The house is dark. "I don't think so."

"What if she doesn't hear the doorbell?" Leah worries.

There's only one way to find out. One of us presses it. After a minute passes with no response, I knock. Loudly.

Soon we hear footsteps. Fingers trembling with excitement, I press the play button on the boom box and the strains of a Swedish holiday folk song fill the starry morning.

"San-ta Lu-ciiiia, Santa Lucia."

When the chorus starts, we sing along as Sylvia, wearing a bathrobe and looking sleep-rumpled, opens the door.

***

As mothers-in-law go, Sylvia is a keeper. She's easygoing, loves to spend time with my girls, and never criticizes my housekeeping. But we are very different. She's a go-getter; she has loads of friends, and is usually out with one of them — seeing a play, attending a quilt show, or biking a wooded trail. I, on the other hand, have a few close, trusted friends, abhor busyness (and biking), and can easily spend hours in the bathtub reading a book. At times, our differences have led to misunderstandings.

Several years ago, Sylvia planned a picnic. We were to drive an hour to a park where we'd spend the morning with my husband's sister and her family. When the day arrived, everyone was ready to go except me. It had been a busy week, and I needed time to refuel. My husband was fine with my last-minute decision to stay home, but when he returned from the picnic, I found out that Sylvia hadn't been.

He repeated part of their conversation: "Doesn't Sara like us?" Sylvia had asked. "Why doesn't she come to more family events?"

"Of course she likes you," he had said. "She just needs a lot of alone time."

I pressed my husband for details. "What did she say to that?"

"I don't think she understood," he said. "You know what she's like; she hates being alone for more than a few hours."

I felt hurt, defective, and a bit anxious — not the best state of mind for resolving a conflict. But remaining silent had caused problems for me before. That's why, when Sylvia stopped by later that evening, I took a deep, wobbly breath and confronted her.

"I hear you think I don't like you."

She looked uncertain. "Oh, it's not that. I just... I just don't understand why you don't come to things sometimes. Explain it to me."

So I tried to explain my introverted personality. In the end, she accepted what I said. But in spite of the hug that ended our conversation, I was left with a nagging inner need to show my affection for her.

Several months later, my daughters and I visited the American Swedish Institute in Minneapolis. On our tour, we learned about St. Lucia Day, celebrated on December 13th in Sweden.

In the Swedish tradition, the oldest daughter in the family wakes her parents on St. Lucia morning (one of the darkest days of the years) by singing to them. Wearing a white dress and a crown of candles on her head, she serves buns, cookies, and coffee. Other children in the family carry candles or star-tipped wands.

I'd heard about this holiday from Sylvia; she had celebrated it years before at the Swedish Lutheran church in her South Dakota hometown. Often, she'd recounted how she'd worn the crown (lit with real candles!) and served cookies to the ladies of the church on St. Lucia Day — which also happened to be her birthday.

Remembering that, I had an idea on the way home from the Institute: "Girls, wouldn't it be fun if we showed up at Grandma's door on St. Lucia morning?"

I bought white dresses and a crown online and borrowed a Swedish music CD from the library. We baked pepparkakor and luciakatter — ginger cookies and saffron-flavored buns — and picked up Scandinavian-blend coffee beans at the grocery store. On St. Lucia Eve, we laid everything out, ready for an early start the next morning. It was going to be an excellent surprise.

***

But now, as we wait for Sylvia to answer the door, I feel a pang of uncertainty. Will she think this is as fun an idea as I do? After all, we are so very different.

Her reaction puts my fears to rest.

"Oh, oh, oh!" she cries, her face beaming as she reaches out to hug us.

Inside, we sit around her kitchen table. While munching cookies and buns and drinking coffee with lots of milk and sugar, the girls excitedly rehash every moment of the morning for Sylvia: what time they got up, how we worried she might not be home, how cold it was standing in her driveway. After laughing and talking for an hour, we go out into a frigid, sunny morning, feeling warmed by her declaration that we've given her the best birthday surprise ever.

That was four Decembers ago. We've been "surprising" Sylvia ever since, and we intend to continue. The tradition has changed a bit over time; we sing the song ourselves (in English) instead of playing it on the boom box, the girls trade off wearing the candle crown, and we all go out to breakfast at our favorite pancake house afterward.

However it looks, our December 13th visit to Sylvia's house has become one of my favorite holiday traditions. Besides being unusual and celebrating my daughters' ethnic heritage, it gives me a chance to remind my mother-in-law that, even though I'm not a social butterfly, I like being with her.

Even at six-thirty in the morning.

~Sara Matson

Nice and Ugly

*Thanks for going to the holiday office party in a
Christmas sweater that's more embarrassing
than my behavior.*
~Author Unknown

My dad knew that Mom only wanted one thing for Christmas: clothes. But my poor father had no idea what to buy her. The year before she had returned almost every present he had given her.

He decided I would help him. I was fifteen years old, opinionated and fashion-minded. We set out on a shopping expedition and it was going great. We had spent the entire day buying clothes Mom would love.

Then Dad saw the display of Christmas sweaters. They were hideous—some red, some green, some glittery, others depicting cute, fuzzy forest creatures in the snow.

Dad said that his one success every year was when he bought Mom the ugliest, gaudiest Christmas sweater he could find. Over my objections, he purchased one with a Christmas tree that lit up and played music.

On Christmas morning, Dad and I exchanged glances as Mom began to open the ugly sweater. She gasped and I thought, "Ah ha! I knew it!" I smirked at my father.

"How cute!" Mom said, and lifted the sweater from the box, holding it in front of her. She swooned when Dad showed her the button that lit the tree up and played the "O Christmas Tree" tune.

Dad grinned at me and winked.

Mom loved all her presents that year. The pants fit. The dresses were the right color. The blouses were age appropriate. So every year thereafter, my father and I would hit the malls together and spend the entire day shopping for Mom's Christmas presents. As I got older, married and had a child of my own, our tradition still continued. This was an annual father-daughter date.

Years after that first Christmas shopping trip for Mom, Dad and I stood in the department store arguing over Christmas sweaters, yet again. I had spent every one of the last eleven years attempting to stop my dad from buying ugly Christmas sweaters for Mom.

"Your mom doesn't think they are ugly," he would always say, and purchase one anyway.

This time, I had found an elegant, expensive Christmas sweater—a black silky cardigan embroidered with small red and green beads forming a beautiful pattern of poinsettias on the right shoulder. It would look beautiful on my mom.

Dad insisted on the sweater he was holding. It featured six different multicolored fabrics sewn together with a different dancing snowman on each color block, and it didn't even look Christmassy. "That sweater looks like a kindergarten teacher's dream, Dad. Please, no," I pleaded.

"Tell you what. You buy your fancy-schmancy sweater, and I'll buy this one. She will open both and we will see whose sweater she likes better," he proposed.

"Deal," I said, confident I wasn't losing this bet.

On Christmas morning, my family arrived at my parents' house to celebrate and eat. The time to open presents came and we gathered around the Christmas tree. Mom opened my present first.

"It's nice," she said and smiled. "I love the material."

I smirked at my father, who pretended not to notice.

Then she opened Dad's. And gasped.

"It's adorable! Where did you find it?" she exclaimed. She stood up and pulled the dancing snowmen on over her shirt.

She looked down at the red, orange, purple, yellow, black and blue color blocks, the snowmen appearing to dance to celebrate their victory.

Dad smiled and winked. Words were not needed. I knew I lost. I didn't know this woman better than this man. They had been married for thirty-five years.

Dad passed away from cancer before the next Christmas. Mom still wears all the ugly Christmas sweaters Dad bought her, and somehow they don't appear as ugly to me as they once did. I smile when I see her donning the sparkly green argyle, the kitten popping out of the present, or the multi-colored snowmen. Now I tell her, "You look nice, Mom."

~Mary Anglin-Coulter

44

Flex Time

The funny thing about firemen is, night and day,
they are always firemen.
~Gregory Widen, Backdraft

M y husband Howard was a volunteer firefighter who later worked his way up to Captain. We knew that our holidays were going to be disrupted by other family's emergencies, so we devised a plan. To assuage our young daughter's worries, we wrote to Santa and let him know that "our" Christmas was going to be celebrated on a different day every year. Santa obviously received the letter, because he never missed filling our Christmas stockings on the appointed mornings!

On "our" Christmas Day we stayed in our pajamas for hours, like other families, while the turkey went into the oven and the gifts were opened. We enjoyed a lovely Christmas meal and went to bed happy with our uninterrupted "special" family holiday.

On the actual Christmas Day, the firehouse would hold a "family" dinner for the on-call firefighters and paramedics. A few police officers in our small town also joined us. Our family attended many of these meals, and just like clockwork, as the turkey and gravy hit the table, the 9-1-1 alarms would sound and all the first responders would rush out, leaving their hot dinners and their disappointed, yet understanding, families.

We taught our daughter Ariel that it is not the specific date that makes the holidays. Years later, she became a volunteer firefighter/paramedic, too, so our two-Christmases tradition continued at home and at the station.

Now that Ariel is married with children, our holiday "tradition" continues because her husband's job demands that he work most holidays. Because our family doesn't care which day we celebrate Christmas, my son-in-law volunteers to work on Christmas and he makes time and a half. We've turned our family flexibility into a benefit that takes all the stress out of the holiday and makes our holidays together even more special.

~Mary Ellen Angelscribe

The Joy of Christmas

Holiday Memories

Memory... is the diary that we all carry about with us.
~Oscar Wilde,
The Importance of Being Earnest

45

The Envelope

Rich the treasure, sweet the pleasure.
~John Dryden

My brother Brandon and I had opened all of the packages under the tree. All that was left was an envelope. We knew that envelopes usually contained cards, and if we were lucky they also contained gift cards or cash.

My dad looked almost like he'd forgotten about the envelope as he casually handed it to me. I broke its seal and discovered inside a 3x5 index card with a border of glitter surrounding a poem.

Of course, I don't remember the poem by heart, but its mysterious rhyming message instructed us to go downstairs. We were excited. Maybe we were getting those skis we had wanted.

What we found downstairs was another envelope, containing another index card with a border of glitter surrounding a poem. This poem told us to go to Dad's car. Were the skis already in the car, ready to go?

Nope. There was just another envelope containing another glittery index card. This one told us to go to Mom's office downtown. Neither of us was old enough to drive. This meant we had to implore our parents to hurry up and get dressed and finish drinking their coffee and get going. They took forever.

Eventually, we made it to Mom's office where we found — you guessed it — a glitter-bedecked poem telling us to go somewhere else.

This time it was to KATU, the TV station where Dad worked. By now, our curiosity was stretched to the limits of our imaginations. Were we meeting someone famous? Were we going to be on TV? It absolutely didn't make sense to keep skis at the studio — Dad had a desk in an open area shared

with the other reporters.

We soon found out, however, that such a desk is a lovely place to keep a 3x5 index card complete with glitter and a poem. The instruction on this poem perplexed us more than any other. It told us to go to an unfamiliar address. Fortunately for us, our parents knew how to get there.

The car stopped in front of the unknown house. It felt like the end of the hunt. My dad handed us the final envelope. The final poem told us to knock on the door and say, "Merry Christmas! Is Humphrey here?"

This is where faith in our parents came in. We didn't know who would answer the door, and we didn't know what a Humphrey was. They shooed us along as they lingered by the car. We peered back to see their smiling faces and built up the courage to knock on the door. As anticipated, a stranger opened. After we recited the greeting, the smiling woman wished us a Merry Christmas and invited us in. We looked to our parents for permission — they were beaming. We were confused. We passed the threshold, and the stranger disappeared down a long hallway. Mom and Dad moved closer to the front door.

While we waited, I examined the room. The yellow, brown and orange couch looked decades old. Across the room, there was a large faded portrait of a well-groomed lap dog. Then I heard a weird sound — like a miniature thunderstorm. And then I saw something coming down the hallway toward us at top speed: a pristine cloud of white fur.

Dad was standing behind us by then. "Merry Christmas," he said. "He's yours." And the woman, who turned out to be a breeder, handed us the puff of fur.

That was the day that Humphrey, a ten-week-old Maltese, became part of our family. It was a gift far surpassing anything I could have imagined — including a set of skis.

~Chelsea Hall

46

A Stocking for Tammie

The happiest moments of my life have been the
few which I have passed at home in the
bosom of my family.
~Thomas Jefferson

I had just finished hanging the last stocking when our oldest son, Jeff, walked into the living room with his new girlfriend Tammie. Tammie and Jeff had known each other since the fourth grade and had dated in high school until we moved away during their junior year.

Their paths had crossed again recently. Both were parents by this time, but no longer in relationships. It looked like a meant-to-be love story.

Now Tammie said, "Aw, I want a stocking up there, too." She was looking at the long line of red and white stockings that reached from one end of an enormous beam to the other. My husband had sanded and polished this beam to perfection, then mounted it to the wall with gigantic wooden braces.

Each of our children, their spouses, and their children had a stocking, and each stocking holder was different, representing something unique to that person.

That wooden beam has always been the main attraction in our living room, where it extends the entire length of one wall. I display my most treasured photos on this shelf and it's considered to be a badge of honor to make it onto "Mom's shelf."

At Christmastime, you know you've made it when your stocking is added to the long parade of red and white tacked onto that shelf.

Now Jeff took me aside so Tammie wouldn't hear and asked, "Mom, do you happen to have an extra Christmas stocking I could use?"

After telling him that I was pretty sure we didn't have one, I inquired as to why he was asking.

He said he had bought Tammie a diamond pendant necklace for Christmas and thought it would be fun to put it in a stocking. I didn't have any extra matching stockings so, instead, Jeff and I fashioned one from a regular man's sports sock. We wrote TAMMIE on it with a black permanent marker and attached a red bow to the cuff with a large safety pin.

Jeff slipped the beautifully gift-wrapped necklace into the foot of the sock and we left it in my bedroom so that I could hang it next to Jeff's stocking on the shelf when Tammie wasn't looking.

On Christmas morning all the kids and grandkids were there early for breakfast before opening gifts. When Tammie walked into the living room with Jeff, she couldn't help but notice the new stocking hanging from our shelf; and there was no doubt that it was hers with the bold handwritten TAMMIE on it.

"Oh my gosh! Oh my gosh! Thank you so much!" she squealed with delight!

She continued her fervent babbling while running over for a closer look, "I love it! It's perfect! This is the best Christmas ever!"

While another girl might have been offended by this stocking, Tammie understood our sense of humor well, and knew it was our way of saying, "You're one of us, and we love you!"

Later when the kids took down their stockings to see what Santa left for them, Tammie was overjoyed with her beautiful necklace; but, quite honestly, I don't think it got quite as enthusiastic a reaction as her stocking.

Tammie and Jeff were married by the following Christmas, and it was a blessing to hang two new stockings on our shelf for Tammie's children.

As our family continues to grow, so does our parade of Christmas stockings. Although I've suggested to Tammie many times that we upgrade her stocking to a lovely store-bought one, she adamantly refuses, claiming hers is the most beautiful one on the entire shelf.

~Connie Kaseweter Pullen

A Heavenly Timetable

*Christmas is a necessity. There has to be at least
one day of the year to remind us that we're here for
something else besides ourselves.*
~Eric Sevareid

After plunking himself down next to me at the breakfast table, my husband Chris gave me "The Look." I knew what that meant; his brain had hatched another big idea! "How about breaking from our normal Christmas traditions this year to take a train trip to Seattle and then across the country to Milwaukee to spend Christmas with my family?" he asked.

I grinned. This was one of his better ideas! We were both captivated by the magical, romantic allure of train travel. With two young sons, ages six and two, I knew romance was unlikely, but I hoped for magical. I didn't have to think twice. "Let's do it!"

On December 21st, we boarded Amtrak's luxurious Coast Starlight in Los Angeles for the first leg of a seventy-four-hour odyssey. When the train departed the station, we were already enraptured.

We spent the first day learning to dine, balance, and promenade successfully without dropping our food, ricocheting off the narrow corridor walls, or rebounding into another passenger's lap. Moving between the jostling cars also required a new skillset. Our boys erupted in belly laughs as they perfected their train legs and learned how to buckle themselves into our sleeper compartment's top berth. We relished hours spent in the spacious lounge car playing games, learning magic tricks, nibbling fancy snacks and Christmas chocolates, and surveying the breathtaking landscape. By day's end we felt like train-travel pros.

In Seattle we departed the Coast Starlight and boarded Amtrak's Empire Builder to journey east. When we stopped in Spokane around midnight, I was grateful to be ensconced safely in a heated sleeper, as the outside temperature registered below zero.

In Spokane we remained on our train and awaited the arrival of another carrying connecting passengers from Oregon. Assured the wait would be short, we went to bed thinking we'd sleep through most of Idaho. But when I drew aside our room curtain at sunrise, the Spokane station sign greeted me. We hadn't budged an inch. Our train was now six hours behind schedule, and we languished for another three hours before the awaited train finally arrived. After those sleeper cars were carefully attached to ours, we departed.

We soon crossed the Washington-Idaho border, turned northeast, and zipped across the Idaho Panhandle. As we neared the entrance to Montana's Glacier National Park, fresh snow lay around us, pristine except for a few deer tracks. The towering evergreens bore mounds of snow on their outstretched, bowed limbs, inviting us into their secluded winter wonderland. To us Southern Californians, it all looked so… Christmassy!

When we emerged from the pristine backwoods into a sprawling meadow, a sprinkling of rustic log cabins balancing geometric-shaped snow stacks greeted us. Some single-story cabins were swaddled in snow to their eaves. They appeared to be hibernating contentedly, patiently awaiting their owners' spring homecoming.

The only thing distracting us from this breathtaking spectacle was our slowing train, which soon screeched to a stop. We peered out windows in curiosity before learning that the rail switches had frozen, which meant rail switching had to be performed the old-fashioned way — by hand. To accomplish that feat, the engineers would shovel through snow and then chop out the ice to access the switches.

My husband and I locked eyes. Quick mental calculations confirmed we wouldn't make our scheduled arrival of early Christmas Eve. I hastened to our room to verify the heat still worked and then tested our toilet's water flow. So far, so good.

After two backbreaking hours spent hacking and scooping in freezing temperatures — while most passengers munched snacks in train car warmth and admired the sublime scenery, and I test-flushed our toilets several times — the crew safely completed the rail switching, and we were once again on our way.

But some fiercely agitated passengers became persistently vocal about their displeasure. Many were making train connections in Chicago for passage to East Coast cities, and now they'd likely arrive too late to enjoy Christmas festivities with their families.

Yet, as their agitation level increased, our family's joy skyrocketed. The train crew didn't have control over the weather, and we knew they were doing their best to get us safely to our destination. Our boys certainly weren't keeping track of time. This was an adventure! And I was determined not to allow a schedule failure to derail our enjoyment.

Finally, to avoid hearing the escalating complaints, Chris and I ushered the boys into our room and shut the door. It was already after dark on Christmas Eve.

As we rolled through North Dakota under a crystal clear sky, I was mesmerized by the spectacle outside our window. A full moon illuminated the ice-clad, iridescent prairie for miles.

The light remained with us as we departed North Dakota and crossed Minnesota and Wisconsin. It illuminated the rails for miles. We felt bathed in it. A sense of glory and power remained, and the fear I'd felt soon melted into a soothing sensation of divine, protective love. It was the next best thing to a caroling Heavenly host! If the train had been on schedule, we would have arrived during daylight hours and missed that radiant Christmas Eve moon.

At 2:00 a.m. Christmas Day, we arrived safely at our destination. Although there was celebration with family yet to be enjoyed, our hearts overflowed with the magical gift of our Christmas train, which traveled on its own heavenly timetable: late, yet right on time to give us a magical Christmas Eve.

~Andrea Arthur Owan

48

Beyond the Arctic Circle

We live in a wonderful world that is full of beauty,
charm and adventure. There is no end to the
adventures we can have if only we seek them
with our eyes open.
~Jawaharlal Nehru

The snow was like a white blanket covering the fields as far as the eye could see. Now and then it glistened in the low winter sun, while the fir trees shimmered in their white coats. Occasionally, the icy arctic wind shook the trees, briefly freeing them of their burden, before the snow started to fall again.

Standing alone in this wintry scene was a house. Smoke curled out of the chimney, making it seem homey and welcoming. I watched as the smoke turned into different shapes and silhouettes.

I was whisked back to my childhood as I entered the house. I couldn't believe that I was here at last and I had to pinch myself to make sure it wasn't a dream. It was an enchanted world filled with sweets and toys, and as I turned to walk to the fire, I finally saw him — smiling, rosy-cheeked and wearing his familiar red suit.

For many years I had imagined visiting Lapland to meet Father Christmas. I had seen vacations advertised on television, and looked at holiday brochures. The more I read, the more magical the trip sounded.

By the way, did I mention that I was in my forties, had no children, and absolutely hated the cold? But did I care? Not one bit! I decided that for once I wouldn't moan about the cold. Of course I could cope with temperatures way below freezing. I would also ignore my fellow travelers if they looked in disdain at this soon-to-be middle-aged woman traveling such a long way just to see Santa.

I was a seasoned traveler and had journeyed to many countries alone. However, I wanted to share this experience with someone, not because I thought I would stick out like a sore thumb, but because the Christmas season is a time to be with friends. My husband couldn't come, as we have a menagerie of animals and nobody in their right mind would want to look after our wonderful, but mostly hyperactive, brood. I mentioned the trip to my friend Clare, expecting a barrage of excuses, but surprisingly she agreed to go with me.

And so, a few months later, I sat excitedly on a plane as it descended toward Rovaniemi in Finland. Looking out of the window, I saw a snow-covered winter wonderland waiting for us, just like I'd imagined. Living in Greece, I don't often get to see much snow, apart from glancing at the mountains from a distance. The scene from the plane's window was spectacular. There was mile upon mile of snow and the fir trees... well, I've never seen so many Christmas trees in my life!

However, as we got off the plane, the bitter wind hit us. Luckily, our first stop on the three-hour ride to the hotel was to be kitted out in a full body suit, with hood and big boots. I felt ready to get out there and find Santa, but we still had a two-hour coach trip further north.

We arrived at our hotel mid-afternoon and it was already getting dark. We had crossed the Arctic Circle. I looked around. There weren't many buildings there apart from the hotel and log cabins and I felt as if I had come to one of the farthest and most deserted places in the world. There is something eerie about it getting dark so early in the afternoon.

We went to see Santa that same day. Our group met in the hotel lobby and I was astonished to see that there were quite a few couples without children. Our instructions were to go and find Santa ourselves, which seemed a daunting task. However, there was help at hand.

As we went outside, we were hit by a blast of freezing air, but this was soon forgotten when an elf suddenly appeared and pointed us in the direction of Santa's home. We trudged through the snow, and with the help of signposts and a few more elves we finally got closer to our destination. By this time, the children in the group were very excited and I must admit they weren't the only ones.

Santa's house looked as welcoming as I had imagined, and it was great to see a couple of reindeer waiting patiently outside for the man himself.

We went in, and within minutes were warm and cozy. There was a log fire burning cheerfully in one corner and sitting close by was Father Christmas, dressed in red, with a long white beard. He was the jolliest man I had ever seen. The kids ran to him while the adults stood near the back, not wanting to spoil the fun. When the elves had calmed the kids down, Santa brought out a pile of letters. Imagine the surprise on the faces of the children when they saw that Santa had the letters they had written to him.

We still had another three days in Lapland after we met Santa. I had always wanted to ride in a sleigh pulled by a team of Huskies and I was excited to get the chance to do it. The dogs were strong and fast, and I was amazed how they managed to pull Clare and me at such speed.

We were also introduced to more reindeer and had a leisurely sleigh ride with them. Then we had a go on a snowmobile, which I must admit I didn't quite get the hang of. Having ridden motorbikes, I went on full of confidence, but unfortunately came off feeling quite shamefaced by my efforts.

We were lucky enough to see the Northern Lights one evening. It was spectacular. What a mixture of colors lighting up the clear night sky.

My trip to Lapland turned out to be everything I had expected it to be. It was a great experience and a fantastic start to the Christmas season.

~Irena Nieslony

49

Chicken Soup for the Soul

The Big Box

After a girl is grown, her little brothers — now her
protectors — seem like big brothers.
~Terri Guillemets

The smell of Norwegian cookies greeted me as I opened the front door to my parents' home and wiped my dripping nose on the cuff of my jacket. The sounds of muted Christmas carols played on the stereo. A fire burned hot in the fireplace with the sound of popping and crackling.

"The wood is damp," my father said to no one in particular. "I had better see where that tarp is leaking." Happy to have a mission, he put on an army-issue parka and his "bunny boots" and headed out the door. He paused. "Were the roads slippery?"

"Not too bad," I lied, as I shrugged out of my coat. My luggage and dirty laundry were in heaps on the landing.

He paused a moment in the kitchen. "Karen's home," he said to my mother and continued his task without interruption.

My mother had just finished brewing a pot of coffee. She came out of the kitchen smiling and was clad in a sweater that was the perfect shade of red for her. She always seemed to look perfect. I looked down at the jeans I was wearing for the second day in a row and my college sweatshirt with the permanent pizza stain on the cuff.

"Hi, Mom," I said.

"Take your laundry downstairs, I'll sort it later. Is this all of it?" she asked as she picked up one of my suitcases. I nodded and we carried it down to the laundry room.

I looked around a little, then peeked in one of my brothers' bedrooms.

"Where's Dave?"

"Outside, bringing in more wood for tomorrow."

"Gary?"

"Around somewhere."

I felt a little letdown. I was a returning college freshman — the least they could have done was greet me with some excitement!

I noticed that my little brother had moved everything he owned into my old room and posters of dirt bikes soaring through the air hung everywhere. I was to stay in the bedroom upstairs — the guest room.

I was starting to feel like a guest in my own home.

I went back to the living room.

"Here, Karen, sit close to the fire," my dad offered. I was chilled now and the fire felt good, I felt the knot in my stomach unwind just a little.

"I checked the oil in your car and added transmission fluid and windshield washer fluid."

"Thanks, Dad."

"I also added some HEET to your gas tank."

"Thanks."

"Lots of snow on your car; the tires are pretty iced."

"Yeah, it's snowing pretty hard out there."

My father looked at me but didn't say much; I knew he had figured out the roads were a lot worse than I had let on. My mom carried in coffee and the fresh Norwegian krumkake cookies she had made. She and my dad locked eyes and smiled at each other.

"You can open that big present early if you want," my dad said, trying not to smile.

I looked. There was a big box under the Christmas tree. It looked like a TV box or a box with a small refrigerator in it. My name was on it in large red letters. Puzzled that they would let me open a present without the whole family around, I paused, but not for long. I ripped the paper off the box, lifted the two flaps on top with shaking fingers, and peered inside.

"Surprise!" My younger brother, Gary, popped out of the box with a bow on his head. "Merry Christmas, Karen!" he screamed amid uncontrollable peals of laughter. My dad started snickering.

I sat on the floor, stunned.

I had just completed my first semester of college. I had struggled with independence, money shortages, and finals. I was exhausted, overwhelmed, and more than a little lost in life. I had expected some fanfare when I arrived home, not people checking tarps, talking about laundry as if I had never been gone, and moving me to the guest room. And now, instead of a big, surprising present, my brother had jumped out and scared me.

I looked at the box and burst into tears. My family stared at me. After I had hiccupped my last sob I looked down at my lap, ashamed of my outburst. I took a krumkake off the plate. I sat and sniffed. I examined the cookie closely, avoiding the eyes of my family.

My dad said loudly, "I used to get terrible headaches after finals."

I started to feel better. My father, in his own way, had reminded me that this was my family; I wasn't a guest in this house. If I fell apart here, they would still want me around. It was okay — I was okay. They were glad I was home, no matter what kind of emotional wreck I was. My father dove into a discussion regarding the maintenance he planned to put my car through the next day; my mother brought me another krumkake and a cup of "de-caf" as she put it.

My little brother came up to me with the bow still in his hair, brown eyes serious.

"Wanna play *Monopoly*?" he asked. "You can be the car if you want."

"But that's your favorite piece," I said as we sat down in front of the fireplace.

"It's okay. You can have it. But only today and only because you cried."

"Thanks." I smiled and ruffled the bow out of his hair. I lifted an eyebrow. "Thanks for the early Christmas present too."

"No problem," he said. "Merry Christmas." He took a huge bite out of my krumkake.

Looking back I cannot imagine how my little brother felt when I started crying. My parents told me that he missed me when I left for college. He had spent hours planning and wrapping the big box. He had put a festive Christmas bow on his head and watched for my car in the driveway. He raced to the box, tucked himself inside and waited patiently for the better part of an hour while I hauled laundry downstairs, talked cars with my father and, in general, took my time.

My little brother, in his heart, had given himself to me for Christmas.

Now, as a mother, my heart is touched in many ways by the hand of a child. But I still remember the Christmas of the Big Box because it was the first time I realized how much children really give of themselves and how easy it is to damage their small spirits.

I tease Gary about giving himself to me for Christmas, because after all it's my job as his sister. He denies, with embarrassment, having done so. I realize now how sweet the gesture was, and how much he cared that I was returning home for a visit. I often wonder what his response would be to the teasing now if I had been more mature when the original gift had been offered, if I had embraced him and given him the big kiss he deserved.

~Karen J. Olson

50

Chicken Soup
for the Soul

The Best Gift of All

Any mother could perform the jobs of several air
traffic controllers with ease.
~Lisa Alther

L arry was seven and I was five and we were obsessed with dinosaurs. When we saw the plastic dinosaur models at the toy store, we wanted them more than anything else.

I wrote a letter to Santa, asking him to please, please bring me a Stegosaurus model kit. Larry wrote a similar letter, asking for a Tyrannosaurus Rex model. We both wrote in our letters that we had worked awful hard to be good that year, which we had, and if Santa could just see his way to bringing each of us a dinosaur model kit, we wouldn't ask for anything else.

When my mom read our letters, she looked at us and asked, "Are you sure you're both old enough for a model kit? Those things can be hard to put together."

"We can do it!" I told her, envisioning how I would snap a few pieces together, put a dab of glue here and there, and voila, my Stegosaurus would be staring at me with all the prehistoric coolness only a gift like that could bring.

"Not a problem!" my brother Larry said, probably imagining how ferocious and mighty his easily put together Tyrannosaurus would look once he spent five minutes or so slapping it together. The smile on his face grew even wider than before.

"If you think you can really do it," she said, looking unsure. "I'm sure Santa would be glad to bring you model kits for Christmas."

"Dinosaur model kits," my brother said. He showed her an ad we'd cut out of the toy store's catalog.

"Stegosaurus and Tyrannosaurus Rex," I added, pointing to pictures of the specific kits.

Mom looked at the pictures. "There sure are lots of little bitty pieces," she said softly.

"It'll be easy!" I said confidently.

Well, Christmas Eve came, and my brother, sister and I went off to sleep, although I didn't do much sleeping. Somewhere around 5:00 a.m., Larry and I slipped out of bed and crept downstairs to find that Santa had come and gone, and under the tree were two big presents for my brother and me!

I tore the wrapping paper off mine and jumped for joy. My model Stegosaurus! Santa had brought me the toy I had wanted more than anything. My brother got his Tyrannosaurus Rex, too. We danced around the living room, then ran to the kitchen table and opened up our model kits... and stared at what looked like a million pieces of plastic. There was a big, fat manual that had instructions on how to put the model together. It might as well have been a manual on how to fly to the moon. My brother and I sighed at the same time.

Still, we were excited and we set about twisting and bending the pieces out of their plastic holders. When we were through, it seemed like there was even more pieces than before.

"You two are going to put those things together?" my sister asked, looking at the immense pile of plastic on the table. "You can't even match up your own socks."

"We can do it!" I said, grinning at my brother. I grabbed the tube of glue that Santa had been nice enough to include and had Larry read me the instructions from the manual.

Half a day later, all we had was a bunch of sticky pieces, some that were glued to the table, some to the instruction manual, and some to my brother and me. There was no sign of two ferocious, mighty dinosaurs.

And so, my brother and I did what any dynamic duo would do when stymied by an impossible project: we began to cry. Larry and I cried our eyes out over the mess we had made and the pile of plastic sitting before us. Our mom dried our tears and handed us other presents to distract us, but we kept looking back at the pile of dinosaur parts and our eyes would well up again.

That Christmas night I felt as if a wonderful dream had turned into a nightmare. I don't know how long I lay there in my bed, dozing on and off, but somewhere in the middle of the night I heard a series of clicking sounds. I got up from bed and wandered into the living room, and this is what I saw: my mom was at the kitchen table, sorting through all the dozens of pieces, wiping off the old glue with a washcloth, and slowly gluing them together.

I stood and watched her patiently work, our secret elf who would make Christmas magic again. I couldn't keep my eyes open, and a part of me wondered if it was a dream. I wandered back to bed not knowing.

In the morning Larry and I sadly stumbled into the living room. We were prepared to toss the plastic mess in the trash and call it a failed experiment. We walked up to the kitchen table, looked for those heaps of sticky plastic parts, and we gasped. There, standing before us, was the most magnificent pair of model dinosaurs we had ever seen. My Stegosaurus and Larry's Tyrannosaurus Rex stood whole and proud and awesomely ferocious.

"Santa must have come back last night and fixed them for us!" Larry shouted, picking up his dinosaur and hugging it.

"That must have been what happened," Mom said, coming into the living room looking a little tired, but very happy.

I looked at my mom, and noticed that there was a small piece of plastic stuck to her pajamas. I ran up to her and hugged her tight, knowing that she had given us a truly wonderful gift: the gift of her time, her patience, and her boundless love. It was the best Christmas gift of all.

~John P. Buentello

51

Chicken Soup for the Soul

Having Mercy

Dogs act exactly the way we would act if
we had no shame.
~Cynthia Heimel

My father and stepmother, Polly, had owned many Boxers, each with a distinct personality. Their latest Boxer, Mercy, joined the family a couple of months before Christmas.

Dad and Polly watched her carefully when they set up the tree and started putting wrapped gifts under it. Some of their previous dogs had been drawn to the tree and the gifts, but not Mercy. She seemed oblivious, even when they placed edible gifts under the tree, including a big, wrapped box of dog biscuits.

A few nights before Christmas Polly woke up while it was still dark and silent, as she often did. As she passed the living room door she glanced in, and what she saw made her stop cold. They'd been robbed. The area under the Christmas tree had been stacked high with colorful gifts. Now every last present was gone. Suddenly Polly was struck by a much worse thought.

Why hadn't Mercy barked? Where was she? Had the thieves taken her, too?

She checked Mercy's bed and found it empty. Mercy was nowhere to be found. In a panic, Polly was about to wake Dad, when she noticed a piece of red ribbon on the living room floor. A few feet away, there was a scrap of wrapping paper and a little further on, some glitter. It all seemed to form a trail, leading to the back door.

For a moment, Polly stood at that door, hesitating.

Should she open it? What if the thief was still there?

Finally she flipped the light switch and cautiously opened the door to the back yard. And there was the perp.

Mercy lay under her favorite tree, surrounded by packages that were chewed, gnawed, pawed and emptied. Mercy had silently carried one package after another, through the house and the doggy door, to where she could pillage in private.

Anything that was edible was gone, including chocolates, cookies, fancy breads, candy canes, and four pounds of Milk-Bones. Beautifully wrapped boxes now had gaping holes and were damp with dog saliva. And Mercy was in the middle of the mess, looking guilty, sorry... and a little sick.

Fortunately, nature took its course and Mercy didn't need to have her stomach pumped. In the morning, Dad and Polly cleaned up the mess and salvaged what little they could.

"Who needs presents?" laughed Dad, happy that Mercy survived her midnight snack.

For Polly, the loss of the presents wasn't the worst problem. It was identifying who'd sent what.

"How do I send out thank-you notes?" she fretted. "Mercy destroyed all the tags."

In the end, Mercy herself provided the answer. The day after Christmas, Polly returned to her easy chair to find Mercy looking guilty as she licked the now-empty plate where a donut had been. Polly quickly snapped a picture of the shame-faced pooch, and sent a copy with each "thank you for the ??" note, along with the story. Polly was a little embarrassed, but we all got a good laugh and Mercy... well she obtained mercy.

~Teresa Ambord

Across the Years

When love is not madness, it is not love.
~Pedro Calderon de la Barca

I t was 11:00 p.m. on New Year's Eve 1986. After fourteen hours I'd had enough of trudging around that 400-meter track. I would normally have worn a dressy outfit and celebrated with dinner and dancing. Was this really what I had in mind for New Year's Eve, especially since it took place on my honeymoon?

I had spent two frenzied months getting ready for Christmas and finalizing the plans for my wedding. We had the traditional gift exchange and meals with family. There were holiday parties, as well as bride and groom showers adding to the festive atmosphere.

We were married two days after Christmas in a small church filled with beautiful crimson poinsettias, magnificent organ music and loving friends and family.

Our honeymoon began in Phoenix, Arizona. We had entered a "fixed time event," a foot race where the objective is to travel as far as you can in the time set for the event. This one, "Across the Years," was a twenty-four-hour race. The idea was to spend New Year's Eve traveling by foot from one year into the next.

We woke New Year's Eve morning to a beautiful sunny day and went to Washington High School for the pre-race briefing. We headed to the 400-meter track, our home for the next twenty-four hours. As we stood listening to the race director explain the rules, we could see palm trees and majestic Camelback Mountain in the distance.

At 9:00 a.m. we began. Alan and I gave each other a quick kiss and we each went at our own pace around the track.

As I went round and round during the daylight hours, the distant palm trees and Camelback Mountain became friendly reminders of the "normal" world that I would return to when this was over. When darkness enveloped us, I withdrew into myself as my world shrank to the small area of track and field.

After fourteen hours of mostly walking, my spirits were low and I couldn't muster much enthusiasm. As Alan walked up beside me on the track he said, "Hello, Mrs. Firth."

I wanted to respond with a smile at hearing my new name, but instead I whined, "Why am I doing this? Romantic honeymoon, huh?" He smiled as he squeezed my hand.

It was New Year's Eve and there I was in sweatshirt and tights, a bandana tied around my hair and sneakers on my feet, slogging my way around a gravel track with other athletes. It was certainly the most casual New Year's Eve outfit I had ever worn.

At midnight, Alan caught up with me again and we held hands as we walked a lap together, watching the fireworks in the distance. Then a sweet noise floated across the field. The race director was playing "Auld Lang Syne" on his clarinet. My tears began to flow.

As we continued hand in hand, I realized these were tears of joy and a release of the tension that had accumulated during the hectic holiday and wedding planning months. They were symbolic of saying goodbye to my life as a single woman as I embraced life with my new husband. When the tears dried enough for me to speak, I looked up at Alan and said, "What a lovely honeymoon. I'm so blessed that we're married."

The song ended and Alan jogged away, leaving me with my thoughts. After "crossing the years" I decided I'd had enough, so I told the timekeepers I was going for a rest. The timekeepers were generously spending their New Year's Eve sitting in the cold counting our every lap.

I napped in the back seat of the car for a while. I woke later and did a lap to stretch my legs. It hurt, but not nearly as much as when I went to the toilet. Sitting down and standing back up was excruciating.

A little while later Alan suggested I do some more serious laps in hopes of finishing in first place for females. He was trying for first place overall. I resisted. But as the sun came up, my spirits lifted and I agreed. I once again went round and round, putting in more miles.

At 9:00 a.m. on January 1, 1987, it was thankfully time to stop. Alan finished second overall with 79.2 miles. I finished fifth overall (out of six runners) with 45.4 miles, and was the first female. There had only been two women and the other lady had stopped due to an injury.

All the finishers lined up for the photo, each holding a long sleeve T-shirt, our "prize" for having competed. We didn't expect or need more. The actual doing of it was the reward.

After sharing a beer with the other runners at our "party," we said our goodbyes. We returned to the hotel for champagne and a gloriously cooked breakfast. We had only eaten snacks for twenty-four hours and we were famished. We crashed and slept all day.

Once it was over, the sense of accomplishment was incredible. I also found I didn't really need to get all dressed up for it to be a celebration of turning loose the old and embracing the new. When I look back there's no doubt it was an exceptional New Year's Eve, one I will never forget.

Thirty years later, Alan and I are still celebrating our Christmas wedding anniversary and still holding hands on New Year's Eve.

~Mary Stewart-Firth

53

Chicken Soup for the Soul

An Unexpected Gift

*I was in a Nativity play as a kid. Back
then, I played the donkey.*
~Tatiana Maslany

I t was early afternoon on Christmas Eve when I called my family in London, England. As each person came to the phone I heard the creak of a 300-year-old door and the distinctive click, click of heels along the oak floor of the hallway.

I could almost smell the floor polish. I knew the scene intimately. I could hear the distinctive tick tock of the commanding grandfather clock in the corner, partially hidden by an enormous Christmas tree laden with gifts. I could see the spiral mahogany staircase where, as children, we sat on the steps guessing the contents of the small wrapped packages dangling on the Christmas tree.

A wave of nostalgia swept over me. I gazed through the dining room window of my new home in America. I looked out over rolling acres and a long, sweeping driveway, reminding myself that we bought the ranch because it reminded us of the English countryside.

Suddenly, I spotted a large truck parked across the bottom of our driveway. A man was opening the gate to the pasture. Surely, they weren't rustling cattle in broad daylight on Christmas Eve. My husband was not home, so I phoned the sheriff.

Then I went out the side entrance of the house, where I had an uninterrupted view of the yard and driveway. The commotion seemed to involve two men chasing what appeared to be a very large dog. The man holding the gate open helped chase the animal into the field where the cattle were grazing. Then he quickly closed the gate. I watched in horror as the animal trotted toward the herd and disappeared among the calves. He was as large as the calves and a big dog would cause chaos in the herd.

Mopping his forehead with a handkerchief, an older gentleman walked toward me. "I'm sorry Ma'am," he said. "I'm a neighbor. Mind if I sit for a moment? That critter just about wore me out." I brought him a glass of water; he got his breath back and continued the story. "The boys will catch him," he said. "We won't be troubling you much longer. The critter got loose, ran up the road and turned into your driveway."

Having put on my eyeglasses I saw more clearly the activity in the pasture. An hour went by and the "critter" still ran free. Reinforcements arrived; ten people were now in the pasture. "He likes an apple, cinnamon pancakes or a slice of toast," said the neighbor. "You wouldn't happen to have a bite we could tempt the critter with, would you?"

I toasted four hamburger buns and sliced up an apple. I was not prepared to make cinnamon pancakes for the critter.

The critter gobbled up the apple and toast, skillfully avoiding all attempts at capture. "Darn it," said the neighbor, after another hour had passed. "I've had enough. That critter is yours, for free, if you want him."

We shook hands on the deal, the neighbor and his helpmates disappeared back down the driveway, and the critter strolled to the pond for a drink.

On Christmas morning I cooked cinnamon pancakes. After breakfast my husband and I took the pancakes and some apple slices to the pasture. The critter trotted hesitantly toward us, snatched a pancake, stepped back, crunched an apple slice, another pancake and eventually allowed us to scratch under his chin. "What are you going to call him?" said my husband.

"Gabriel, of course," I said, caressing Gabriel's back where the hair formed a distinctive black cross that extended down the center of his back and across his shoulders. "What other name would you give to an eighteen-month-old miniature donkey that arrived unexpectedly on Christmas Eve?"

~Josephine Montgomery

54

Chicken Soup for the Soul

Memory Lane

Christmas is the day that holds all time together.
~Alexander Smith

My husband and I had decided we wanted to do something special to mark our first Christmas together. We went to one of the fancy department stores and bought an expensive glass ornament. It was beautiful — painted gold and covered in sparkles, with what looked like a burst of golden fireworks hanging in its hollow center.

The next year, we bought a delicate glass ball with an angel suspended in the center. The following Christmas we found a red velvet birdhouse with a small teddy bear looking out the door. He held a wrapped gift in his hand, and we knew our two-month-old daughter would love it when she was older.

Our annual ornament tradition continued, and with each addition came a story. The unfortunate, gangly, ten-inch tall snowman made of Styrofoam balls covered in yarn was bought the year we waited until the last minute and found the store shelves picked bare. Our daughter, who had been fussing in her stroller while we searched, smiled when she saw the snowman, and after that we went through a period when our kids seemed to pick our ornaments.

That's how we ended up with the brilliant red glass mouse topped with wild yellow hair, and the corn husk country mouse, complete with cowboy hat and guitar, whose head repeatedly fell off.

As time passed, we chose ornaments to remind us of a major event from that year. The clear globe filled with sand and tiny shells was from the summer we went to the Outer Banks for a family reunion; the decorated miniature rolling pin commemorated the year we tore the house apart and moved the kitchen; and the bear swathed in scarves, hat, and snow pants was from the year we moved from the wintry North to warm Florida.

There are special ornaments for the years our son and daughter were married, and there are ornaments for the years each of our four grandchildren were born.

Each year, when I hang the ornaments among the lights, I take a trip down Memory Lane.

Next year, we will have been married fifty years, but there will be only forty-nine ornaments to unpack. It has always been that way — one ornament fewer than the number of years of married life. That's because we spent that first Christmas nearly 9,000 miles apart — he in a canvas, wood-floored tent in Vietnam, and I in a room rented from an elderly woman.

For our fiftieth anniversary, we'll do what we weren't able to do that first Christmas of our marriage: search together for the most important ornament of all — one that represents the beginning of our lives together.

~Michele Ivy Davis

Endings and Beginnings

Year's end is neither an end nor a beginning but
a going on, with all the wisdom that
experience can instill in us.
~Hal Borland

Every New Year's Eve, we had breakfast at Aunt Dot's house. Aunt Dot lived three blocks from us, in a ranch-style home bursting at the seams with shelves of books, photo albums and ceramic trinkets she had collected over the years. Colorful pots of spider plants and philodendron lined her kitchen windowsills and movie posters for classics I had never seen covered the walls in the living room. I remember thinking *Gone with the Wind* must be a movie about a tornado.

Although the food was delicious, pancakes with bacon and home fries, my most vivid memory of the meal was the centerpiece that Aunt Dot always arranged on her kitchen table — seven sets of ceramic salt and pepper shakers. There was a pair of winged Valentine Cupids, an Easter Bunny with a large pink egg, a leprechaun with his pot of gold, a duo of star-spangled, red, white, and blue Uncle Sam top hats, twin orange jack-o'-lanterns, two turkeys wearing pilgrim hats, and Mr. and Mrs. Claus.

It wasn't until years later, when I was home on break my senior year of college, that I finally asked Aunt Dot about the unusual centerpiece. She was now eighty-seven years old and she still invited us to the last breakfast of the year.

I had come over early that morning to help with the meal preparations and Aunt Dot was enthusiastically stirring pancake batter as she replied to my question. "What are you talking about?" she said. "I put those salt and pepper shakers out every single year."

"I know," I said, setting plates on the table. "But why? What's the reason you always put them out on New Year's Eve morning?"

"Well, my dear," Aunt Dot said thoughtfully. "It helps to remind me that even though the holidays are over, there's another whole year of them coming."

I nodded. "I guess that makes sense."

"Let me tell you something," she said. "I have learned over my many years that nothing really stops; every ending in life is really just another new beginning." She pointed at me with the batter-covered spoon. "Remember that, my dear."

"I will," I told her.

In the spring of that year, after a short illness, Aunt Dot passed away. She left her book collection to my mom and the movie posters to my sister, but I was surprised to learn that I got the holiday salt and pepper shakers. I guess Aunt Dot wanted to make sure I remembered her philosophy.

I continued Aunt Dot's breakfast tradition at my own apartment with the salt and peppers shakers centerpiece in place.

Now, a couple of decades later, every New Year's Eve morning, my parents, my siblings, their spouses and children still come to my house for the last breakfast of the year. The pancakes are never as good as Aunt Dot's, but the center of the table is covered with those old salt and pepper shakers, reminding us all that every ending is really just another beginning.

~David Hull

The Joy of Christmas

Through the Eyes of a Child

*There's nothing sadder in this world than to awake
Christmas morning and not be a child.*
~Erma Bombeck

A Christmas Recruit

The manner of giving is worth more than the gift.
~Pierre Corneille, Le Menteur

Early one December many years ago, I realized something horrible: my parents must have been on Santa's naughty list. I was quite young at the time, but I had seen the shows and heard the stories. I knew that the better you were, the more presents you were given. My parents hardly ever received gifts from Santa.

The idea that my parents could be bad people was hard for me to stomach, so I went to the only source of truth I could trust: my older sister.

She walked me very seriously to the middle of the stairs. That was the ultimate private place in our house. Not only could nobody hear us, but it was also easy to spot anyone approaching.

"Mom and Dad aren't kids," she told me.

I rolled my eyes. Everyone knew that.

"And Santa," she continued quietly, "is all about kids. He doesn't worry about adults."

I felt a pressure loosen in my chest. That made complete sense. Of course, my parents weren't bad people. They just weren't kids.

"But," she said, "there's more to it."

"What?"

"Santa is always looking for helpers."

Have you ever had a moment where you feel like the world is opening up around you? This was one of those times. I sat on the cold wooden staircase and listened as she explained that Santa wasn't greedy. He didn't want to be the only one allowed to give gifts. In fact, he loved the idea of us picking up the slack, especially when it came to parents.

During our next trip to the mall, my sister staged a distraction so I could make a purchase without Mom noticing.

That Christmas morning, my parents each had a special present from "Santa" under the tree.

I know what you're thinking. How could they not have noticed the shaky writing on the notes? Why didn't they question why Santa had brought them each a box of cheese?

I don't have answers for you. All I know is that I spent that Christmas morning in suspense, waiting for them to discover their presents. When they finally did, I could barely contain myself. Their faces broke into wide smiles. Then, as they tore the giftwrap away and realized they were cheese boxes, they laughed and shouted "Thank you, Santa!" My dad opened his to share the cheese with everyone.

I felt like my heart would burst.

It is one of my clearest and happiest memories of my childhood Christmases, far outstripping any gifts that I ever received.

I knew right then and there that I would spend the rest of my life working for Santa.

~Patrick Matthews

Reality Check

The best of all gifts around any Christmas tree:
the presence of a happy family all
wrapped up in each other.
~Burton Hillis

I stared at the pages of magnificent Christmas decorations and sighed. The tables covered with delicious-looking foods and fancy desserts in *Better Homes and Gardens* were enough to make anyone drool.

How could I possibly prepare these fantastic holiday dishes for my family? I had three small children and no time for such luxuries. I barely had time to clean our home, let alone design beautiful decorations and cook sensational meals.

I wanted to make this year's Christmas celebration memorable, but I was still recovering from last year's miserable failure. I had spent days creating a gingerbread house as well as gingerbread men to hang on our tree. But as Christmas approached, the decorations kept disappearing and the house eventually collapsed.

As the holidays neared, I began to feel mounting tension in my arms and neck. My head ached, and I was miserable. Instead of looking forward to Christmas, I was beginning to dread it.

Wasn't Christmas supposed to be a joyful time? Well, something had gone wrong. I had somehow lost sight of the real meaning of Christmas amid all these elaborate ideas. I had been allowing the experts to tell me how I should celebrate our holiday.

I decided to consult the only "experts" who really mattered — my children. I wanted to make the big day special for them, and so I needed to find out what they really wanted. "How shall we celebrate Christmas?" I asked them on the way home from the store the next day.

My eight-year-old daughter replied, "Let's have spaghetti. Spaghetti would be perfect for Christmas because it's red."

I felt better already. Spaghetti was easy to make, and it was my daughter's favorite meal. I knew she would be happy with that choice.

My six-year-old son suggested, "Let's decorate the tree with candy canes."

I could purchase candy canes anywhere, and they were inexpensive. I could easily buy extra candy canes for the ones that went AWOL, although I would urge my family not to eat them until after Christmas. I planned to sweeten the deal by promising them a party with hot chocolate and other goodies to go along with the candy canes.

My three-year-old son said, "Let's have a birthday cake for Jesus. I like the chocolate one in the box. We could play games in the afternoon."

All their suggestions seemed easy to accomplish. I could certainly make chocolate cake from a mix, and I knew the children would love to "decorate" the cake themselves. What a relief! I wouldn't have to spend time creating fancy foods or elaborate decorations to make my children happy.

For the first time in weeks, I began to smile. Instead of fussing, I could spend this special day playing games and relaxing with my family. This was truly going to be a fantastic, memorable Christmas!

~JoAnne Check

58

Chicken Soup
for the Soul

O Wholly
Overwhelming Night

A child is a curly dimpled lunatic.
~Ralph Waldo Emerson

The Christmas Eve children's service overflowed with little ones, laughter, and anticipation. Kids squirmed in holiday dresses or once-a-year ties in the crowded pews. To entertain the families squeezed into every possible seat, piano students pounded "Silent Night" or "The First Noel" on the choir director's piano. When their turns ended, they rushed back to their smiling parents and grandparents.

My little family missed most of this. We decided to forgo getting seats at the children's service in favor of a shorter wait time beforehand. Our younger daughter, two-and-a-half-year-old Mary Claire, has been nicknamed "Our Lady of Perpetual Motion." She needed room to roam so we were off standing at the back of the church anyway.

We strolled into church just before Father Jim began his procession. Twinkling lights and Christmas hymns greeted us. I spied an opening near the low baptismal font. It provided some breathing room, perfect for a toddler on the move. A few minutes later, my husband came in from parking the car and we stood together, holding hands, for the opening prayers.

When Father Jim called the children forward for the Christmas story, the real magic began. Each Christmas Eve, he creates a giant flannel storyboard on his vestments and robes. The little ones place felt pieces of the story — cutout sheep, shepherds, baby Jesus — on his vestments. By the end, Father Jim is covered with fabric, the children enjoy the story, and the congregation giggles at the show.

Our older daughter, a kindergartner, grinned with excitement. She was in charge this year, and took her role seriously. Throughout December she had "practiced" reenacting the Christmas story with our toy nativity set. She'd perched her little sister on her lap and told the story — with a few fractured carols sprinkled in — over and over. It always ended with a rousing rendition of "Happy Birthday" to Jesus.

I watched nervously as our girls walked hand-in-hand down the long center aisle for the children's message. Kids poured out of every pew, clamoring for a seat on the altar steps. We were on high alert, afraid Mary Claire might make a run for it. We didn't need to be. Our daughters sat sweetly side by side in their fancy holiday dresses and hung on every word. My eyes were damp when Father Jim finished and the girls ran back toward us. I hugged them tightly. What a special Christmas this was becoming!

Yet as the service continued, Mary Claire's patience wore thin. She hadn't napped enough that day. My husband sent me "the look." He thought it was time to go. I waved him off. I was high on Christmas spirit and didn't want the joy to end.

"Look at Father Jim," I whispered quietly into Mary Claire's ear. "He is saying prayers for Baby Jesus!" She watched for a moment. I pointed toward the lights on the Christmas tree. "Aren't they pretty? Look at all the colors!"

The distractions worked. Soon her hot baby breath whispered questions into my ear. Pleased with my solution, I caught my husband's eye and smiled. "See!" my confident smile said. "We're good. I've got this!" In my smugness, I wasn't paying attention when a few moments later, another question came.

"Mama, who's that?" she whispered, while her chubby finger pointed toward the large stained glass window on our left.

"That's Jesus," I answered.

"What's he doing?" she hesitantly asked.

And then I did it. Unthinkingly, and with complete disregard for the not-even-three-year-old sensibility, I answered, "That is when he dies."

A quiet moment settled over the church. Then she erupted.

"He DIES?" she shrieked. "Baby Jesus DIES? HE WAS JUST BORN!"

My mind raced to catch up as she shouted louder and clearer than I thought was possible.

"Noooo!" she sobbed. Every person around us turned to look while I frantically tried to undo what I'd done. "Of course he was just born! Today is Jesus's birthday! Yay! Hurray for Baby Jesus!"

It was too late. She sobbed with all the grief a child can muster. Tears slid down her flushed round cheeks faster than I could wipe them. Despite the understanding smile and stifled chuckle of the grandmother nearby, I knew it was time to go. I looked toward my husband, who already had our five-year-old bundled up and the activity bags packed. I had never been more grateful to him as we made our quick exit.

At home, with presents under the tree and carols in the background, we returned our little family's attention to the celebration of the season. Bedtime stories and cookies for Santa restored the magic. With the kids tucked into their beds, my husband and I laughed and laughed over the evening's events and the unpredictability of children.

~Katie O'Connell

A New Home for SarahRose

Christmas... is not an eternal event at all, but a piece
of one's home that one carries in one's heart.
~Freya Stark

In 2012 our local paper ran a winter photo contest. I carried my camera outside that day and snapped a few pictures of our "Little Cabin in the Big Woods" and actually anticipated winning the contest. That seems a bit amusing, looking back. After all, we live along the Front Range of the Rocky Mountains and every single day people photograph the spectacular scene — breathtaking photographs of wildlife, the Garden of the Gods, Pikes Peak, and the like. But when my photo was chosen as the winner, I wasn't surprised at all. This was a photo of my home... and I loved it.

There wasn't really anything spectacular about our little log cabin. Built in the 1940's as someone's summer vacation home, it appeared tiny next to the ancient pine trees that surrounded it. But, it was our cozy home of twenty-seven years. We fell in love with the place as a young family looking to escape the confines of city life. Here we raised our children and figured that even though "Whispering Pines" had its faults, we'd stay there forever — because it was home.

Growing up in a military family, I had the privilege of traveling extensively around the world. In those days, I was perplexed to hear statements of longing to "go home." Wasn't "home" the place you went to sleep at night? Wasn't it where your mail was sent? But I had noticed many people referred to their "home" as someplace they were not currently living. How odd — a distant place called "home." That was when I noticed that "home" was not just a noun, but more of an emotion, as in "I feel at home here." Home is where you feel protected, embraced, and understood.

So there it was. The place called home by our family for nearly three decades.

What our cabin lacked in square footage, it made up for in charm. And it was host to a wide variety of events over the years, including impromptu dance and drama presentations by the seven rowdy children who grew up there. Weddings, baby showers, graduation parties, music recitals, and other holiday celebrations were held within its walls.

Then, on June 11, 2013, Whispering Pines vanished along with more than five hundred other homes in the Black Forest Fire — still counted as the most destructive fire in Colorado history.

Fortunately, we had time to gather the children, pets, some photos, computers, and important documents ahead of the flames. At the time of the mandatory evacuation, we unknowingly checked in to the same hotel where firefighters from across the country were staying while helping to battle the blaze.

Over breakfast each morning we thanked them for their service and chatted with fellow evacuees. The fun of the evacuation evaporated when the official news arrived that our address was among those listed as a "total loss."

Our youngest daughter, twelve-year-old SarahRose, exclaimed after a long deluge of tears, "I'll never dance again." This was the child who was such a joyful dancer that her grandfather had often commented to whomever might be listening, "Someone should really teach that girl to walk."

It was still early summer, but our devastated daughter was already thinking ahead. "This will be the worst Christmas ever!" she cried.

The idea of celebrating Christmas anywhere else seemed impossible, and pretty improbable as well. Many of our family, friends, and neighbors had lost their homes in the fire, too. It seemed that there would be no joy in this holiday season for SarahRose.

In an attempt to reclaim some element of normal life, I encouraged SarahRose to attend her regularly scheduled summer dance programs. "It will do you good to focus on something else," I told her. But she was reluctant. "Maybe it will help," I said.

Expectations were low, emotions were volatile, and stress levels high. We knew moving forward was our best option but we weren't sure how to do so. Logically it seemed to me that if SarahRose were spending all day with her friends doing what she loved, those were steps in the right direction.

By the time her summer programs were over and the fall semester began, she was beginning to feel excited about dancing again. Looming large over all the dancers at that time of year is the upcoming *Nutcracker* season. Cast lists typically appear toward the end of August and eager eyes scan the corkboard for postings.

We have long been a family of traditions. Stockings hung by the chimney with care, the Advent log, and other favorite activities were repeated year after year. As a family with three dedicated dancers, our girls have been dancing toy mice, soldiers, dolls, sugar babes, party girls, sugarplums, garland girls, angels, marzipan, flowers, and probably some parts we can't remember. Yes, *The Nutcracker* is a huge part of our holiday every year.

But things seemed different that year. There was no chimney on which to hang our homemade stockings, and although a friend made us a new Advent log, we had no mantel on which to place it. So many traditions were changing for us, whether we wanted them to or not. Feeling a bit apprehensive, SarahRose decided she would dance only in the Youth Ballet's production of *The Nutcracker* that year. Although sometimes it's fun to be part of two or three *Nutcracker* productions in the same year, she thought that would be too stressful when we didn't even have our real home anymore.

The chatter around the Ballet Society studios was all about *The Nutcracker* casting. A few people had commented to SarahRose, "I bet you'll be Clara this year." or "I hope you get to be Clara this year." She thought they were all being especially kind and encouraging because of the fire and she didn't expect to get the lead role. She figured she was too tall, because the prior year she had been in the correct age/height group for Clara.

Surprisingly, SarahRose was cast in the coveted role for the Colorado Youth Ballet's production! Her tears turned to laughter and she enjoyed every one of those rehearsals. It was one of the highlights of her life, giving her a new home for the holidays — the ballet studio — right when she needed it.

~Donna Lorrig

Photo by: Ted Mehl of A Better Image Photography, courtesy of Colorado Ballet Society

60

Manners Mishap

Politeness is the art of choosing among
one's real thoughts.
~Abel Stevens

We bundled up in our coats, mittens and hats to head out the door to Grandma's house. We loaded the wrapped gifts into the trunk and I saw that the kids were all buckled into their car seats. As we began to pull down the driveway, the kids were animated in their discussion of what awaited them at their grandparents' house.

"I bet Nana made cinnamon rolls!" Kyle said.

"And Grandpa will probably get out some shrimp later!" said Karen, matching his anticipation.

There's not much that's more heartwarming than listening to eager children on Christmas morning. Before they got too much further into their holiday chattering, I thought it would be a good time to launch into my annual conversation about good manners. "Be sure to say 'please' and 'thank you' at Grandma's today — at all of the meals and when you open your gifts — even if you don't like something," I lectured.

"Okay," they responded, as if they were wondering how I could be thinking of something as boring as manners on an exciting day like Christmas.

"How grown-up of me!" I chuckled to myself.

We finally arrived at the house and the kids dashed inside. They would only ask fifty times when it would be time to open gifts and I would only remind them fifty times to mind their manners.

Finally, the moment they'd somewhat patiently waited for arrived. We all gathered in our designated spots. The kids helped their grandmother and various aunts and uncles pass out the gifts. Then it was time to unwrap the gifts, one at a time as everyone watched.

Every year, my grandmother created handmade gifts. This particular year, she had knitted rainbow-striped cardigan sweaters. My daughter's was made with beautiful pastel yarns and my son's was made with primary colors. As they opened their sweaters, I watched as my young, elementary-aged son pulled his out of the box, held it up with an awkward look on his face, and said, "Thank you! Even though I don't like it!"

I was mortified as giggles broke out around the room. I couldn't really discipline my son because he'd done exactly as I'd instructed him. He said thank you even though he didn't like the gift. He just missed the context a bit.

Oh well! Out of the mouths of babes. Even my grandmother got a good laugh out of it and commented later that maybe the colors weren't quite suited to a young man. Kyle gave the sweater to his sister, who was very grateful to have two! Her enthusiasm for the sweaters and the group's laughter more than made up for my son's unfiltered but obedient comment.

~Stephanie Davenport

61

Chicken Soup for the Soul

A Gift from the Heart

*While we try to teach our children all about life, our
children teach us what life is all about.*
~Angela Schwindt

It had been a tradition for my husband to give me a box of
Nutchos chocolates at Christmas. They don't make them anymore, but at the time, they were delicious: a swirly mound of
milk chocolate filled with ground nuts.

In one of my "woe is me" moments, facing the first Christmas
after my husband and I had separated, I moaned and asked who was
going to buy me my Nutchos that year.

Days later, I took the kids to the local department store and handed
them money so they could do their own Christmas shopping. They
had been instructed to stay together, and we had a set time and place
to meet before we headed home.

A short time later I saw the kids lugging their purchases. It made
me smile to see their excitement with their first foray into holiday
shopping. But as we walked home, I saw one of my son's purchases
hanging out of his bag.

It seemed that instead of using the money for gifts, he had spent
the money on a huge bag of Doritos or some sort of junk food for
himself. I was annoyed, thinking that was not the giving holiday spirit
I was trying to teach him.

"Why did you buy chips?" I asked. "That money was for gifts for the family, not for you to buy yourself a snack."

He looked at me, his sad eyes looking hurt, holding back tears. "They're not for me," he said. "They're for you. You wanted to know who was going to buy you your nachos, and I wanted to make sure you got some."

Nutchos… made from chocolate and nuts. Nachos… a chip made by Doritos. I guess they could sound very much the same to an eight-year-old boy.

I gave that thoughtful little boy a big hug right there on the sidewalk.

~Deborah Lean

62

Chicken Soup for the Soul

Perfectly Presented

What's in a name? That which we call a rose by any
other name would smell as sweet.
~William Shakespeare

Even if I'd won the lottery, I wouldn't have sounded as excited as my daughter did that day. She had just come home from school and she stood at the door, grinning from ear to ear and holding a shopping bag.

For over a month, my daughter had worked extra chores around the house in order to earn money she could spend at the school's Christmas shopping day. The teachers transformed the cafeteria into a store where the children could buy inexpensive gifts. They would learn how to pay for items and receive change while shopping for their friends and family.

"Did you have fun?" I asked, remembering how ecstatic my daughter had been when she left for school that morning.

"You should have seen all the stuff, Mom," she squealed. "Hurry, come see what I bought everyone."

We quickly slipped into her bedroom, away from prying eyes. My daughter's hands shook from excitement as she gingerly removed the first item from her bag and slowly unwrapped the tissue paper that surrounded the gift.

The unwrapping took forever, but finally a miniature, tan burlap banner with a stamped picture of a rainbow trout and fishing pole emerged. Under the picture in small black letters it said, "Grandpa, world's best fisherman!"

Even though my father wasn't a fisherman, I knew he'd love it simply because my daughter had gotten it for him. "Wow that's nice," I chimed in. "Grandpa will love it!"

"But it's not for Grandpa," my daughter informed me. "It's for Uncle Paul. He's the one who loves to go fishing."

I could see why she'd gotten it for my brother — an avid fisherman, but hadn't she noticed the word "Grandpa"?

Upon unwrapping the next item, out popped a sparkling fabric coin purse with tiny letters that said, "To an aunt who is 'sew' sweet." Inside the purse I found brightly colored threads, a needle, and the tiniest pair of scissors I'd ever seen. While an adorable and useful gift, I knew my sister would never use it. Other than a sewing class in junior high school, my sister had never sewed or mended anything in her life.

Of course I told my daughter her aunt would love the sewing kit. "It's not for Aunt Jan," she replied. "It's for Grandma. She's the one who loves to sew."

At first I found her mistaken gift choices humorous, but carefully contained my laughter. What had I expected from a first grader who had shopped by herself? I couldn't blame the school. I asked my daughter if the teachers had helped her pick out her items; she said they had offered to help, but she wanted to shop on her own.

The next item was an abstract, black and white paperweight stamped with "World's Best Uncle."

"Is that for Aunt Jan?" I asked, now that I understood what my daughter had done. Aunt Jan loved black and white and had recently decorated her bedroom in those colors. My daughter answered, "Yes."

She unwrapped a white coffee mug sprinkled with black musical notes that simply said "Dad" on it. "Grandpa's present?" I asked, since my father loved playing the piano. She nodded yes.

As she pulled out the remaining presents, any humor on my part evaporated as I stared at my daughter's collection. In later years, my daughter and I would laugh about her first solo shopping trip, but at that moment my heart melted when it hit me how much love and care had gone into my daughter's shopping spree.

I could not have picked out more thoughtful or perfect gifts and she'd done it all on her own. I had no idea she'd known all about her family's hobbies and passions, but she'd shopped from her heart, making sure each gift perfectly matched its recipient.

As she lovingly wrapped her gifts, my daughter confessed that initially she'd picked out presents that she would want someone to give to her. Then, she remembered that Christmas was about bringing happiness to others and put them back. Those words alone made me feel the school shopping experiment had been a huge success.

Christmas morning I opened the present my daughter had gotten for me, a beautiful tiny fabric rainbow banner with the word "Grandma," and below it, "You're my pot of gold." The gift would hang on my wall until it rotted and fell apart.

But the greatest gift I received that Christmas was the joy on my daughter's beaming face as she watched her family open the presents that she had bought with her hard-earned money and carefully chosen. All by herself she'd discovered the joy in giving to others, a discovery that would last her a lifetime.

~Jill Burns

Sibling Secret Santa

We can only be said to be alive in those moments when
our hearts are conscious of our treasures.
~Thornton Wilder

It was Christmas of 2006 and once again we were planning our Sibling Secret Santa. My six-year-old brother Eric wanted to be included this year, despite the fact that his eight older brothers and sisters always gave him piles of gifts. Participating in Sibling Secret Santa meant he would receive only one gift.

The rest of us, who ranged in age from eighteen to twenty-seven, warned him that it would be his only gift to open Christmas Eve — a fact even some of us "adults" struggled to accept. Eric assured us that he was okay with this but we didn't believe him. My oldest sister had picked his name from the hat and decided to have a little fun with it. Our mother was famous for painting a piece of wood with a cheesy saying and giving it to us as a "present." So my sister gift-wrapped a wooden sign that read "God Bless America" and placed it in the pile for Eric. Hiding in the back bedroom was his real gift — a new bicycle.

During our annual Christmas Eve party, the nine of us gathered as we always did in the living room with *A Christmas Story* playing on the TV in the background. We all expected Eric to be disappointed by his wooden "gift." Some of us sat on the floor, some in chairs dragged in from the kitchen. Eric sat on the couch sandwiched between his two older brothers, giddy with anticipation. One by one we opened our gifts from our Secret Santas: new clothes, glassware for our houses, and other thoughtful and fun items.

Finally, it was Eric's turn.

We handed him his gift and waited for the meltdown. A six-year-old used to receiving stacks of toys and treats on Christmas Eve would no doubt be disappointed with a piece of wood. He began to recklessly tear though the snowflake paper, tossing shreds to each side. I will never forget his adorable little face as he unwrapped that painted sign and smiled bigger and brighter than I've ever seen. He beamed as he held the sign up, proudly showing off his gift to his brothers and sisters. I realized then that this little boy didn't care what that present was; he was just so happy to be a part of our Christmas tradition.

I was so proud to be a part of my family at that moment and I was reminded of how important our family traditions were. And I've never seen someone more appreciative of a gift — that is, of course, until his new bike was wheeled out!

~Jamie Kopf

The Best Present

*Good judgment comes from experience, and often
experience comes from bad judgment.*
~Rita Mae Brown

My seven-year-old eyes gleamed with envy when I saw my friend's new Disney watch. Hour and minute hands slowly marked time as Cinderella's face peeked from behind them. A soft pink leather band encircled my friend's arm. It was perfect.

That's what I wanted for Christmas.

"You're not old enough for a watch yet." My mother's voice brooked no argument. "What else would you like for Christmas?"

I hung my head. "Nothing." I dragged my feet as I walked away.

Looking back, I realize my parents had no money to waste on something I would likely lose. The market wasn't flooded then with cheap disposable trinkets as it is now. A watch was something we kept for years. Still, I wanted that watch.

When presents began materializing under the tree, none matched the size and shape of a jewelry box that might contain a watch. However, one with my name on it did pique my curiosity. About six inches tall, it had irregular contours — no straight edges or boxy corners. Mama had wrapped it well with thick paper, and the few times I could sneak to the back of the tree to check it out failed to give me any clues about its identity. My curiosity grew. Christmas seemed so far away.

One day, I could no longer stand it. While Mama cooked dinner, I pulled my four-year-old sister Shelly into the living room and pointed to the mystery gift. "Do you know what that is?"

Shelly nodded.

"What is it?"

"Mama told me not to tell you," she said.

I put my arm around her and used my best conspiratorial voice. "Let's make a deal. I'll tell you what I got you for Christmas if you tell me what's in that present."

Shelly brightened. "Okay. Watch."

I watched her. Nothing happened. "So what's in the present?"

"Watch."

I frowned for a moment and then comprehension dawned. "You mean a watch? They got me a watch for Christmas?"

She smiled and nodded.

I stared at the gift. It wasn't the right size or shape for a watch, and Mama had already said I couldn't have one yet. Shelly must have gotten mixed up. Or could they have changed their minds? Maybe...

Shelly stomped her foot. "I told you. Now you tell me. What did you get me for Christmas?"

I continued to study the present. "A coloring book," I said absently.

Shelly wandered off as I pondered the possibilities. Finally, I decided she was wrong. It couldn't be a watch. Whatever was under the bright wrappings would have to remain a secret until Christmas morning.

The big day came, and I headed straight for that gift. When I tore off the paper, I found a ceramic Cinderella figurine on a pedestal. In front of her, sat a beautiful Cinderella watch with a pink band. I squealed. "You got me the watch! Shelly told me you had, but I didn't believe her." Then I gasped and looked up.

The room suddenly became silent.

"Shelly," Mama said, "come here."

I froze, too horrified to speak.

"Why did you tell Tracy about her watch?" Mama asked.

Shelly, of course, spilled the entire story and received a lecture on keeping secrets. In turn, I got a well-deserved scolding for my deception. What hurt more was the disappointment in my parents' eyes. Not only had I ruined their surprise, but I had conned my little sister into doing something she wasn't supposed to do. I couldn't have felt any worse.

Mama and Daddy let me keep the watch. I wore it, but Cinderella's pretty face no longer held the same charm for me. Instead, she served as a daily reminder that I had violated my parents' trust.

Years later, I realized how much that reminder helped me stay on the straight and narrow. I never wanted to disappoint my parents like that again, but more importantly, it wasn't the kind of person I wanted to be, one who would use deceit and trickery to get what she wanted. The scolding, not the watch, was the best present I could ever have received.

~Tracy Crump

The Epiphany

*Other things may change us, but we start
and end with the family.*
~Anthony Brandt

As a young girl, I started writing my Christmas list in July, and by December I was mailing status reports to Santa about what a good girl I was. Every year on Christmas Eve my father stayed on Santa watch, and at the first sound of sleigh bells or reindeer hooves on our roof he would shuffle me off to bed as quickly as possible. My mother acted as my door guard to prevent me from sneaking out to see Santa at work.

Christmas morning was always the best. As soon as the sun peeked over the trees surrounding our small country house, I would race from my room, dash around the corner, and slide to a halt in our living room. The gas logs were always lit; the stockings were full; our beautiful Christmas tree was glowing; and Santa's gifts were displayed in plain sight.

Christmas morning was special because it was just my parents and me. We would see the rest of the family in a few hours, but the morning was all ours.

But then one Christmas my father wasn't there.

It was a harsh winter that year, one of the coldest that I remember. My father was a hard-working employee of the Department of Transportation. He was on call most nights, and risked his safety during some dangerous situations — lightning storms, hurricanes, ice storms, and even fatal car crashes. That Christmas we experienced one of the worst ice storms the community had seen in years. On Christmas Eve, just before our family dinner, my father was called out to work in order to help clear the roads during the storm. I wasn't too sad. I knew he'd be back soon.

He wasn't.

As the hours went on, I pestered my mother with questions regarding whether Dad was going to make it home for Christmas. She smiled each time and told me he'd be home as soon as he could. A few hours into the storm, we lost power. I asked my mom if Santa would be able to make it through such an awful storm. She assured me he would; after all, he had Rudolph leading the way.

Mom let me stay up past my usual bedtime to wait for Dad. By midnight, he still wasn't home. With no Christmas music, no Christmas lights, and no sign of Dad, I reluctantly gave up and was headed to my room when Mom said we could have a campout in the living room instead.

She sang Christmas carols and found every blanket and pillow in the house for us. Then she had me lie down on the couch, bundled up against the cold, and she told me stories — stories of past Christmases, stories about Santa, the story of Christ's birth, and even stories of she and Dad sneaking Santa's cookies. Before long, I fell asleep, wrapped in my mother's warm blankets and hanging onto her happy stories about Christmas.

When I opened my eyes, Santa had come. The presents were there and, for a moment, I felt a giant grin spread across my face. Mom suddenly appeared next to the window and drew open the blinds. We were still without power, but the storm had subsided. The morning sun was bright, and it made the winter landscape left by the storm glitter like a scene from a Christmas card.

With a happy but tired smile, Mom handed me a present. I hesitated, and after a moment asked if we could wait until Dad got home. Christmas morning was our family's time. It was the best part of Christmas, and it didn't feel right without him there. She hugged me tightly and sat next to me on the couch. For the rest of the morning we sat there together, huddled under a mountain of quilts, and entertained each other. We sang, we laughed, and bit-by-bit I felt my missing Christmas spirit return.

By early afternoon, the power came back on and the phones resumed working, too. We called the family to wish them a Merry Christmas. Travel was too dangerous, so our family gathering was postponed until the roads were clear.

As the late afternoon sun moved across the sky, a truck door slammed shut outside. Seconds later I heard footsteps crunching through the ice and pounding up the stairs to our front door. The door swung open and my father came bounding in. He was cold and tired, but at the sight of me he broke into a smile and shouted a hearty "Merry Christmas!" I raced into his arms and relished the warm bear hug that only my father could give.

Happy to finally have us all together, my excitement returned. We spent the rest of the day opening gifts, telling jokes, and enjoying each other's company.

I snuck a glance at my parents as they talked. In that one moment, even as a child, I realized the blessing that I had experienced. We were together, and that's all that mattered.

~Whitney Woody

The Hanukkah Gift

I brought children into this dark world because it
needed the light that only a child can bring.
~Liz Armbruster

It was clear from the moment I entered the toy store that I was a different kind of shopper. I was surrounded by people with lists — people who were on specific missions. I, on the other hand, had not a clue as what to buy. I had asked my son's former home therapist to help me pick out a Hanukkah present for him and she had enthusiastically agreed.

I realize it sounds strange, requiring assistance in selecting a gift for my own child; but Josh is on the autism spectrum and doesn't play with toys. Don't get me wrong — he has interests. He loves swimming, reading books, music, *Sesame Street* and the Muppets. He adores being tickled, jumping in bouncy castles and going on amusement park rides. But board games, doctor's kits, action figures… they're not his thing. I've never had a problem buying books or DVDs that reflect his passions, but I buy those things all year long. I wanted to buy him a Hanukkah gift that would be special — something he would both enjoy and actively play with.

"What about this?" my shopping companion asked, holding up a box of plastic animals.

"Won't work," I responded. "Josh will either mouth them or bang them against the wall." We passed the sporting goods section where

I recalled buying many items for occupational and physical therapy: a deep pressure vest to help Josh feel physically grounded, a beanbag chair for flopping, and a trampoline for when he was feeling especially jumpy.

After rejecting toy cars, pretend kitchen paraphernalia and other items that had failed to capture Josh's interest in therapy sessions, we settled on an oversized construction table that would fit in the corner of our living room. It came with large plastic bolts that fit in the table's surface, a plastic hammer and saw, and sliding doors in which any extra equipment could fit.

I went home and wrapped it to the best of my abilities, which wasn't saying much. Living with autism had made me a lot less focused on things like how a gift was presented. The important thing was to try out this gift. Even if Josh never played with that construction table he would remember that his father and I gave it to him. That had to count for something.

When my husband Aaron came home from work on the first night of Hanukkah we gave Josh his gift. Josh went over and examined it, feeling it out and banging his hammer. He then quickly gravitated toward the bubble wrap that had encased the table and proceeded to happily pop it with his hands and feet, giving himself the needed sensory input that so many on the autism spectrum crave. None of this surprised us; we knew our son well enough to know that this was a likely occurrence, and we accepted it. "At least we know he likes part of the gift," we joked, making light of a situation that we knew bothered us deep down. As we had with other items we'd bought for Josh in the past, we decided to keep the construction table in its designated corner. We had previously bought Josh toys that he hadn't shown interest in until months, even years later.

The days went by uneventfully. Holidays are often difficult and lonely for people with children on the spectrum, and we are no exception. Big parties can be overwhelming, often isolating us from family gatherings and public celebrations. We lit Hanukkah candles when Aaron got home from work while Josh was sleeping; we knew having an open flame would be a safety issue, and while it wasn't how we wanted to approach the holiday, we understood it to be necessary. Later that week, however, my holiday observance took a wonderful turn.

I went to check my e-mail one day before Josh got home from school. In my Inbox was a message from one of the teachers at Josh's school who runs the Jewish Affiliations Group. Since a formal Jewish education is impossible for Josh, this group gives children like him a chance to participate in activities and parties that mark the major holidays on the Jewish calendar. Most importantly, it creates an opportunity for these students to relate to a given holiday on a level that they can understand and enjoy, which makes the holiday experience at home far more inclusive than it would be otherwise. It meant the world to me.

I opened the message that read:

> Josh had a great time at the Hanukkah party today!
> Here are some pictures of him playing Pin the Candle on
> the Menorah and decorating a dreidel! Happy Hanukkah!

I clicked on every photo attachment; each one was better than the next. In the first one Josh was holding a candle made of oak tag, smiling brightly. In the next he held that same candle up to an oversized oak tag menorah that hung on a bulletin board while carefully placing it into its designated slot. In another, he was intensely engaged in decorating a cardboard dreidel. It wasn't just that he was celebrating Hanukkah that got to me — it was how utterly engaged he was. His expressions of delight and intense concentration in those photos overwhelmed me with joy; and his active participation in each activity translated through every image on my computer screen.

When Josh got home from school that day I gave him a huge hug and opened his backpack. Inside I found a tin menorah that he had painted in school. That evening, after sundown, I brought Josh to the window to light his creation and recited the accompanying blessings. It was the second blessing that deeply moved me: "Blessed are You, G-d, King of the universe, who has wrought miracles for our forefathers, in those days at this season."

It had been quite a while since holiday rituals felt more than obligatory. At that moment my son was able to connect to Hanukkah in a jubilant, meaningful way. In my mind, that was a miracle that needed to be celebrated as well. As we watched the candles flicker in the darkness I looked down at Josh, kissed the top of his head and smiled. "Thank you," I whispered, offering up a silent prayer of gratitude; for there was no better Hanukkah gift that any one of us could have asked for, let alone receive.

~Jennifer Berger

The Joy of Christmas

Holiday Decorating

*An informal survey shows that what most people want
for Christmas is two more weeks to prepare for it.*
~Bob Stanley

67

Confessions of a Holiday Hoarder

Later is the best friend of clutter.
~Peter Walsh

I live in a modest home, but we have enough decorations to deck the halls of a strip mall. Think I'm kidding? We have two trees, three manger scenes, snowmen of all shapes and sizes, and enough holiday teapots to host the Mad Hatter.

We only actually purchased two of these items — the smallest tree and the humblest nativity scene. We were newlyweds and we had nothing — at least, for one merry minute. Then, recognizing that we had nothing, everyone gave us gifts and hand-me-downs until we had more Christmas decorations in our small flat than I had furniture.

When we became new parents, people gave us "Baby's First Christmas" items — personalized ornaments, commemorative angels, more snowmen. This repeated with each additional child.

Then, my children entered the bauble and doodad factory that is kindergarten and grade school. Dozens of endearing holiday creations came our way — clothespin reindeers, Popsicle stick wreaths, papier-mâché Christmas piñatas. Most bore the monstrous scrawl of a kiddo just learning how to write, often under the wandering inscription of "I love Mom and Dad."

Ask any parent of a teenager — these things are more precious than gold, frankincense and myrrh.

When our grandparents moved to smaller living quarters, they gave us even more decorations, some very fine and some very corny. But they all have sentiment and meaning to us.

My husband and I are sentimental people but we never intended to be "Holiday Hoarders." Every January I vow to clean out the maimed and lame, but then I hold onto something my grandmother gave me or something my seventeen-year-old made when she was three.

Heck, I struggle to get rid of the stuff even when it's broken. The year my grandmother's tree passed out on the living room floor, she was dying in hospice. I couldn't bring myself to toss it, so I repurposed it. I took several boughs and used them to wrap around our staircase railing as a garland. That was two years ago and I am still doing it.

To atone for my soft heart, I organize like a curator. Everything has its place, even if its proper place should be the recycling bin. We have our original Christmas tree upstairs and my mother-in-law's tree downstairs, an ornament gracing every bough. I have a table just for snowmen and another for teapots. I even have my own island of misfit toys for all the decorations that have no theme. The funny part is, when it's all out, the place looks downright jolly.

It didn't cost me much, except my crawlspace. And, one day when these kids of mine marry, it will all be theirs. They will probably toss most of it, but then again, they might not. After all, I already gave them something — my genes.

~Nicole L.V. Mullis

68

Chicken Soup for the Soul

A Magical Time

Christmas waves a magic wand over this world, and
behold, everything is softer and more beautiful.
~Norman Vincent Peale

To say Mawmaw liked decorating her home for Christmas is a vast understatement. That would be like saying Santa thinks cookies are okay or Frosty somewhat enjoys a snowy day. My grandmother was the Queen of Christmas Decorating, second only to Mrs. Claus herself.

Every October Mawmaw would begin to purge the storage shed of its Christmas artifacts and fill the already crowded house to the brim. Patience was not a virtue when it came to Christmas. Plus, Mawmaw liked to perform this extreme home makeover by Halloween in order to, as she put it, "give the Devil a black eye."

Many of my favorite childhood memories are set in her tiny, cozy home filled with treats, tinsel and trees. As soon as I entered her house it was as if I were transported to the North Pole. Bright red, shiny wrapping paper covered the door, making it look like the biggest Christmas present ever. The family room was overflowing with nativity scenes in all sizes and styles — large and porcelain, small and crystal. Mawmaw had two Christmas trees. One was more traditional, and the other was a bright white artificial spruce complete with pink ornaments, the vast majority of them hearts. You could see both trees at the same time in her small house.

My favorite decoration was a Christmas clock that she never took down. It played carols every hour, on the hour, the entire year.

This is a warm, fuzzy scene no matter your age. But seen through the eyes of a child, its magic was magnified.

The years went by, and after my grandpa passed away Mawmaw moved to a senior living community. I was worried that Christmas as I knew it was over.

My first visit to Mawmaw's new place put that fear to rest. The nursing home displayed an enormous tree in the lobby near its floor-to-ceiling windows. They also had plenty of large wrapped presents for decoration. It felt warm, cozy and homey.

Mawmaw's room was completely her. She had a lot of her most important possessions there, including Christmas decorations. A large, fuzzy snowman welcomed everyone into the room. The tree was now one foot tall and made of shiny plastic, but it was still there. The nativity scenes created a unique, miniature skyline across her windowsill against the snowy landscape outside.

And my favorite decoration? The Christmas clock? Mawmaw gave it to my parents. Now, when I visit my childhood home and hear a Christmas carol ring out every hour, I'm reminded of the permanence of Christmas. Places and circumstances change, time moves forward, but Christmas, family and the love that permeates them remains, no matter what.

~Traci Clayton

Our Alluring Tree

*Perhaps the best Yuletide decoration is
being wreathed in smiles.*
~Author Unknown

There was only one weekend left before the big holiday, and we were running out of time to get our tree. My husband, Paul, begrudgingly accompanied me to a local tree farm and we sawed down a blue spruce tree. Paul hastily dragged the tree through the snow to our pickup and hoisted it into the bed, oblivious to the nostalgic value of this occasion. In less than five minutes we were home, rushing so that Paul wouldn't miss the big game on TV.

Luckily, our son Reed was home when we arrived, so he seized one end of the tree and helped Paul push and shove the tree through our front door and then wedge it into the tree stand. I didn't dare suggest spinning the tree to be certain the bare side wasn't showing or the crooked trunk revealed. In a flash my two helpers disappeared into the basement to resume their preferred project, preparing the fishing tackle for winter storage. While they watched the Steelers, Paul and Reed changed or sharpened hooks on hundreds of wooden and plastic fish facsimiles.

I stood by the aromatic spruce, resignedly pinning on the lights and questioning why I was doing this alone. As I descended to the basement to retrieve the musty old boxes of ornaments, I observed

Paul filing the hooks on a bumble bee, a ten-inch oblong lure, painted like its name with mustard yellow and black stripes, a brilliant crimson streak just under the plastic lip. In that instant my mind conjured a Christmas tree display I had visited last year at our local library. Each tree portrayed a unique theme. Some trees wore items that weren't even actual ornaments, but collections that the decorator had acquired.

I spoke impulsively. "Why don't we decorate our tree with musky lures this year?" It worked! Within the hour, our tree was bedecked with grandmas, believers, and spinners in kaleidoscope colors. I had never seen the guys participate with such enthusiasm in any holiday activity prior to this.

Conveniently, the lures come right out of the tackle boxes with built-in hooks, so there were no boxes to open, no tissue paper to unwrap, and no hauling boxes from the basement or attic. Most of the lures spend the winter hanging from little ledges in our basement.

We selected the lures for the tree based on color, their unique designs, or their nostalgic value. Just as families reminisce about traditional ornaments and their history, we talked about which lures worked in which lakes, the lure on which Reed caught his first fifty-inch musky, the lure that was lost in the bottom of a lake and found a year later by a friend of ours, and so on.

We also talked about the next year's fishing vacations and which lures to retire or get repainted by Sandy the lure painter. Our tree looked beautiful with the radiance of a glitter perch, a mother-of-pearl shad, and a hot orange crawdad nestled among the boughs in the glow of twinkle lights. No garland was necessary either. We had the feathery pink, chartreuse, and iridescent gold streamers of the spinners to add texture and elegance.

Now that the tree was so macho, Reed even agreed to have his photo taken by the tree with his date for the Christmas dance.

The musky lure tradition persisted for sixteen years, with the exception of one year when our black Labrador retriever was a puppy and we feared he would be hooked. I simplified the holidays in other ways as well. Over the course of subsequent years I eliminated cookie baking, mailing greeting cards, and excessive shopping. I give gift cards, lottery tickets, and coveted cash — not so imaginative, but apparently appreciated. If need be, Amazon will ship all the toys I need for my granddaughters.

In 2011 the inventory of musky lures relocated to Ontario, now stored in Reed's garage and used for fishing the St. Lawrence River. No sparkling glass balls or commercial trimmings could ever supplant those lures as prized Christmas tree ornaments.

~Cinda Findlan

70

Tin Can Christmas

You give but little when you give of your possessions. It
is when you give of yourself that you truly give.
~Kahlil Gibran

W hen I was eight years old, my father moved our family from New Jersey to Massachusetts to start a business in the town where he'd grown up. At first, my brothers and I were unhappy about the move because it meant leaving our friends and classmates. The relocation was especially hard on my mother, as it placed her hours away from her mother and sisters for the first time in her life.

Once landed in our new home, my brothers and I occupied ourselves with making friends, tackling schoolwork, and playing with cousins we'd never met before. It was harder for Mom, though, to meet new people. On top of that, we were short on funds while my dad worked to launch his business.

As fall turned into winter and money remained tight, my parents were arguing more than ever and Dad was scrambling to work odd jobs while he got his business off the ground. Gifts were not really in the budget that year, and Mom's spirits grew as gray as the skies.

On top of all this stress and sadness, we discovered that most of our Christmas tree ornaments had broken during the move from New Jersey.

My mother, ever resourceful, took an unexpected action. On a mild day in early December, my brother and I came home from school to find Mom in the back yard, assembling an impromptu crafts station on the picnic table. "We lost our Christmas ornaments," she proclaimed, "so we're going to make our own." Mom had gathered spray paint, sequins, and glitter to adorn the unlikeliest of decorations: tin can lids. She'd spent the past week removing and saving the lids after meals, and that day she eagerly waited for us kids to arrive before cutting them with tin snips into stars, bells, angels, and trees.

My brothers and I got to choose our shapes and decorate them as we laughed, sang carols, told tales about our new teachers and classmates, and basked in Mom's renewed cheer. That December afternoon at the picnic table was more memorable than most Christmas mornings full of shiny paper and expensive gifts.

To this day, my brothers and I speak fondly of our "tin can Christmas" as we point out the few surviving ornaments on our parents' tree. Primitive, yet crafted with love and hope, they are more precious than most of the glittery, store-bought new ones.

I recall that ornament-making party in the back yard as a glowing example of my mother's creativity, resilience, and ability to bring love and light to our days no matter how dark her own were. Struggling with three kids, financial hardship, persistent migraines, part-time jobs, and a business to co-manage, Mom didn't have much time or space to explore her passions during my childhood. But she was usually up for fun, and sometimes went out of her way to create it.

The magic of that particular Christmas came directly through my loving mother, who could turn tin cans into angels, and darkness into light.

~Kim Childs

71

Perfectly Imperfect

The heart, like the mind, has a memory. And in it
are kept the most precious keepsakes.
~Henry Wadsworth Longfellow

My mother-in-law was never particularly sentimental. When she passed away at ninety years old, after living for sixty-five years in the same house, she had one thin photo album, some dusty slides, and a small box of photos. A tiny enameled tin held a locket and a pair of baby shoes from her first child, Carolyn, who'd died at age one.

Still, her Christmas decorations — spare though they were — stayed the same from year to year. A white porcelain nativity set. A garland across the mantel, adorned simply with a few flocked red birds. A Santa candleholder. And — peculiarly, I thought, for someone whose house was always impeccable — three ceramic elves, each holding a letter of the alphabet: N, O, and E.

Once, she saw me looking at them and shrugged. "The L broke years ago, but I just like them," she said.

Had she held her baby daughter, and later, her two sons, up to the mantel to look at the merry row of elves? Was my no-nonsense mother-in-law just a wee bit sentimental about those ghosts of Christmas past?

The last time my children and I spent with Ma was Christmas. After dinner at her house, she wanted to get out the old slides, which had been buried in boxes in the closet for years. Nearly blind with macular degeneration, she had to stand with her nose nearly brushing the screen to see the images, but we spent hours with those memories. Afterward, we all agreed it had been our best Christmas together, ever.

She died that February. When we cleaned out the house, I saved those three little ceramic elves, still smiling and holding up the holly-

sprigged letters N, O and E. The next Christmas, I put them out, but somehow it bothered me. Their message seemed to be: "No L." I wondered again about Ma's loyalty to the damaged set. Why hadn't she thrown it out or given it away like so many of her other imperfect or unneeded belongings?

Now she was missing from the family circle, just like her daughter. Just like that long-broken L. Had she looked at it as I now did, seeing a once-complete set that was forever missing a necessary piece?

Year after year, I lined up the elves. But I never learned to accept the gap at the end.

Nearly five years after Ma's passing, I packed up the set with the other Christmas decorations. The holiday was over for another year. But this time, I had a thought. Maybe if I searched the Internet, I could find a vintage elf, holding up the letter L.

It was a crazy idea.

The elf set was at least sixty years old. Why would anybody save one letter all those years? And, if they had, what would be the odds of it being the only letter I needed? Who would they expect to buy it? Someone named Linda or Leonard?

Still, I figured it was worth a try.

For hours, I searched and clicked. "Vintage ceramic Christmas elf letter L."

Many results cranked forth. Ceramic elves, plastic elves, modern elves, gnomes and pixies. None of them holding any letters whatsoever. My eyes blurred from scanning through them.

Suddenly, one line jumped out: "Ceramic elf, vintage. Holding letter L."

My hand shook. This suddenly felt like something inexplicable was happening. I clicked.

There he was. A perfect, perky little Christmas elf, holding up the letter L, just as if he had been waiting to offer it to me.

He looked the same. Could he possibly be from the same set? The size looked right. The color looked right. The letter even had the holly decorating it, just like the others. I knew he'd be right at home with the rest.

Without further debate, I clicked "Buy."

Several weeks later, a tiny carton appeared in my mailbox. Impatiently, I clawed at the packing tape and pulled out the tissue paper packing.

There he was — saucy and smiling. The elf with the L.

But when I got out the rest of my set, my heart sank. This guy was just slightly smaller in scale. He didn't really match.

So maybe it wasn't the after-Christmas miracle I'd thought it was. But when I lined them all up the following holiday season, weaving their way through a bed of pine, they looked pretty darn good. "No 'L'" had once again become "NOEL."

The set wasn't perfect. When we lose someone, nobody else can ever really take her place. My mother-in-law went on to have those two boys after Carolyn died, and her life was again complete, but never the same.

Now she, too, was gone. We'd add other family members, including her great-granddaughter, born on what would have been Ma's 100th birthday. However, without her, our family would never be as it once was.

But that was okay. And the elves were okay. I knew Ma would

have been delighted with her great-granddaughter. And I knew, with her love of order, she'd have been delighted to see NOEL marching across the mantel again.

~Susan Kimmel Wright

Christmas Glow

The words light and Christmas are close together
in the dictionary of our hearts.
~Author Unknown

I blame *National Lampoon's Christmas Vacation* for my husband Derek's reluctance to attempt outdoor lighting and decorations during the holiday season.

Watching the movie is an annual tradition in our home, but I fear Clark Griswold's electrical mishaps may have installed a wariness of Christmas lights in my own "Sparky."

Each year, the day after Thanksgiving finds me knee-deep in red and green storage bins and tinsel as I deck our halls. My usual décor comes off the walls and is replaced with framed Santa prints and holiday sentiments.

Glittering candles gleam from every surface. Candy canes fill Christmas mugs. Our fifteen-year-old son Sam constructs a gingerbread house. The nativity set is carefully unpacked and surrounded by a heavenly host of angels I've collected over the years. The stockings are hung by the entertainment center with care and our plain white dinnerware is packed away, replaced by elegant holiday-themed dishes.

Though the inside of our home may seem like a winter wonderland, the only visible evidence of the season outdoors are two dispirited wreaths flanking the front door.

I'm not alone in my wish to have the outside of our home reflect its indoor cheer. Sam has been hankering for outdoor lights for years. "Please, can we just have a few?" he asks. "I'll help you hang them. I'll make sure our house doesn't look Griswoldy!"

"We'll see," his dad replies. Every child knows "we'll see" means "no" in dad-talk.

But this fall, Derek and Sam discovered several boxes of lighted holiday displays while helping my mother-in-law clean out her garage. "What should I do with these?" his mom asked. "We haven't put them up since your dad died."

Sam seized the moment. "We'll take them!"

"But…" Derek started to say.

"Of course you can have them! Papa would love to know you're using them," said Grandma.

A father's objections are no match for a grandma and grandson combo.

So, this year while I unpacked the bins from the basement, Sam went to the shed and lugged out boxes filled with deer, a star, a nativity set and a Christmas tree.

He manfully untangled wires and lights and assembled various parts of reindeer anatomy. However, Sam insists they are not reindeer. "The boxes say 'deer,'" he said. But I'm at a loss as to what regular old deer have to do with Christmas, so I'm calling them reindeer.

In true Griswold fashion, the lights on the middle part of Dancer (yes, I named them) refused to shine. Enter Derek, who spliced some wires and sliced his thumb and soon all was bright.

Then it was the Christmas tree that kept collapsing and Dasher who tipped sideways like he'd tipped back one too many rum toddies. By this time Derek was sweating and I could see why he'd been reluctant to take the holiday lights plunge.

Sam, however, had enough enthusiasm for the both of them.

Finally, they hauled the decorations out to the front yard and departed to the hardware store to buy electrical cords and timers and whatever else they needed before the big reveal.

I've learned much about hardware store trips over the years. Enough to know one trip is never enough. I also surmised that getting hundreds of lights to twinkle may take a lot of time and may involve language I prefer not to hear. So, while they were at the store, I headed out to have dinner with friends.

The sun set and I prolonged my outing with a few errands, uncertain what I'd find when I returned. Would fuses be blown? Tempers lost? Light bulbs smashed?

I needn't have worried. As I rounded the corner to our home, a soft glow beckoned. I followed the light and it led me to a shining star suspended beneath our front window. On the lawn below, the nativity set sparkled with jewel-toned lights, while a pair of mostly-lit reindeer kept watch. The lighted Christmas tree shimmered nearby.

It was tasteful. It was beautiful. Papa would be proud.

"Great job, guys!" I said, as I entered the house.

Derek and Sam grinned. "Yeah, it turned out pretty nice," my husband said. "But you know, we could add more. Maybe some angels, candy canes, some more deer…"

Sam joined in the dreaming. "They put all this stuff on sale after Christmas — we could get some great deals!"

Their voices followed me into the kitchen as I poured a cup of cider. "Trains! Snowmen! Santas!"

Once again I'm reminded, 'tis the season to be careful what you wish for.

~Cindy Hval

Saving Father Christmas

If you had duct tape, you were prepared for anything.
~Annie Barrows

The arm twisted free, thumped down to the floor, and slid under the Christmas tree. I wrestled both legs and the lower torso almost back into place. Just as I yanked up the pants, the legs did an acrobatic flip and rolled off the chair. "What else can go wrong?" I muttered.

Loud tapping on the store window startled me. I jerked and grabbed the head to keep it from joining other fallen body parts. Peering into the darkness outside, I discovered a laughing group of my old high school friends. Where was the Woman's Christian Temperance Union when I really needed them? They used to make stores cover their windows when there was any dressing or undressing of mannequins.

I gave an exaggerated bow to my new audience and continued to put Santa back together even though his preference seemed to be falling apart. Turning this store window into a charming Christmas scene had sounded so simple when the store manager suggested it. His only request had been to include a reclining chair, which happened to be on sale, in the display. The tree and decorations practically put themselves together. Even the two mannequin children in their red and green pajamas had cooperated and were peeking into the room.

Santa, reclining in the chair, was supposed to be taking a little nap, even though his painted-on eyes would remain open. I retrieved the wayward arm, reattached it, and added a strip of duct tape just to make sure that arm didn't escape again. Duct tape — what a wonderful invention to come out of World War II. More of my beloved duct tape secured Santa's legs. On went the red suit. I was on a roll now. To create a belly that shook like a bowl full of jelly, I rammed bed pillows in the shirt and pants and buckled his belt. Lastly, I used duct tape to anchor the beard and hair. The hair sort of resembled a cheap toupee, but fortunately, the hat covered most of it.

I stepped back to examine my work. Nice. Another tap on the window made me look out. Five thumbs pointed up.

~Sharon Landeen

74

Chicken Soup for the Soul

Camel Herder

*One camel does not make fun of
another camel's hump.*
~Ghanaian Proverb

It was a month before Christmas and I was in my attic surrounded by boxes of holiday decorations. Luckily I had labeled each box with a marker. When I spotted the box labeled "Nativity Scene" my heart skipped a beat. My children and I have always looked forward to unwrapping the delicate figures of Mary, Joseph, Baby Jesus, and the Three Wise Men, along with a stable full of animals. Carrying the box downstairs, I was greeted by applause from four excited children.

As soon as the box was opened, eight little hands started pulling out its contents. Then I heard my son Scott sobbing. "Look, Mom, my camel has no legs."

He was right! The camel that had served us for years by standing watch over Baby Jesus was legless. "I'll fix him; don't cry," I said.

In the meantime, we set up the nativity scene on the floor, to the right of the fireplace where the cradled baby would be kept warm.

I carefully glued Mr. Camel's legs back on. It didn't work. Scott cried when the legs fell off for the second time, and the third. "Don't worry, I have an idea," I said.

I called and e-mailed my friends about my camel dilemma. I had high hopes that a replacement camel would turn up. Someone just had to have an extra camel they could spare.

My husband, who is a true believer in Christmas miracles, said, "If you tell one person you are looking for a camel, you'll probably end up with fifty."

The next day a neighbor arrived at my door holding a tan camel in her hands. "I had two camels which fought all the time," she said, laughing. "It's time to separate them."

Her camel was a bit larger than I hoped for, but how could I refuse this kind gesture? I placed the camel in back of the stable. Then I explained to my children that some camels are big and tall while others may be short and pudgy, like people.

I was given a chipped beige camel by another neighbor. He was the front-runner so far because of his perfect size, but he was pretty ragged looking, as though he had just walked across the desert following the Star of Bethlehem.

"He needs a bubble bath," my daughter suggested. We wiped him down, but it didn't make any difference.

A good friend e-mailed me saying she had a purple camel that would be the talk of the town — Bethlehem, of course. I couldn't wait to pick it up. The camel had a purple shiny lacquer finish, and a gold and red etched seat with a matching harness. This was the one!

When I brought the statue home, there was no putting it down. It flew in and out of little hands, like a hot potato, and then around again. Yes, the purple camel would watch over Baby Jesus in our crèche.

In two weeks time I amassed thirteen camels. My nativity scene was surrounded by a caravan of camels that were standing, sitting, sleeping and arching their necks. My kids enjoyed playing with the different sizes, shapes and colors of the camels, marching them up and down the living room floor and around the Christmas tree.

Next year I plan to label another box of Christmas decorations that will say "Camel Caravan." Who would have thought a purple camel could bring so much joy into our lives?

~Irene Maran

75

Barely Decorated

*I love Christmas, not just because of the presents but
because of all the decorations and lights and
the warmth of the season.*
~Ashley Tisdale

I grew up in Ohio, where cold and snow were a big part of the Christmas season. When I struck out on my own as an adult, I moved to Florida. As the holiday season approached that first year on my own, frosted window panes were replaced by Santa in sunglasses and Bermuda shorts and flamingos draped in twinkle lights.

Growing up, the first Sunday after Thanksgiving was tree-cutting day. We'd pile the entire family into the station wagon and head off to a local tree farm. There, we'd meet up with several other families we knew who collectively called themselves "The Brunch Group." We'd all tramp out into the fields and each family would select its own version of the perfect tree. Afterward, we'd all head to one family's home for hot chocolate.

Christmas in Florida, on my own, was a far different experience. That first year in a new city there were no friends to meet, and no nearby farms to cut my own Christmas tree. Undeterred, I set off to the lot at the corner supermarket and selected a tree like the ones I'd grown up with, a six-foot tall blue spruce. I'd already shopped for a stand and several strands of lights. Even alone, I was excited to get home and decorate.

It didn't take long, once I returned to my railroad flat apartment, to get the tree straight in the stand and cover it with strand after strand of colored, blinking lights. I stood back, turned off the lamp, and admired the twinkly glow of my handiwork. For a moment, it looked and smelled just like Christmas.

That's when I remembered that there was no attic to go to and no boxes of ornaments to retrieve. I hadn't even thought about ornaments.

For the next few days, each time I entered my home, I looked at that bare tree. Yet, I refused to head to the local stores to purchase ornaments. In my family, ornaments were never purchased in bulk. Each ornament was purchased, on its own, during a trip or adventure. Each one had a special memory attached to it. As we hung each ornament we got to relive family trips and personal accomplishments. A dozen store-bought red balls certainly wouldn't do.

When I arrived home from work about a week after I'd assembled my first tree, there was a box on the porch. I loved getting packages and mail, and I rushed inside to open the parcel. It was from my mother and it came with a simple note: "I thought you might need these."

Inside was a selection of some of the familiar family ornaments I'd grown up with. My mother had selected a few dozen of "my" ornaments, those that held a special meaning for me from my childhood, like the snowman with the frilly collar, the bass playing Santa, a chipped, plaster dog painted brown, and a silver bell with my own smiling second grade face. At the bottom of the box, unwrapped, but with a blue bow, was a small box. Inside was a new "one-of-a-kind" ornament. A shiny key dangled from a little house with the inscription: "My First Home: 1987."

One after the other, I hung the few treasures on my very big tree. Those few ornaments didn't make a dent in all those empty branches. But, for me, it was the most beautiful tree ever. It was my first Christmas tree on my own.

~Gregory A. Kompes

76

The Barbie Christmas

Children make you want to start life over.
~Muhammad Ali

My five-year-old granddaughter, Anna Grace, was sitting on a child's wooden bench in my living room and staring at the decorated Christmas tree. It was most unusual for her to be silent. She hadn't said a word in an hour and I was wondering if she was okay. Her big blue eyes were larger than ever.

Finally, she turned to me and said, "GG, why didn't you tell me?"

"Because I wanted to surprise you."

"Where did you get all the Barbies?" she asks. "And all the pretty dresses?"

"I was shopping at Goodwill. Someone dropped off fourteen Barbies in pretty dresses. I thought they would be beautiful on a Christmas tree and you would love it. I decided to search for more after that."

After discovering the first fourteen dolls, I kept looking for secondhand Barbies in party dresses for the Christmas tree. At Salvation Army and Southern Thrift, I found more dolls and plastic bags filled with sparkling clothes to dress the Barbies we already had. My plan fell into place. I had a variety of forty Barbies ready for the tree — all dressed beautifully.

Anna Grace enjoyed the tree throughout the Christmas season. At year's end she was delighted to take it down. She placed the Barbies in a line on the floor, counting each one. It was time to play with the best Christmas decorations ever.

Anna Grace played with the Barbies for hours. We dressed and undressed them, cut and styled their hair, named them, and went on imaginary adventures with them. They were swimmers, gymnasts, shoppers, and explorers. They had Ken dolls to escort them to fancy parties or the beach. I don't know which one of us had more fun playing with our collection of thrift store Barbies.

Months later, Anna Grace said, "GG, I have beautiful Barbies somewhere at my house, but these thrift store Barbies are the ones we played with the most."

It's been eleven years since the Barbie Tree Christmas. Our family and friends still talk about it. Now, the Barbies wait in their pretty dresses, tucked away in tissue-lined boxes. A few will be selected for a small Christmas tree. It's a grandmother's tradition and a story I've told over and over and over.

~Gloria Hudson Fortner

77

The Sad Little Tree

Never worry about the size of your Christmas tree. In
the eyes of children, they are all thirty feet tall.
~Larry Wilde

I t was later than I had realized. The sun was beginning to set
and the farm would be closing shortly. I bundled up our three
daughters quickly as my husband warmed up the van. We
arrived at the farm with just fifteen minutes to pick out a tree
and cut it down.

Cutting down our own Christmas tree had been a family tradition
from the time my husband and I were newlyweds. As our family grew,
so did our excitement for going on our annual adventure to find the
perfect tree.

As we walked through the rows of trees, my youngest daughter
Kimberly piped excitedly, "There it is, the perfect tree!" My two other
daughters agreed in unison, "Yes, that's the one!" My husband and I
looked at each other puzzled. We were surprised the girls thought that
straggly little tree was perfect. Its branches were misshapen and the
trunk was visible through the spots where there were no pine needles.

We tried to coax our daughters into changing their minds by
showing them what we thought were better trees. We soon realized
there was no changing their minds. With the clock ticking toward
closing time, we had no choice; the sad little tree would be ours.

We tied the tree to the roof of our van and headed home. As we slowly drove through the whirling snow, we joyfully sang Christmas songs until we reached our front door. My oldest daughter, Heather, hopped out of the van first. With eyes wider than saucers, she announced, "The tree isn't on top of the van!" We thought she was kidding, but no, the tree wasn't there. It must have fallen off along Route 537 during our chorus of Christmas songs.

The girls were so disappointed. We had our entire evening planned around decorating the tree. Hot cocoa, more Christmas caroling, and reading the book *The Night Before Christmas* were on our agenda. "We'll get another tree tomorrow," I said, secretly hoping the new tree would be prettier. But the girls gave us the look that no parent can resist, complete with pouting and quivering lower lips. There was only one thing to do — backtrack and find that tree.

About five minutes into our drive, our headlights shone on our tree off to the side of the road. "There it is!" we all shouted together. As we got closer, it was apparent that it had been run over by something big, perhaps a truck. As my husband and I lifted the tree, we saw that a big portion of the tree was ripped off, but we took our little broken tree home anyway.

Once at home, we all agreed that the flat broken side would go up against the wall. That night, as we decorated our tree, something magical happened. We didn't realize it at the time but we were making a very special family memory. By the time we were done, I had to admit, it didn't look sad after all. My daughters all agreed that the tree was beautiful. "This is the best tree we ever had. It's perfect!" my daughter Samantha said with excitement. My husband and I couldn't have agreed more!

Now as Christmases come and go and we gather around our Christmas tree, we always say, "This is one of the prettiest trees we've ever had!" Then we reminisce about our little broken tree! One by one, we chime in and tell the story of that very special Christmas almost twenty-five years ago.

~Dorann Weber

78

Lights, Camera, Action

*The child supplies the power but the
parents have to do the steering.*
~Dr. Benjamin Spock

ecorating for Christmas has always been a highlight of the
year for me. When I was young and still living in my parents' house, I pleaded to get the decorations out as soon as
Thanksgiving dinner was over.

Every time a "Christmas" box was pulled down from the attic,
my eyes lit up. There's just something about Christmas — especially
the lights — that brightened my spirits on the gloomy days of winter
when it gets dark so early.

My sweet, eleven-year-old son, Colton, knew how much I liked
decorating for Christmas. One year, we got all the Christmas boxes
out with the intention of putting up the lights and decorations a little
at a time each night after I came home from work. But Colton wanted
to surprise me, so he did it himself.

He couldn't wait to show me how he carefully wound the white
lights around each baluster and each railing on the deck of our second
floor apartment. He was so proud of himself! I gave him a big hug and
told him how much help he was to me.

After dinner, we decided to go out on the deck and enjoy his
special holiday decoration surprise. He wanted me to sit on the chair
while he plugged in the deck lights. When he did, they were so bright

I thought I was on a television stage. He had not strung one set of lights... but four. I couldn't bring myself to tell him I thought there might be too many lights. I didn't want to hurt his feelings.

I continued to give him kudos about what a good job he had done. We sat outside basking in the overwhelming glow of all those white lights. When we decided to head inside for the night, he begged me to leave the lights on.

This routine went on for a couple more nights until one night there was a knock on the door. I looked through the peephole and there stood the apartment maintenance man. He politely told me that the people on the deck next to ours were complaining about all the light. This was not because they were Scrooges, according to the maintenance man, but rather because our lights were so incredibly bright that they were keeping the poor couple awake at night even with their blinds closed!

After he left, I drove around to the loading dock of the Home Depot behind our apartment complex to check out our lights from that distance. There happened to be workers unloading a truck at the time. I pulled up, got out of the car and looked back toward our apartment. I mentioned to the workers that the enormous glow in the distance was from my apartment and they told me they had wondered what was going on over there. There were other Christmas lights in our complex but none as bright as ours. They joked that there was maybe a Hollywood movie crew shooting a sequel to *Christmas Vacation*.

I spent the short drive back deciding how to explain to my son that we would have to remove some of the lights. Not wanting him to feel bad, I gently explained that we did not want to "outshine" our neighbors. That evening, we took photos of what a magnificent job he had done decorating the deck for Christmas, after which I helped him remove several strands of lights.

Last year Colton sent me a photo of how he had decorated the sidewalk up to the apartment he now shares with his wife. He had penguin and candy cane lights along the walkway, five inflatables on the small grassy area, a wreath on the door and miniature white lights framing his doorway. I guess he never really forgot how good it feels to decorate for the holidays. And even though it's been twenty-three years since my genuinely sweet son went delightfully overboard in creating his Christmas surprise for me, I'll never forget the year that he put us on center stage in the "Hollywood Lights."

~AimeeAnn Blythe

The Joy of Christmas

Taking Care of Each Other

The joy of brightening other lives, bearing each others'
burdens, easing other's loads and supplanting empty
hearts and lives with generous gifts becomes for
us the magic of Christmas.
~W. C. Jones

The Last Christmas

It is the personal thoughtfulness, the warm human
awareness, the reaching out of the self to one's fellow
man that makes giving worthy of the Christmas spirit.
~Isabel Currier

I t was an unusually warm and sunny day for early winter in Minnesota, with a fresh coating of snow gently blanketing the ground. The air smelled of a crisp pine scent coming from the fragrant evergreen trees nearby. Crowds of people were gathering on the lawn of a house, the driveway and the nearby road. They quickly decorated the outside of the house and the nearby trees with ornaments, ribbons, and wreaths.

A local news station had picked up the story and was filming the activity. Friends and neighbors set up tables offering homemade Christmas cookies and hot apple cider. A talented local art teacher was selling special Christmas pins painted by her art students to raise money for the family inside the house. And then Santa arrived bearing a glorious red sack full of toys and gifts. He rang the doorbell.

All this commotion and good cheer was the result of a top-secret mission to bring Christmas early to the family inside that house: my good friends Michael, Nicole, and their four young children. Michael was nearing the end of his battle against an aggressive form of oral squamous cell cancer. Radiation and chemotherapy treatments had bought him some precious time, but the cancer was in his lungs and lymph nodes now.

It had been surprisingly easy to coordinate this event by using technology. We were able to spread the word to family, friends, neighbors, community and church. People e-mailed and called by the dozens and asked what they could bring and how they could help. In just one week's time, the word had gotten out that there would be a spectacular Christmas celebration on Michael's front lawn in the middle of November!

Now, Santa was ringing the doorbell and we were waiting for our guest of honor. Michael slowly opened the door and the crowd began to sing Christmas carols. He choked back tears at the same time that he was smiling. In that brief moment, it seemed like the cancer had disappeared.

The news crew captured the entire event as it unfolded. Michael stepped out onto the porch where he was greeted by Santa Claus and a multitude of people that he had touched in one way or another. As he slowly waded through the crowd, he happily shook hands and gave out enormous hugs. He exclaimed, "Man, this is awesome… this is crazy." The caroling began again as people reached for each other's hands.

A couple who owned a nearby reindeer farm had also heard of the family's hardships. They pulled up to the house with two of their most beloved and exquisite reindeer! The stunning pair wore jingle bells on their halters as they stood majestically in the driveway. Michael's children squealed in delight as he watched their small faces light up like Christmas light bulbs. As he reached out his hand and gently stroked the reindeer, he realized that he had been given an extraordinary gift in this tribute. He had wanted his family's last Christmas with him to be a special one, and the community had come together to make it special not only for him, but for his wife and children. This was something they would remember forever, a lasting legacy from a beloved husband and father.

More than two hundred people converged on the family's lawn that day toting an abundance of Christmas spirit for one exceptional human being and his family.

Michael passed away peacefully in his bed with his devoted wife by his side a few weeks later; his wish for a final, meaningful Christmas became a reality.

~Rita Kaye Vetsch

The Mean Old Man Next Door

Christmas is most truly Christmas when we celebrate it by giving the light of love to those who need it most.
~Ruth Carter Stapleton

When my wife, Ann, inherited her grandmother's house we were excited to be moving into our very first home. It needed some repairs but it was spacious and comfortable. Our two girls were thrilled they would no longer have to share a room.

The couple across the street had a rambunctious freckle-faced boy the same age as Karen, our seven-year-old, and he offered to show her around when school started. Judging by how often Tommy teased Karen, I — remembering my own childhood crushes — decided that he had developed an instant crush on her. They played together every day and she soon stopped longing for the friends she left behind in our old neighborhood.

On our left side was a single mother with twin girls who were five years old. She immediately offered to trade off babysitting duty with Ann. In a few weeks she and Ann were well on their way to becoming good friends. Everyone we met seemed to be amicable and approachable. Except for the older gentleman next door on our right.

Ann and I were doing some yard work in the front of the house the first time we saw him. He came out of his house, leaning heavily on a cane, and slowly made his way to his mailbox. "Hi!" Ann called out cheerily and I raised my hand in greeting. He continued on his way to the mailbox without any sort of acknowledgment at all. Ann gave me a quizzical look and I shrugged my shoulders. Our houses were close together and I didn't see how he could not have seen us or heard Ann's greeting.

"Maybe he's having a bad day," I said lamely.

Ann's usually smiling mouth slid down into a frown. "Or maybe he's just a mean old man who doesn't like kids moving in next door."

A few days later Karen and Tommy were playing roller ball in our front yard. Just as Tommy hurled the ball toward the bat near the edge of the yard, Ann called them inside for ice cream. They didn't see the ball roll past the bat and end up a few feet into the old man's yard. When they went back outside they saw the old fellow slowly nudging the ball back into our yard with his cane.

"Thanks for returning our ball," Karen said politely, running to snatch it up, as the old man seemed to be having difficulty pushing it back into our yard.

Without looking up, the old man replied. "Make sure it stays over there. I can't have a bunch of toys cluttering up my yard."

When the kids related the incident to Ann she was outraged. "Why make such a fuss over one little ball?. My first impression was right. He's just a mean old man."

After that we always referred to him as "the mean old man next door." We warned the kids to stay clear of his yard and we made no more friendly overtures toward him. When the kids went trick-or-treating on Halloween we skipped his house, taking note of the one dim light that shone from the rear of the house. No lights on was the universal hint to kids that no candy would be offered at this house.

From time to time we would see the old man as he made his way to his mailbox or sat on his back porch in nice weather. We never saw visitors and figured that was due to his sour disposition. Ann noticed that when he was outside he often appeared to be watching the kids at play. "Probably making sure that no toys or kids end up in his yard,"

Ann said, frowning.

Shortly before Christmas I got laid off from my job. How do you tell small children that Christmas will be scant? But what good are new toys under the Christmas tree if the colored lights won't glow because the electric bill wasn't paid? "We'll just have to do the best we can and hope they don't notice," I said.

Ann scowled. "They'll notice that the other kids got far more than they did and they'll think that they must have been naughty."

My heart sank. I couldn't bear the thought of my sweet girls thinking that they had been bad.

I was in the yard raking up the very last of the fall leaves, mainly to keep busy so I wouldn't dwell on how fast Christmas was approaching. Out of the corner of my eye I noticed the old man standing in his yard. I tried to ignore him but when he continued to stand in the same spot I lifted my head and made eye contact with him. To my surprise he motioned for me to come over. Feeling more curious than friendly, I put down my rake and approached him.

"I have something to show you," he said, his eyes twinkling with excitement.

I followed him inside as he led me to a large closet at the end of the hallway. He smiled at me and opened the door. "I think it's about time I let this stuff go. I want you to have it for your little girls."

I stared in disbelief. The shelves were laden with beautiful dolls of all sorts, games, puzzles, and a huge array of toys in mint condition. I looked over at the old man and his eyes were misty. "They all belonged to my little girl before I lost her and her mother in an automobile accident when she was only six years old. I heard about you losing your job and it seemed wrong for me to hold onto these things when you have two little girls who could be enjoying them."

He sighed. "I love to watch your girls play. I hope I didn't upset them when I asked them to keep their toys out of my yard. I can't see or hear very well anymore or pick up my feet like I once could. It's easy for me to trip and once I'm down I can't get up without help."

"How can I possibly thank you?" I said in a thick voice. My girls would have a nice Christmas after all, thanks to the mean old man next door.

"Let me help wrap them," he said, looking at me hopefully.

"I'd like that."

The mean old man next door is now our favorite neighbor. Because of his generosity, our girls had a wonderful Christmas and we have a frequent guest for Friday night dinner.

~Joe Atwater

The Most Wonderful Shopping Trip

Be a rainbow in someone else's cloud.

~Maya Angelou

My husband was finishing up college and we were using every available means to earn an income and to spend frugally. There was no money left over to buy Christmas gifts for our two young daughters.

Most of our friends were in the same situation. We would all have to make the best of it.

The college wives had a group that met every month for activities and friendship. At the November meeting, the leader made an announcement: "Our church ladies are sponsoring a gently used toy giveaway. Each college wife will be able to come to our event and 'shop' for Christmas toys."

Of course, we buzzed with excitement. We couldn't wait for our "shopping" trip. It was the answer to our prayers.

We arrived at the appointed house on the appointed night. I don't know what we expected, but we entered a toy wonderland. Every inch of the living and dining rooms, den, garage, and even part of the kitchen were covered in toys so gently used they could pass for new.

For the first round, everyone could choose a toy for each child. What a great time we had choosing the perfect gifts. Some of the women chose a toy per child and left, not realizing there would be enough left over for another round. I stayed because one of our church ladies pulled me aside and said, "I have something special for you if you can stay until last." Of course I could stay.

We all did a second round of shopping and there were still toys left over. More of the women left. We all had selected two toys per child, so it seemed like enough.

The ladies from the church invited us to do a third round of shopping. Meanwhile, I lingered, waiting for the "special something" that I had been offered.

Finally, only a few wives remained. The lady returned and asked me to follow her into another room. I didn't know what to expect. She presented me with a beautiful, white doll cradle in pristine condition.

"The person who donated this wanted it to go to a special home. I believe it's perfect for your little girls."

I was overwhelmed. This was an expensive toy, far nicer than the already great toys I had been allowed to choose that night. But that wasn't all. Another lady gave me a set of vintage doll bunk beds, complete with mattresses, pillows, sheets, and handmade quilts.

I didn't know what to say. I felt so blessed and so humbled. They wanted my daughters to have these because they were "such good little girls" and because I "worked hard and didn't complain." I surely didn't feel I deserved them but everyone else was gone. So I thanked them over and over again as they helped me load things into the car. On my way out, they plied me with more leftover toys.

We had one of our best Christmases ever. Our little girls were thrilled. I don't know why God decided to bless me that way, that night, but bless He did, through those wonderful ladies. The toys were eventually outgrown and passed down to other children who would enjoy them as much. My granddaughter now has the bunk beds in her playroom. I will never forget the love and caring of those ladies and the most wonderful "shopping trip" of my life.

~Sandra Holmes McGarrity

In Security

The greatest happiness of life is the conviction that we
are loved; loved for ourselves, or rather, loved
in spite of ourselves.
~Victor Hugo

We had been married for nine months, and I was still learning the ways of my in-laws. It was my first Christmas away from my family and our familiar traditions, and my heart ached for home.

My in-laws are lovely people, in every sense of the word. Their home belongs in a magazine, with hardwood floors and chic country-home decor. My mother-in-law is always perfectly dressed for every affair and my father-in-law is a beloved pastor of the largest church in their town. I felt even more insecure because my brother-in-law had married his high school sweetheart so they had known her for years. I was the new person—a short geeky science nerd who had never been out in the country.

My husband told me not to worry so much. Everyone would like me. But I still felt out of place. I didn't know all the people they knew and I didn't understand their insider jokes. I couldn't even learn the family games quickly enough, and I felt as though every misstep I made was being recorded in their minds whether they were conscious of it or not.

On Christmas morning, I called my family to wish them a happy

Christmas morning, I told them I loved them, hung up and started to cry. I felt like a failure in every way: a failure as a daughter-in-law and a failure as a daughter to my parents by not being with them on the most special holiday of the year.

I crept downstairs, trying to blend in with the perfectly decorated walls. They were all gathered at the table eating... fresh cinnamon rolls. Just like at my parents'. With real cream-cheese frosting. And there was a plate waiting for me.

"Happy Christmas morning, hon!" said my father-in-law.

"Your stocking is over here," said my mother-in-law.

My mother-in-law had put out stockings sometime during the night. She had handmade every one herself. And there was mine, with my name stitched across the top in red thread, with a little heart woven beside it.

My insecurity disappeared. I finally felt loved. But I suddenly realized it wasn't the first time — they had loved me the whole time. I looked up at my mother-in-law, and I saw in her eyes the same hope I had: that I would love and accept them back.

The best present I received that year was the other half of my family, and I've been reminded of my good fortune every single Christmas since.

~Nan Rockey

How the Grinch Tried to Steal Our Christmas

Always give without remembering and always
receive without forgetting.
~Brian Tracy

I stared at the empty parking space where our car had been. It had been such a good day, too. For the first time in several years, we'd actually had a little extra in our budget for Christmas, and we had spent the morning shopping for each other. We left the Christmas-crazed shopping mall with a packed car and decided to stop at a handy fast-food spot for a quick taco.

Twenty minutes later we were standing in stunned disbelief looking at the oil-splotched patch of pavement where our loot-filled old Subaru should have been waiting.

For me, it was like my heart was a giant balloon, and someone had just poked it with a pin. I could feel myself deflating and the world around me turning grey. Like the scene in the movie when the Grinch's heart grows three sizes... but in reverse. Deflated, defeated, depressed. Suddenly everything, including Christmas, sucked.

Suddenly, I noticed how much my feet ached.

Not only had our entire gift budget been in the back of that car, but also a thousand dollars worth of groceries for our church's holiday breakfast, which I was supposed to be cooking the next morning. They had given me the cash to pay for all the food.

The moment passed, the rain continued to fall, and people kept coming and going around us, but my mind remained in an endless loop of, "What am I going to do…what am I going to do?"

My wife went back into the restaurant to call the police, while I made the call I'd been dreading. Pastor Doug answered, and hearing the tone of my voice, immediately asked what was wrong. I told him about the stolen car, the lost gifts, and worst of all, the loss of a thousand dollars worth of groceries and gear for the big breakfast.

Doug asked if he could pray with me, which he did. He asked me how much I'd spent on all the stuff in the car, and I told him. Finally, he asked me where I was, promising to be there shortly to pick us up and take us home.

I went back inside, and sat, staring grimly out the rain-splattered window, feeling my heart shrinking three sizes, as my wife valiantly fought tears in the seat beside me. The police came, took our report, and left. I drowned my sorrows in another taco. Forty-five minutes later, I saw my pastor's familiar white pickup truck swing into the parking lot, followed by a car I didn't recognize.

Doug and one of our church elders came in and plopped down in the seat across from us. Sighing and shaking his head, Doug threw an arm around me and assured me that everything was going to be okay. I felt terrible. Everyone had trusted me with this event, and I had blown it.

Then he reached into his jacket and pulled out an envelope, which he passed across the table to me.

"I called a couple of the guys," he said with a smile, "and they called a couple of guys. You feel like doing some more shopping?"

I opened the envelope and found a thick stash of cash, more than I needed to cover the stolen food. I realized there was an extra thousand dollars in that envelope, for us.

"Doug," I said, my voice quavering, "I can't…"

"Yes, you can," he interrupted. "This is what family does. We bless each other when things are good and we let ourselves be blessed when bad things happen."

Then he tossed me the keys to the car that our elder had followed him in, telling me that we could borrow it until we got ours back or got a new one.

I was shocked and overwhelmed. I could feel the tears welling in my eyes as I thanked him.

Only a moment before, everything had been hopeless, dark and cold, and then, just like that, the clouds parted and the sun was shining again.

Late that night, when I finally collapsed, exhausted, into bed, I reflected on how it wasn't only gifts and food that had been stolen, but also our joy. Through the kindness of our church family, that was only a temporary loss.

I was reminded, just when I needed reminding the most, of Dr. Seuss's Grinch and his own discovery that "Christmas, in fact, doesn't come from a store. Christmas, perhaps, means a little bit more."

It's something that cannot be stolen, no matter how big your Grinch is.

~Perry P. Perkins

The Children's Christmas

*Christmas, in its final essence, is for grown-ups
who have forgotten what children know. Christmas
is for whoever is old enough to have denied the
unquenchable spirit of man.*
~Margaret Cousins

I'd been up since the crack of dawn preparing a Christmas feast that would feed twenty-one friends and family members plus the three of us. It was almost noon, and the delectable aroma of turkey and stuffing permeated the house. I'd already prepared two gigantic pots of peeled potatoes and diced fresh vegetables. The glazed ham, roast beef and meat pies sat waiting to be popped into the oven.

I put the finishing touches on the appetizers, carefully storing them in the fridge beside cranberry sauce, salad, condiments, and other side dishes I planned to serve. As holiday music played softly in the background, I measured spices for my gravies and set the table.

Though the plates and cutlery didn't all match because I was feeding so many, everything gleamed and looked picture-perfect. Poinsettia centerpieces with matching crimson candles lay nestled among breadbaskets I'd fill at the last minute. I was admiring my work when the call came. It was my younger brother's girlfriend.

"We can't come," she groaned into the phone. "We have the stomach flu."

"Oh dear," I gushed soothingly. "Get back into bed and try to rest. If you like, I can send some food over later." The gagging sound she made before quickly hanging up suggested it was the wrong offer to make.

The phone rang again. This time it was a friend. She'd just had a heated argument with her sister, another of our invited guests, and her husband. "Jake and I refuse to sit at the same table with those two and their annoying brats," she hollered, hanging up with a loud slam.

A second later a call from her sister came, saying basically the same thing. Before I could tell her it was safe to come, the dial tone hummed in my ear. I was down four adults and three kids.

I was just about to ask my fifteen-year-old son, David, to clear and dismantle one of the folding tables when the phone shrilled a fourth time. I picked it up warily.

"Mary, it's Janice. I'm so sorry, but we can't make it today. Glen's mom had a heart attack. We have to get to the hospital. I'm dropping all three kids off at my cousin's on the way."

I clucked sympathetically. As I was telling her I would send good thoughts, my call waiting beeped. With a quick "stay strong" to Janice, I switched over to hear my older brother announcing there was a blizzard in Ontario, and that they had no choice but to stay home. In the span of three minutes, my guest list had dwindled by nine more people. I could feel a headache rapidly approaching.

Seconds later, I heard my husband Don stamping snow off his boots in the foyer.

"Honey, I have bad news," he hollered.

"Who bailed this time?" I bellowed back, dragging my feet into the living room.

"Ursula called on my cell while I was walking the dog. She, Frank, and the four kids are all down with bad colds. They don't want to come and make us all sick," he said. "What's wrong?" he added when he saw tears starting to slip down my cheeks.

"Everyone cancelled!" I wailed. "It's only the three of us left! What am I going to do with all this food? I was expecting two dozen people."

He caught me in his arms right as I started to sag and sob at the same time.

"Shhh," he soothed. "We can always freeze the leftover food. It's not the end of the world."

He was right, of course. Except for two couples, everyone had a perfectly good reason for backing out. I was instantly ashamed of myself for feeling "inconvenienced" when people I loved were so sick. As for my brother in Ontario, if anything had happened to him while traveling through the snow, I'd never have forgiven myself.

My son got up from the couch and handed me a tissue. I smiled at him through watery eyes.

"It's Christmas," I hiccupped. "Let's make the best of it. I'm sorry I reacted like a baby"

"Mom," David began, "can I invite some of my friends for dinner instead? A lot of them have no plans. Some of them are pretty poor and have nothing special for dinner either — and we have all this food…."

Don and I stared at each other, both nodding at the same time.

"Of course. Go ahead and call them," I told our son.

"How many can come?" he asked.

"I have food for twenty more people… maybe thirty. Some may have to eat off paper plates," I warned, "but everyone is welcome."

The doorbell began buzzing at 2:00 p.m. By three, twenty-one teenagers and two of their little sisters filled my home. The kids proudly handed me a bouquet of flowers they'd all chipped in to buy, thanking me politely for inviting them. I pushed back tears at the sweet gesture, and shooed them all downstairs to wait for dinner.

The volume on David's stereo went up several decibels as heavy metal music drowned out carols, but Don and I didn't care. The house was alive with laughter and the spirit of the holiday. Many youngsters dribbled in and out of the kitchen offering to help, and as I delegated small chores, we chatted.

That Christmas dinner was one of the best we ever had. Our table was packed with hungry kids who demolished the twenty-pound turkey and the roasts, digging into the vegetables as if they were eating ambrosia. No one muttered about diets, indigestion or allergies. They simply enjoyed and appreciated every morsel of food that went into their mouths. As I watched them eat, any thoughts of leftovers being transformed into potpies, hot sandwiches or midnight snacks rapidly disappeared, but it didn't matter.

After dinner, those kids banished our family to the living room while they pitched in and cleaned up my kitchen until it was spotless. Someone had brought a newly released movie and before I knew it, my living room floor was covered with fifteen- and sixteen-year-olds, generously allowing the "old people" to sit on the couch and watch the movie. The two little girls curled up on either side of me, cuddling close. After passing out bags of microwave popcorn and canned soft drinks, we turned off the lights to enjoy the film.

By 10:00 p.m., everyone began to leave, but not without warm hugs and sincere thanks that made my eyes well up yet again. That night, I turned to my husband in bed. "Why is it we never thought to invite David's friends for Christmas dinner before?"

"I don't know," he replied sleepily. "You always hear that Christmas is for kids, but we seem to make the meal itself more of an adult occasion, picking and choosing who we want at the table."

"Not anymore," I vowed, remembering the grateful young faces that saved our day from being a quiet, lonely disaster.

~Marya Morin

The Spirit of Santa

They err who thinks Santa Claus comes down through
the chimney; he really enters through the heart.
~Charles W. Howard

The opulence took my breath away. Long tables draped in ivory and gold filled a room lit by a hundred candles. The smell of turkey and pumpkin pie filled the air as a huge fire crackled in the fireplace. Ah, Christmas Eve.

I smiled at the irony. Three different projects had failed that year and we were careening toward bankruptcy. I'd miscarried and was still deeply mourning. Our own Christmas dinner would be a turkey roll from Walmart. But, the saddest part of all was explaining to Matthew, Mary and Katie that Santa would not be coming that year.

At ages eight, six and three, they were unfazed by my warnings. "Don't worry, Mama," they'd assured me. "Santa won't forget us."

The warm pajamas and used books I'd hidden away would not compare to the bounty they had received in the past.

So when my friend invited us to dinner and a visit from Santa at her house, I was grateful. As we dressed up, I'd told the kids that a visit from Santa was worth far more than presents and that they were the lucky ones of all the kids in the world.

Dinner was wonderful. Good food, fine wine, and the companionship of people with open hearts. And, when Santa came, even I was excited.

This was no store Santa either. His white beard and round belly were all home grown. And his eyes twinkled with a light that came from his pure, loving soul and radiated clear around the room. Indeed, this was really Santa.

Eight-year-old Matthew took one look, ran to hide and had to lean on us to make his way back to meet the jolly man. Six-year-old Mary, on the other hand, leapt into his arms. And the jolly old man caught her with an open belly laugh that assured her she was right where she belonged. "Oh, Santa, it's you!" she cooed as she gently stroked his beard.

But, despite the wonder and joy of the moment, I could not hide my sorrow at our plight. This should have been a time of joy for my children, and all I could think of was what was lacking. I tried to get Santa aside to explain our situation before he talked to the kids.

But, I never got the chance and as Matthew sat reciting his list Santa promised and promised and promised, then left to "begin his evening rounds."

Soon, we said our goodbyes and piled into the car for the five-minute ride home through the snowy streets. The DJ on the radio announced that Santa had been spotted over our town.

Mary squealed and looked up at the sky as she searched for her new friend.

But as Mary cheered, Matthew cried, "Oh no, oh no, OH NO!"

"Honey, what's wrong?" we asked.

"He's here and I'm not asleep!" Matthew began ripping at his clip-on tie as he wiggled out of his shoes.

"It's okay. He knew you were at the party," I consoled.

"No. He told me to be good and go to bed tonight. I'm up. I'm being bad! He'll never come!"

"But, remember," I said, seizing my chance. "You got to see him tonight, and he gave you your truck. He may not be able to come to your house too; he has so many other children to see tonight."

"Silly Mommy," laughed Mary in the midst of all the chaos. "Santa always comes."

"But, honey…" I began as we pulled into the driveway, and then there it was.

"Look kids," Steven pointed. "What is that?"

"Santa!" they yelled.

And it was. For there, on the deck, was Christmas. A big red sled sat by the front door. Propped up inside were trucks and telescopes, Barbies and plush toys... and magic. For the second time that night, a scene had taken my breath away.

There, in the cold and snow, we knelt down to explore the miracle. Tears flowed down my cheeks as my babies shrieked and giggled in wonder. Clearly Santa knew my kids and had brought them each a special, personalized treasure.

Then, shy Matthew, who had been so afraid to see Santa at the party, ran out into the middle of the yard, lifted his hands to the sky and yelled, "I love you, Santa Claus!"

The next morning, when the tree held warm jammies and a book, the kids were thrilled. They declared it the best Christmas ever.

Today, it is still our favorite Christmas.

It was a lesson in faith, and simple joys, and sharing. It was a gift that our family now "pays forward" every year.

Maybe it was only a few gifts tucked into a sled. But for me, it was the truth of the world. It was the spirit of Santa. And, it changed me forever.

~Susan Traugh

86

An Open Heart Every Day

*A single act of kindness throws out roots in
all directions, and the roots spring up
and make new trees.*
~Amelia Earhart

One December day I was hurriedly moving along to get
out of the extreme cold when I encountered an elderly,
white-haired man. At first he solemnly shuffled along,
seemingly lost within himself. His white bearded chin
was lowered to his chest — giving me the impression his spirits were
even lower. Yet something in his plump stature implied a regal grace
even though he was wearing a frayed coat and baggy old pants that
made him look like a derelict.

I felt sorry for this lonely looking stranger and wanted him to
know someone cared. I smiled and said, "Isn't this weather something?
It's so cold today that even the animals have ceased to play."

Ignoring me, he kept right on walking.

Then... he abruptly stopped, swung around, and said, "I'm glad
you spoke. Or today this old man would have forever given up hope
on his fellow man's ability to communicate friendliness."

"I beg your pardon?" I said.

"You have nothing to be pardoned for," he exclaimed. "It's those
who scurry about never acknowledging others who should ask to be
pardoned. I've been searching this whole month to find one friendly

person to engage me in some kind of cordial conversation… no matter who or what I appear to be. Instead, I receive hasty handouts of money. Apparently, these people seem to feel that's all I'm worthy of."

After hearing his sad words, I looked around us at the people who were rushing here and there. He was totally right. They were all intent on getting where they needed to go, as if they had tunnel vision.

"Furthermore," he continued, as his face portrayed sorrow, "I couldn't even find a smiling face. People just scurried about with deadpan looks. Nor did they bother to even say hello to anyone they didn't know."

As he talked, I searched his broad face with its dimpled cheeks for a sign of joviality. And then, suddenly, his pale blue eyes began to twinkle.

"And wouldn't you know it," he exclaimed, "I'm also negligent of losing my gladsome perspective. I got so caught up in my own thoughts and actions, that I, too, almost missed my chance to befriend someone."

A smile warmed my face, but a shiver clutched at my heart. Not from the elements of the weather, but from the thought of someone emotionally pained over not being acknowledged as a human being, no matter what his station in life.

I asked him if he would like to share lunch with me at a nearby café. Laying his gloved finger aside of his impish nose, he gave me an affirmative nod, and then hastily grabbed my arm to direct me. At first, I had thoughts of being hustled, and then I felt ashamed. After all, I was the one who first spoke to him, because he looked like he needed some human contact.

After an hour of laughter and pleasant conversation with this memorable elf-like man, I reached for the lunch check. Immediately, my guest sprang from his chair and grabbed the check from my hand.

"Oh, no, you don't! This is my gift to you for restoring my faith that there's still congeniality in the hearts of mankind."

As we left the café he surprisingly gave me a hug, and then exclaimed while bounding away, "Merry Christmas, *fidus Achates* (trusted friend)."

~Sylvia Bright-Green

Kindness of a Stranger

If we could all hear one another's prayers, God might
be relieved of some of his burdens.
~Ashleigh Brilliant

It was Christmastime, and I had promised my son, Joshua, a bicycle. But that was months ago, and life's little catastrophes had claimed my bike savings again and again. I stood at the bicycle display and my heart sank. I had not imagined little bikes were so expensive.

Surely, there must be one that I could afford. I walked back and forth in front of the display, as if I could will one into existence. "Please God," I prayed silently. "I promised him a bicycle." I stopped and stared as the truth became evident; there was not a single bike within my budget.

A man walked up beside me and began to make small talk about the bikes. He was excited about making his selection. He wanted to know which one I was getting. I told him that it wasn't for me and explained the promise. And then I told him my dilemma. I wondered aloud if I might find them cheaper at another store. "No," he said, "they're all about the same." I really didn't want to hear that. "Which one were you going to get?" he asked. I pointed to a lime green one, my son's favorite color. The man agreed that it was a nice one, sure to make a little boy happy.

He stared at it for a moment and then reached underneath the shelf and picked up a big box. "Come on," he said to me, "I'll carry this to the register for you."

"I can't!" I said. "I don't have enough money."

"I know," he said, "I'm getting it for you."

"What? You can't get this for me."

"Yes, I can!" he replied, already walking to the front of the store. I followed, protesting, even as he got in the checkout line and paid.

"Now which way to your car?" he asked, walking out of store.

A million concerns as to his motives raced through my head, but I walked to my car, sputtering disbelief and gratitude all the way. My cash was in my hand. "Let me give you the difference!"

"You can't pay for it," he said, "unless you can pay the whole amount."

"But I don't have the whole amount," I said.

He ignored me and slid the big box into the trunk. Then he turned to me, said, "Merry Christmas!" and quickly disappeared in the parking lot.

I sat in the car, in awe of what had just transpired, and gave thanks to God for answering a mom's prayer once again.

I planted the generosity of that man's deed in my heart, and over the years tried to be sensitive to what I could do for others.

Fifteen years later, I found myself standing in that same store, my financial circumstances much improved. I heard a pregnant woman in the next aisle quietly lamenting that she couldn't afford what she needed for her unborn baby. I smiled and said to myself, "I'm on it, God!"

~Edie Schmidt

Operation GOLD

*Coming together is a beginning. Keeping together is
progress. Working together is success.*
~Henry Ford

We had always spent Christmas Day at my grandmother's house and it was never the same after she passed away from ovarian cancer. Listening to Christmas tunes became depressing, and decorating the house with lights, trees, and wreaths became a chore.

I needed something to focus on besides missing my grandmother. Having survived my own cancer as a child I thought it would be wonderful to create a holiday gift program for children who were battling cancer. My children could get involved from home and it would also help them understand a little bit of what I went through when I was their age and how fortunate we are to have good health.

It was only a couple of months before Christmas, so I began social networking on my computer to find the children who would receive our gifts. Parents from all parts of the U.S. began responding to the idea, and soon I had the wish lists of twenty children with cancer for my Operation GOLD holiday gift program. Although twenty children seemed like a small number compared to the number of children battling cancer, it was enough to get the program launched and help make a difference.

With the first step accomplished, I had to find twenty families to donate presents to those twenty children. After spending multiple hours on the Internet and on the telephone, I was able to find twenty volunteer families that would provide the gifts.

In just four weeks, my plan had come together. The volunteer families would purchase items from their assigned child's wish list and mail them directly to the child's home. I even set aside a child with cancer for my family to buy for. I'm so glad I did because my two sons were able to participate and relate on a kid's level. We picked out presents, wrapped them, and shipped them to the child with cancer. It was a process that meant a lot to me and hopefully to them.

Since the program was based on trust and a verbal agreement, I did feel a bit worried at times, but I had to remind myself to trust that everything would work out, and that's exactly what happened!

Little by little I started receiving thank-you e-mails from the parents of the sick children. Some of the children were still in the hospital and unable to celebrate Christmas at home. One child passed away the day before his presents arrived. This was the harsh reality of childhood cancer and it reminded me of how lucky I am to have survived.

Overall, the program was a huge success. I felt like my grandmother and I were doing something together for the other children and families touched by cancer. I had transformed my sadness into something wonderful.

~Kristen N. Velasquez

89

Kindness Re-gifted

I don't think Christmas is necessarily about things. It's
about being good to one another, it's about kindness.
~Carrie Fisher

I t was Christmas Eve as I embarked upon a depressing adventure with my debit card at the store. I had only a few hundred dollars remaining to get me through December, so I purchased a few necessities and tried not to look at the stacks of pricey cookies, pies and candies. From the store's PA system, Nat King Cole reminded me that turkey and mistletoe could make everything bright. I couldn't afford either.

All the way home, my cantankerous Buick spat and sputtered, stalling at nearly every intersection. "Get me home, you old clunker," I muttered. "You're not going to the mechanic today! You know exactly how broke I am!"

She knew all right, but she didn't care. She let out a huge belch and stalled a few blocks from home. I yelled at her. I threatened her. I pounded her steering wheel. Finally, I took a deep breath and asked her to get me home, promising a trip to the repair shop after unloading my groceries. The Buick roared back to life.

I got to the repair shop twenty minutes before they were closing for Christmas Eve. But the receptionist in this small, independent shop cheerfully greeted me and agreed to have the mechanics examine my vehicle. A skeleton crew of three men was still on the clock, enjoying some well-deserved cookies and camaraderie before checking out for their holiday. Without complaint, they proceeded to the bay to diagnose the demon I had dragged to their doorstep.

I sat in the waiting room sweating profusely. How was I going to afford this? The receptionist offered to make me a cup of coffee in the pot she had just cleaned and put away. I politely declined and wrung my hands in desperation.

At 4:30, the receptionist locked the front door. I apologized over and over again for ruining her plans, but she assured me that everything was fine and that it was important to have a car that could get me where I needed to be on Christmas. I sat back down, feeling guilty but also feeling a bit of warmth creeping into my heart.

Thirty minutes later, the head mechanic returned to the shop and handed me my keys. "She's all ready, Mr. Ramsey." He proceeded to recite a string of mechanical terms describing my car's ailments and her treatment plan. I understood very little.

I trembled as the man listed everything on the bill. I visibly shook as I reached for my wallet and extracted my weathered bankcard. In a few moments I was going to throw up. The mechanic and the receptionist glanced at the clock, then glanced at each other and finally looked at me. "It's on us, Mr. Ramsey," the receptionist announced cheerfully. "Merry Christmas!"

"Thank you," I mouthed as I fought back tears.

Both employees smiled as I headed for the door and exclaimed in perfect harmony, "Merry Christmas!"

* * *

I never forgot that Christmas Eve and I've been paying it forward ever since. Recently, I had a chance to help another young man when the fall semester was ending at the college where I work part-time.

I had graded the online submissions of students who had obviously worked through the early hours of morning to meet their deadline, but Ignacio was one short. He had completed five of the assignments, the last of which had been stamped at 4:57 a.m. He was now standing before my desk, looking a wreck with dark circles under his eyes. The quiet freshman was nervously wringing his hands together. He looked like he was going to throw up. He barely spoke except to weakly whisper, "good morning," as he shook my hand.

"Wow, Ignacio!" I proclaimed. "You sure were burning the midnight oil! You got a lot turned in! Way to go!"

"Uh, about that..." he choked, unable to finish. He swallowed and tried again to no avail.

"Listen," I offered quietly. "You've been such a great student this semester. I really appreciate you being in every class and always participating. You know, my grades aren't due until next Saturday. What if I give you until Friday to get the rest of the work done?"

I could see the tears forming at the corners of his tired eyes. He trembled a bit and let out a sigh of relief. He mouthed the words, "thank you," and shook my hand again.

"Merry Christmas, Ignacio!" I hollered as he headed to the door. "Now, go home and get some sleep!"

~Tim Ramsey

The Joy of Christmas

Holiday Traditions

Christmas! The very word brings joy to our hearts. No matter how we may dread the rush, the long Christmas lists for gifts and cards to be bought and given—when Christmas Day comes there is still the same warm feeling we had as children, the same warmth that enfolds our hearts and our homes.
~Joan Winmill Brown

90

Chicken Soup
for the Soul

Washing Our
Hands in Money

*A partner is someone who makes you more than you
are, simply by being by your side.*
~Albert Kim

"What were you thinking?" I asked my husband, Larry, in frustration. "You KNOW I invited Ashley. You KNOW they're separated."

Larry had run out to the supermarket to get a couple of last-minute items for me. He had bumped into Joe, Ashley's estranged husband.

"How could I not invite him?" he said. "I was at the checkout and noticed him with little Joey, eating at the counter. They were having chicken nuggets, for crying out loud! Chicken nuggets on Christmas Eve while we're having a banquet?"

He added, "The kid was crying for his mom. They both looked miserable."

That sold me. Larry's big heart sometimes gets us in trouble, but this time he was right.

We got back to work preparing a turkey dinner with all the trimmings. Larry "helped" between football games, but at least he had prepared the stuffing in the morning. The prior year I had lost a diamond from my wedding ring when I made the stuffing, so I didn't want to touch it this year and have the same thing happen to my new ring.

In the afternoon, our son Jim arrived with his wife Cindy, and our granddaughters, Christina and Lindsey, nine and twelve. By then the turkey was baked and resting. Things were under control.

Ashley came with her seven-year-old Annie, bringing a loaf of homemade Italian bread.

Then my mom, who lived with us, took all the kids into her room. The sweet sound of their melodious voices could be heard as Mother, who adored children, taught them Slovakian Christmas songs.

Larry served eggnog as the adults settled into the den by the Christmas tree. Ashley privately confided to me that she and Joe were sharing the children for the holidays. She got Annie and he got Joey. It was a depressing arrangement.

How could I tell her that the husband she had been complaining about was about to ring our bell?

Finally, Larry blurted out: "I ran into Joe and Joey and invited them here for dinner."

"You didn't!" she exclaimed. I thought I detected a small measure of hope in her voice.

Joe soon arrived with their five-year-old, Joey, who, upon seeing Ashley, ran into her arms crying, "Mommy!" with such joy it warmed my heart.

Joe sat down across from Ashley. We made small talk and before things got too personal I distracted everyone with my family's Slovak tradition: "Washing our hands in money."

Mother and the kids joined us. Christina ran upstairs to get Larry's substantial dish of change, which he added to daily. It was her annual chore, which she relished.

I rinsed the coins and transferred them into a pretty glass bowl with clean water and before dinner we all "washed our hands in money."

Everyone always got a kick out of this tradition, which was supposed to bring luck and prosperity in the coming year.

We'd tease the kids, saying all pockets would be frisked to ensure that no change disappeared mysteriously. This good-natured ribbing always produced giggles.

When we had "washed our hands in money," we took our places at the table.

As we held hands and bowed our heads, Joe said grace. He spoke about the meaning of Christmas, family, friends and the love of God. I was impressed. His prayer was touching. Larry and our granddaughters did their usual good-natured routine of squeezing hands and sneaking silly, furtive glances at each other during the prayer. Well, as long as they prayed I didn't mind.

The conversation at dinner was spirited and cheerful. I watched Joe and Ashley as they observed the kids' easygoing interaction with each other and the admiration and respect they showed the adults.

As the kids cleared the dishes for dessert, I noticed notes under each place setting.

"I grew up in an Italian family," Joe explained "There was not much money for gifts. Our tradition was for the kids to write a note of thanks to the adults. These notes were placed under the plates at Christmas."

Larry read his note first. It was from Christina. "Poppy, thanks for having Daddy because otherwise I wouldn't be here. Ha ha."

My note made me tear up as I read Annie's childish scrawl, "Thank you for giving us Mommy and Daddy for Christmas."

All the notes were heartwarming, but the best one came in the mail a few days later. It was from Ashley and read:

Thank you for showing us the true meaning of Christmas. Your warmth and kindness made us appreciate that there's nothing more important than family. I realized that a temporary setback is no reason to quit. We have decided that we love each other too much to separate.

P.S. Joe landed a great job. Maybe washing hands in money really works.

I wasn't sure about the last part but who knows?

Ten years and another child later, Joe and Ashley have a solid marriage.

Side note: After dinner as I rinsed the bowl of coins in which we had washed our hands, what should I find but the diamond that had fallen out of my ring a year ago? It had been in Larry's change dish all year. It was just a material thing but finding it added a certain radiance to an already meaningful Christmas.

~Eva Carter

91

Chicken Soup for the Soul

The Dad Club

I once bought my kids a set of batteries for Christmas
with a note on it saying, toys not included.
~Bernard Manning

The countdown is on. Soon, garages across the continent will be hosting frustrated dads who are trying to assemble every manner of contraption the toy company geniuses can conceive.

Christmas Eve is unique in its power to create an experience shared by so many dads at the same time. Since the dawn of time, dads have been waiting for the kids to fall asleep so they can open boxes, spread out parts, and read vague directions in dim light.

Screws are turned. Fingers are pinched. Pieces are lost. Beer and blood are spilled. This is how it goes every year in countless man caves from coast to coast.

Christmas morning will come and the kids will be excited. Dads will be appreciated by moms. The swearing and smiling and sweating and searching for that single, yet vital, little nut that rolled away someplace will all be worth it come Christmas morning.

I remember my own initiation into the club several years ago. It involved a complicated battery-powered tractor and a tricycle. I spent several hours on raw knees constructing those treasures, which now lie broken and rusty from being abused and left outside in the rain.

I had help that first night from the other members of the club, the heroes who came before me: my dad and grandpa and uncles. The men I loved and admired most helped me. They operated those screwdrivers alongside me and they got out the "magnet on a stick" to retrieve the lost screw from under the workbench.

I finally understood things about my own dad I had never known before. I am glad I understand now. My life would be less without appreciating his sacrifice and efforts to bring a smile to my face on Christmas morning.

So, this Christmas Eve I will renew my membership in the club. I will follow the directions step by onerous step. I will peel off layers as I heat up and I will stretch my sore back. I will say, "No, thanks" when my wife asks if I need any help. She will close the door and walk away relieved, as the ream of paper from the instructions and the too-many-to-count pieces sprawled across the concrete floor can be overwhelming.

I won't mind. This will be my time to be a good dad. I will be at my absolute best in those pre-dawn hours when the final bolt is tightened and the last decal goes on.

In the morning, I will sit red-eyed and oily, smelling like antifreeze and lawn fertilizer. I will have a cup of coffee in my hand and a grin on my face. When my seven-year-old daughter asks why I have Band-Aids on three fingers, I will say a beautiful little lie to her pretty little face. And when she follows up with, "Does it hurt?" I will reply, "Not much, sweetheart, not much." And this won't be a lie. I'll be too happy to hurt.

~Dave Markwell

The Gift of Time

Children make your life important.
~Erma Bombeck

The M&Ms were sorted by color in individual bowls. They sat next to a tray of red licorice sticks and candy canes. Six tubes of decorator icing, each one a different color with its own uniquely shaped tip, lay scattered on the kitchen table.

I looked in from the dining room doorway. "We need a bigger table." The room reminded me of what Mrs. Claus's kitchen might look like. The rich aroma of cinnamon and ginger filled the air. Even with the leaf inserted, the table overflowed with foil trays. Each tray contained an undecorated gingerbread house, twenty-one in all. They were ready for the friends who would be visiting us over the next few days.

For several years, my husband and I had offered the gift of time to various families each Christmas season. Couples would leave their young children with us, usually on a Saturday morning. Then they would gratefully slip out to spend the day Christmas shopping without the pressure of prying eyes.

The grandfather clock in the living room struck ten. Even though the morning sun streamed through the windows, I turned on the lights of our Christmas tree. Then I hit the play button and Christmas music filled the room. Right on time, a car pulled into the driveway and moments later the doorbell rang.

Four children rushed through the door and immediately began to peel off their coats, gloves, and boots. Their parents trailed behind them. After hugs and kisses all around, Ken and Roz waved goodbye and stepped back toward the door. The kids barely noticed the departure as they took their seats at the table. They remembered the drill, even though it happened only once a year.

"I'm ready!"

"Can we start now?"

"Can we, please?"

"Pretty please?"

Four upturned faces pleaded to begin. While they talked about their planned masterpieces, I set an assembled but undecorated gingerbread house in front of each child. Organized chaos soon reigned.

"I need the white tube!"

"Wait — I'm using it first."

"But I need it now!"

I picked up an errant M&M from the floor, and walked over to the kitchen table. "Remember the rules. We share the different colored icings and take turns."

"But she'll use up all the white and I need it for the snow on my roof."

"You already have snow! It's my turn!"

I opened another tube of white icing and screwed on a decorating tip. "There's enough for everyone." Actually, there was more than enough. The looks of pitiful disappointment when I ran out of one color the previous year were enough to teach me to stock up.

For an hour or two, the kids plastered the unadorned gingerbread houses with gobs of icing: white, red, blue, and green. Then they covered the icing with handfuls of candy. There was an unspoken rivalry to see who could attach the most candy to their house without it falling off. Their creativity was fun, intensely focused, and fiercely competitive. Once they found their rhythm, silence prevailed for a brief time, occasionally punctuated by bursts of satisfied giggles as they surveyed their progress.

With each Christmas, the children grew more creative. In the beginning, they simply covered every inch of the gingerbread with icing and candy. But they quickly became proficient in handling the tubes and identifying the various tips available for each color. Within a few years they were decorating their houses with intricate icing patterns as they sought to have their handiwork match their vision. The older children even learned to use the icing and candy to add chimneys, shrubs, fences, and snowmen to the basic gingerbread structure.

When they were finally satisfied with their achievements — or when the candy ran out, whichever came first — we photographed the children with their architectural creations. Then we cleared the table and moved the houses out of reach to allow the icing to harden. Next, we ate lunch, although they weren't usually hungry, probably because much of the candy never made it onto the houses!

When lunch was done we shifted the activity from the kitchen to the living room.

"Can we watch *Rudolph the Red-Nosed Reindeer*?"

"No! *March of the Wooden Soldiers*."

"I want *A Christmas Carol*."

"We watched that last year."

That last comment always surprised me. They even remembered which movie they had watched the previous year!

After the movie, we played games and later examined their houses to make any necessary "repairs." Depending on the time, we watched another Christmas special. We could only stall so long before our guests wandered over to the Christmas tree. With an impressive nonchalance, they surreptitiously checked out the wrapped gifts, examining the gift tags. With a bit of approved snooping, they quickly spotted their names and the presents were distributed. Soon the only sounds we heard were the tearing of paper and laughter… lots of laughter.

By the time their parents returned, we were all worn-out… but it was a happy exhaustion for all. The children had a full day and their parents returned with a trunk full of presents, but of course, the kids didn't know that. The day's highlight occurred when the children proudly displayed their masterpieces to Mom and Dad. As they piled into the cars, holding their creations on their laps, we would realize, once again, that we had as much fun as they did.

The best part of all? Decades later, we still hear from many of the families. The children have grown and now have children of their own. And they are carrying on the tradition with their own families. Through letters, Christmas cards, and social media, each year they send us photos of a new generation of budding architects displaying their sweet masterpieces.

Funny thing is, all those years ago we thought we were giving the parents the gift of time. Now I realize we were creating lifelong memories... for the parents, the children, and for us.

~Ava Pennington

93

Messages in a Bottle

The flame never dies because the
commitment never ends.
~Author Unknown

I t was 1940 in the small town of Cleburne, Texas. It didn't take long to spot new people there, and it was my mother who spotted the new milkman making a delivery to the house across the street.

When she told me the story, she explained that the milk bottles rattling in their metal cages sounded like music when he carried them, causing her heart to pound like that of a schoolgirl.

She knew this young man in the crisp, white uniform was the man for her. So she waved the sturdy young man to the porch, introduced herself, and made the proper arrangements.

On the occasion of his first delivery, Dad left an empty bottle along with Mom's two-quart order. A piece of paper curled out of its opening. Mother recalls how her heart beat wildly as she read the note: "Would you consider going out with your milkman?"

Would she!

Exactly six months from the day my father delivered the milk along with its bold message, it was my mother who was dressed in white. The man of her dreams waited at the altar as she made her grand entrance into the town's oldest Christian church to marry him.

As a result of my father's first request, my parents had gotten their wish — each other. The tradition of writing down what you wanted for Christmas and dropping it into that same empty milk bottle began during their first year of marriage. My mother decorated the bottle with a wreath and hand-painted sprigs of holly and mistletoe on its outer surface. The bottle was then displayed at the Thanksgiving table, allowing them both a full month to ponder over whatever the other had asked for.

During my parents' second year of marriage, Mom's note had an unusual Christmas request. She asked my father for a child. She asked him the same thing for three years running, the result being the birth of a girl, a boy, and then in the fourth year, another boy — me.

My siblings and I looked forward to Thanksgiving almost as much as Christmas, for that's when the milk bottle would be brought out and the sugarplums would begin to dance in our heads. We were encouraged to ask for something that would be useful to all of us. That didn't seem like much fun to us kids, but we knew our Christmas goodies weren't restricted to our milk jar requests.

Our house was the center of activity for the whole extended family at Thanksgiving. A wave of hungry relatives always materialized to share in our feast, and then to write their Christmas desires on a small note and drop it into the bottle's glass tummy.

As I grew older, I realized that the reason our relatives loved to come to our house for Thanksgiving was as much about putting their notes in the milk jar as it was about the food and giving thanks. An aunt once told me that my parents' unusual custom represented the milk of human kindness rather than the actual giving of gifts. Judging by the family closeness that has continued all these years, and how my own children took to the custom like little tadpoles in a warm pond, I guess my aunt was right.

Some of my older relatives had suffered greatly during the Depression and the war that followed. My mom and dad became a kind of rallying cry for family unity and my mom's tradition seemed to represent the idea that hopes and dreams were still possible and good will and the spirit of giving were never out of style.

After my dad passed away, my elderly mother seemed to treasure the oft-repeated ceremony all the more. It bridged any generation gap we might have experienced over the years and the tradition has now entered into its fourth generation.

Then one day, Mother chose me to be the guardian of the Christmas bottle and its messages. I assured her I would not let the custom die, no matter how silly it might seem to some.

"Our tradition has brought all of us many wonderful gifts," she reminded me. "The best of them has been those from the heart. The ones in which people ask for no more than love and goodwill."

I vowed that her descendants would not let her down and so we haven't.

Much of the original enamel green and red color my mother painted on the milk jar that first Christmas has now peeled away, but every Thanksgiving through Christmas it still occupies a place of honor in my house. The simple quart jar, representative of my parents' love for family and each other, now sits on a bright Christmas doily with a small wreath around its stubby neck.

The little hands of my grandchildren still drop their thoughtful notes into its mouth in hopes that this magical container will make their Christmas dreams come true. And, on behalf of my parents, I see to it that they do.

~Jay Seate

94

A Face Good Enough to Eat

The best angle from which to approach any
problem is the try-angle.
~Author Unknown

When I was in elementary school in Saginaw, Michigan, back in the 1950's, I had a neighbor and classmate named Paul Davis. His birthday was December 16th and every year for his birthday treat he would bring wonderful cookies to school. They looked like Santa's face, complete with raisin eyes and coconut beards.

I would always make sure to walk home with Paul on those days, just in case someone had been absent and he had an extra cookie or two. Somehow, one year, one cookie survived long enough for me to show my mother. She got the recipe from Paul's mother and bought the special cookie cutter at Morley Brothers, our wonderful all-purpose department store.

Over the years, my mother and I continued to make these cookies. After I got married I bought my own cookie cutter. We had three daughters and the cookies remained a must at Christmastime. I was a stay-at-home mother in those days and would make the Santa cookies for my daughters' class parties. Some special teachers would get a plate of them years after they taught our daughters. Eventually, my mother gave me her Santa cookie cutter and I guarded both of them because Morley's had closed years before and we never saw anything even resembling these wonderful Santa faces at any other store.

Several years ago in late December, I had made multiple batches and the two plastic cutters were sitting out waiting to be hand washed and put away for another year. My oldest daughter decided to help out by loading the dishwasher and she put them in there! They both melted a bit and came out totally unusable.

For some reason, I had kept the original paper insert from the cookie cutter box. So, I knew that they were from Aunt Chick's in Tulsa, Oklahoma. Now, it was time to see if that company was still in business. Honestly, I wasn't optimistic but if I couldn't replace them, then a long-standing tradition would come to an abrupt halt.

I wrote to the Tulsa Chamber of Commerce and inquired about Aunt Chick's cookie cutters. I enclosed a copy of the insert that I'd kept for so many years. Within days I received a reply. They even sent me newspaper clippings about Aunt Chick (she had died in 1982) and they told me that the cookie cutters were still available at The Final Touch in Tulsa. They also told me that Aunt Chick's granddaughter, Pat Kimbrel, had taken over the business and it was now called Chickadees Cookery Company, based in Irving, Texas.

I was elated! I phoned The Final Touch and explained what had happened and said that I wanted to buy ten Santa cookie cutters. The woman told me that they were only available in sets (Santa's face, a star, a tree, and a stocking). But I didn't want the other designs.

So, I decided to call Chickadees Cookery Company. I was able to talk with Pat Kimbrel and tell her about the happy memories connected with her grandmother's cookie cutters. She said that she hoped to get them back into distribution once again. Through Pat I was able to buy four Santa cutters. Then, several weeks later, I received a note from The Final Touch saying that they found six Santa cutters and asked if I still wanted them.

I phoned to say "Yes!" and sent a check. So, within a few months I went from having no Santa cutters to having ten of them!

It was wonderful to be able to do business with two women who went out of their way to satisfy a customer. And, now the family tradition of the Santa face cookie cutters continues not only in our house but also in the home of our oldest daughter, who has since married. At this point, it's three generations strong.

So Happy Birthday this December 16th to Paul Davis wherever you are. I'll bet you never knew that your old friend, neighbor and classmate would perpetuate the cookie tradition for nearly a half-century. Thanks to you and your mother and with the help of some dear women in both Oklahoma and Texas, we'll be enjoying our very special Santa face cookies for many years to come.

~Tracy Moeller Cary

95

Chicken Soup for the Soul

Just the Ticket!

Man's mind, once stretched by a new idea, never
regains its original dimensions.
~Oliver Wendell Holmes

"Merry Christmas to us!" Norm tossed two tickets onto the kitchen table.

I picked them up. "Really? The Barnum & Bailey Circus?"

My husband nodded, a boyish grin spreading from ear to ear. Bringing home freebies was the unexpected perk of being a reporter-photographer for one of the local television stations. As newlyweds on a limited budget, we appreciated these free dates, opportunities to attend a variety of events. But… the circus? During Christmas week?

I shrugged. Why not?

The following December, his twinkling eyes rivaled Santa's as Norm handed me another set of tickets and waited for my reaction.

"You're kidding…" I was at a loss for words.

"The pickins are slim this year, sweetie. Do we go?" He waggled his bushy brows.

Female mud wrestling? For Christmas?

I accepted the dare. "Why not!" I shot back.

And so it all began, the most un-traditional of Christmas traditions: to do something each holiday season that we've never done before, perhaps unexpected or challenging. As our family grew to include four children, we hauled them along for the memory-making moments.

One year, I read an article about a performance at a local church, a musical of some sort with a hometown, homegrown cast that included kids. Best of all, admittance was free.

We bundled up and headed out in a raging blizzard. The six of us joined a total of seven others scattered throughout the church's cavernous, pine-swagged sanctuary. We picked a pew right up front, close to the action, where our children could have an unobstructed view. The "concert" turned out to be *Amahl and the Night Visitors* — an... opera. An opera?

Norm perused the program. He glanced down the length of the bench at our kids, his black brows inching upward. "Really?"

"They'll love it," I assured him as the lights dimmed and the show began.

The sound system squawked. The performers fumbled their words. The storyline dragged.

This family needs a growth experience, I reasoned as I shushed my restless four-year-old.

The songs increased in pitch. And vibrato.

This family could use some culture, I determined as I shook my head in warning at our ten-year-old, who was rolling his eyes and barely stifling his giggles.

The music got louder. More dramatic. More, uh, operatic.

I grabbed at the flailing arms of my daughters, aged nine and seven, as they silently mimicked, "A-maaaa-ahl, A-maaaa-ahl, A-MAAAA-ahl!" and gestured broadly in wicked imitation of the actors.

This family needs to... leave, I decided, mortified at the way our youngsters carried on. But our departure would be a huge distraction and, well, we comprised half the audience. I sighed, did my best to control my manic monsters, and suffered through the remainder of the musical.

I'm certain the cast suffered through us.

In the decades since, our yuletides have yielded a long list of un-traditions, a list that includes memorable, Christmas-flavored firsts such as sledding at midnight under a brilliant blue moon, hosting a break-the-gingerbread-house party, and researching and cooking a traditional Bethlehem meal.

We've shivered through an ice sculpture competition, hummed along during a Cranberry Pops concert, built an igloo after an epic snowstorm, strolled through a beggarly Dickens village, ridden a jingling sleigh through snow-hushed streets, watched the scenes of a live nativity — complete with aromatic camels and braying donkeys.

We've witnessed the twinkling festivity of The Plaza in Kansas City, the rollicking pageantry at Dolly Parton's Dixie Stampede in Branson, and the solemn sanctity of Temple Square in Salt Lake City.

We've celebrated Hanukkah with Jewish friends and — most recently — sat spellbound with four young granddaughters during *The Nutcracker* ballet.

Some of these once-in-a-lifetime opportunities were growth experiences. Others exposed us to culture. And, admittedly, there have been a few we've suffered through. But all of them have enriched our holiday celebrations by broadening our horizons and deepening our memories.

Rarely do we search out these occasions. Most seem to find us. This year, kind friends offered us tickets to a holiday benefit for Opera Fort Collins. The evening's entertainment will be a shortened version of their most popular Christmas production: *Amahl and the Night Visitors*.

We've accepted. Maybe we'll invite our children — and their kids.

~Carol McAdoo Rehme

Luminaria

The darkness of the whole world cannot
swallow the glowing of a candle.
~Robert Altinger

White paper bags and candles arrived in a bundle and lay on our front porch. I stared at them, and then read the accompanying note. "Oh," I said, smiling as I thrust them toward my husband. "Look what the city gave us. All we have to do is add sand to the bags, place the candles inside and line our sidewalk and driveway with them on Christmas Eve."

"Why?"

"Well, it says here that it's a traditional custom of lighting the way for the Holy Family called Luminaria. Everyone lights the candles at 7:00 p.m. and turns off their porch lights for an hour."

He nodded. "Sounds nice. Let's do it."

So, in the midst of preparing for our first Christmas with twin baby girls in our new Southern California home, we added Luminaria to our list.

Christmas Eve arrived and so did high winds. As fast as we set the sand-filled bags down, the wind blew them over. We added extra sand to no avail. Our newly landscaped yard had bushes that were barely as tall as the lunch-size bags. As the time to light them approached, we worried that the winds would cause them to turn into torches, burning our new plants.

"We'll just have to stand out there with them," Bill said.

I could see he was right. So we bundled up the babies, put them in their strollers, and went out to light the Luminaria. We discovered that our neighbors up and down the street had made the same decision.

"I'm going to bring out some coffee and cookies," I told Bill.

"Good idea," he agreed. "Bring some of that cider, too."

I piled Christmas cookies on a paper plate, poured coffee into a Thermos and cider into a pitcher, grabbed some festive napkins and cups and put it all on a large tray. We stood by our mailbox and offered the goodies to our new neighbors, who gradually congregated in our driveway to talk between rescuing flaming paper bags.

The next year we put a card table in our driveway and our neighbors, now friends, brought goodies to add to our treats. And the following year we set up a long table with a red paper cloth and a large urn of "Farmer's Bishop," my mother's recipe for hot cider steeped with clove-studded oranges and cinnamon sticks. It drew raves, and so did her sausage balls.

Through the years our evening festivities grew. One family placed large red candles in a huge, elaborate candelabra and ceremoniously marched down the middle of the street carrying it high before placing it on our table. The first time was such a hit they continued the ritual each year. We set up outdoor speakers to play Christmas carols and many sang along, some even wandering down the neighboring streets to invite others to join us. Our next-door neighbor won the city's home decorating contest and we laughed when some of those who drove by to see the lights stopped for a cup of cider and a cookie, as if it were part of the lighting display. It was a fun way to meet other members of our small town.

As our children grew and our community friendships broadened, so did our invitations. Folks from school and church stopped by on their way to or from church or dinner, bringing their out-of-town guests with them and a plate of something for the table.

"It's the perfect way to have a party," I reflected. "Because we're outside, the house stays neat and clean, ready for Christmas tomorrow."

That statement was true until our girls became teenagers and their friends made our Luminaria part of their Christmas Eve celebration, too. As my mother went through the house one year on her way to refill a tray, she returned to the chilly night and pulled her coat around her, murmuring, "Why do the kids have enough sense to go inside while we stand out here in the cold?"

I stepped inside to check. Sure enough, there they were, sprawled on the floor in front of the blazing fireplace, laughing and enjoying the time free from adults and younger children. "Smart," I thought, and quietly slipped back outside.

It had to happen; one year it rained. The Luminaria bags were soggy messes along the driveways. We pulled our hat tree to the front door for wet raincoats and added a bucket for umbrellas. Everyone piled into our not-too-large house, bringing their Christmas cheer with them.

Each year when 10:00 chimed we cleared the table and invited any of those still present to join us for 11:00 p.m. Christmas Eve church service. It was always special to end our party that way, later stepping out of the sanctuary at midnight singing "Silent Night," and wishing each other a Merry Christmas.

With time our guest list dwindled as children grew and families began to travel to be together. Our daughters left for college, and then married and moved away from home. We now attend our grandchildren's church nativity pageant instead of serving cider in our driveway, although cider and sausage balls remain part of our family's Christmas Eve traditions.

Life is full of changes but memories remain and we still receive Christmas cards that mention those happy times at our driveway Luminaria. And today when we leave the house on Christmas Eve we turn on our new electric Luminaria to light the way for the Holy Family.

~Jean Haynie Stewart

97

The Sounds of Christmas

In the night of death, hope sees a star, and listening
love can hear the rustle of a wing.
~Robert Ingersoll

I was an eager ten-year-old the night I led the way up the worn old sidewalk, excited it was finally my turn to summon our audience. I took the steps up to the porch two at a time and rang the doorbell. There was a stirring in the house and in an instant I was back on the front lawn with my fellow Christmas carolers. The porch light flickered on and an elderly woman who had once taught me Sunday school made her way carefully out of the house, steadying herself against the porch railing. I can still remember the smile that illuminated her face as twenty voices came together to serenade her with "Silent Night."

The magic of that night and the joy of the Christmas season stayed with me well into adulthood. A Christmas caroling hayride through the streets of our small town seemed the perfect way to carry on one of my favorite holiday traditions while creating wonderful new memories with my tribe.

The men of the family didn't quite share my enthusiasm for riding on a bumpy trailer while singing songs to strangers in the cold. My son, Josh, opted to ride alongside his dad in the cab of the truck as they pulled a flatbed loaded with hay and cackling Christmas carolers.

As luck would have it, Josh and my husband Joey were the only two musically gifted members of our family. When my daughter Kyley and I joined voices in a heartfelt attempt at "Silent Night," it didn't sound like the magical rendition I remembered from my childhood. The most melodious sound that escaped our lips was our laughter following each song. Our lack of vocal talent didn't keep Kyley and me from making a joyful noise. Our family did, after all, believe laughter to be the sweetest music of all. Oh, the precious memories that were being made!

Our Christmas caroling capers became well known in the area. Each year as the holiday season approached, I would receive phone calls from family and friends eager to join in the fun. While it wasn't our only December tradition, it had become the one that Kyley and I most looked forward to. Well, that and Ky's birthday party.

Born on December 23, Kyley was my "almost" Christmas baby. Every year, despite a full schedule of holiday gatherings and a stint as my church's pageant director, I would brave the throngs of holiday shoppers to buy birthday presents. Two days before Christmas I would go all out decorating our home with balloons and streamers in shades of pink and all of the family would come together to celebrate Kyley.

I was in full-on birthday shopping mode December 18, 2008, when I called Kyley from a Target parking lot and asked her for a few additional gift ideas. I had checked off each item on her holiday shopping list but it didn't look like much sitting on the back seat of my car. "I have everything I need, Mom," she responded. "I'm sure I'll love whatever y'all give me. You don't need to buy me anything else."

I told Kyley that she was a good girl and I was proud of her. We exchanged "I love yous" and I hung up the phone.

It would be our last conversation. That night, exactly one week before Christmas, Kyley died in a car accident just down the street from our home. She was buried on December 23rd, her seventeenth birthday.

There was no Christmas caroling or birthday party that year, or the year after. Our home, which had always been filled with the laughter of friends and loved ones during the holiday season, was now quiet.

I found I could not bring myself to carry on the traditions of our family when one of our members was no longer with us. I did not want to betray my daughter by making new memories without her. Kyley was now in my past and I feared that if I attempted to live the life I had before she left us, I would be moving further away from her.

"You believe in Heaven don't you?" a friend asked me one day. I nodded in response. "Then you have to believe that Kyley is waiting for you in your future. Every day you live brings you one day closer to her." It was a life-changing revelation. This new perspective would allow me to move forward guilt-free.

That December 23rd, for the first time since Kyley left us, I hosted a Christmas caroling hayride for family and friends. I spent hours preparing food, making hot chocolate, and binding homemade songbooks containing what had once been some of our favorite holiday hymns.

As the guests began to arrive, I said a hurried prayer asking God to give me the strength to remember Kyley that evening with more smiles than tears. I thanked Him for the true miracle of Christmas — the gift of His Son, and I asked for one small favor... a sign that Kyley was still with us. I made a quick mental note of all the things that would qualify, in my mind, as divine assurance of Ky's presence. Ladybugs and fireworks rounded out the list as I closed with a heartfelt, "Amen."

Loved ones sat side-by-side on bales of hay, songbooks in hand. We were a more somber group than years before and I felt a responsibility to lighten the mood. I managed a joke about my singing and a few friends joined in with some good-natured ribbing. There were a few chuckles and everyone seemed to relax. As we prepared to sing our first hymn, I realized I hadn't thought to bring flashlights. It was dark and for those without cell phones it was nearly impossible to read the words to the songs. I yelled for my husband to pull up under a nearby streetlight. I took a deep breath as we joined together to sing "Silent Night." The first note to escape our lips was drowned out by a deafening boom. A shower of sparks rained down upon our party as people instinctively scrambled over the sides of the trailer to escape the barrage. And then... silence.

"What just happened?" someone asked.

People turned their illuminated cell phone screens toward the now dark streetlight. Something had caused it to blow at the exact moment we'd started our song.

"Wow! That was crazy! Sounded like someone set off fireworks right above our heads!" Someone else added, "Looked like it, too!"

Fireworks? I thought. Yes, of course! My sign!

A rumble tickled my throat and before I realized what was happening I heard a familiar sound — laughter… heartfelt, sidesplitting laughter. And it was coming from me! The joyful noise grew as family and friends joined in. It was sweet music… the sound of old traditions and new memories being made. It was the sound of healing hearts. It was the sound of Christmas.

~Melissa Wootan

98

Chicken Soup for the Soul

Wishing for a Silent Night

You can learn many things from children. How much
patience you have, for instance.
~Franklin P. Jones

I should start mentally preparing after Thanksgiving, but, like a root canal or gynecological appointment, I prefer not to think about it until I absolutely have to. Sometime during the second week of December, Derek and I will have to attend at least one school Christmas concert.

We're bad parents. We loathe school concerts. It wasn't always this way. When our eldest child was four, we attended our first holiday concert at his preschool. It was delightful. The children were adorable, but none as precious as our own darling boy.

That was eleven years ago. We'd probably still be enjoying holiday concerts except that we've added three more sons since that first experience. Consequently, we've attended about thirty school concerts. We've endured recorder recitals, choir competitions and spring solo extravaganzas, but the bane of our existence remains the Christmas concert.

Have you ever tried to force a twelve-year-old skateboarding "dude" into a jacket and tie? Have you ever spent hard-earned dollars on choir outfits worn only twice? Have you ever shopped for dress shoes with a child who doesn't believe in shoelaces? If you can answer yes to one of these questions, then you'll know why the glitter has worn off the whole holiday concert experience.

The cherub who was sweet as an angel at five becomes an embarrassment at eleven as he scowls from the back row of the choir, with his tie flung behind his neck so as to announce to the world, "You can make me wear it, but you can't make me like it!"

And there's the repetition. The same carols attempted every year. A quick route to a migraine is hearing the Fifth Grade Beginners Band pound out "Jingle... Bells... Jingle ... Bells" in achingly precise 4/4 time.

When our children were little we stayed for the entire concert, even though our kids were in kindergarten and second grade. One year we realized we could skip out after our kids were done, but that was the year the music teachers grew diabolically clever and began interspersing grades, culminating in an all-school grand finale.

I'm all for music education in our schools, just like I'm all for people eating tofu. I just don't want to experience it personally.

Christmas concerts are a way to reward faithful teachers who've labored for months trying to teach music fundamentals to children. Considering what they have to work with, they produce miracles each year. But, can't I just send a dozen roses to the band room?

It got so bad I used to pray for a kid to misbehave, just to liven things up. But that proved to be a bad strategy that I abandoned after my second-born wrapped his shepherd's costume around his face and acted like a mummy during the Virgin Mary's solo. The girl who played Mary alternately smiled sweetly into the audience and glared at Alex, as he approached the manger, hands outstretched in a stiff-legged mummy shuffle.

My outlook might be different if I had a budding Pavarotti or Domingo in the family, but so far all I have is the Pips with no Gladys Knight.

We didn't fully weigh the consequences when we decided to have four children. It looks like we'll be sitting through at least 100 more school concerts. There's just no way to avoid the second week of December. Bah humbug!

~Cindy Hval

A Divine Creature

*Christmas is the season of joy, of holiday greetings
exchanged, of gift-giving, and of families united.*
~Norman Vincent Peale

The painted navy blue swallow, artistically perched on its ceramic nest, caught her eye. My sister Rosemary, being a country girl and no stranger to real diving swallows in her barns, had a passion for the "divine creatures," as she called them.

"I really love it," she said about my new piece of art.

"Thanks. I love it, too."

My two-dollar yard-sale find looked perfect on my kitchen wall, and, although it held little significance, I did think it was a lovely bit of décor. Rosemary always admired it when she came over. I was tempted to give it to her, but it looked great on my kitchen wall.

When the holidays approached, I got busy finding gifts and crossing names off my list. I couldn't stop thinking about how much Rosemary had loved that little bird. She was a single mom with six children and she didn't have a lot of her own treasures.

I had to do it. I climbed up the stepstool and lifted the little ceramic piece off its nail. I found a box and wrote a note: "A true gift is something you really treasure yourself... Love you, big sister. And Merry Christmas!"

When Rosemary carefully peeled back the tissue on Christmas

Day and saw the swallow, she was in awe. Then when she read the note, her eyes welled. We hugged and she promised she would care for "our swallow." If I ever changed my mind she would give it back to me in a heartbeat. I assured her I would not change my mind.

The following Christmas, I opened a lovely square box and pulled back the tissue. The swallow was back! Rosemary's note expressed her thankfulness for having the swallow on her wall for a year.

And so the tradition of the Christmas Swallow began. It has become the highlight of our gift exchange and our children and grandchildren look forward to the swallow exchange every year.

Now, when my year is up, I remove the swallow from my wall and smile. I know it doesn't look nice but I leave the nail empty during the years when the swallow is hanging at Rosemary's.

That empty nail reminds me of the importance of family and how giving from the heart is the best kind of gift. Our little bird has flown back and forth between our homes each Christmas for twenty-four years now. Rosemary and I are not getting any younger but each year when one of us opens "the box" we giggle like schoolgirls.

One year, Rosemary almost forgot to bring the swallow. She had to turn the car around and run inside to take it down and wrap it up. One year, I almost dropped it. But so far, so good. We haven't missed a beat. Who would have guessed that a seemingly insignificant two-dollar treasure could bring so much Christmas joy year after year?

~Glynis M. Belec

California Christmas

*I wish we could put up some of the Christmas spirit in
jars and open a jar of it every month.*
~Harlan Miller

I grew up in Southern California where we're lucky if we don't
have a heat wave for Christmas. We may brag to our friends
back East about spending the holidays at the beach or pool,
but on Christmas Day, many of us yearn for a crackling fireplace and snowflakes drifting down from the sky. That's why a few
residents in my small Los Angeles suburb give our town a touch of
winter magic every year.

Right before Christmas Eve, they drive a pickup truck into the
mountains and pile it high with snow. On their return, they shovel
the snow onto the sidewalk in the center of our little downtown and
build a seven-foot snowman.

Our local Frosty has stick arms, a carrot nose and a large red
muffler. After a hot day, he has sometimes melted enough that his lime
buttons protrude on sticks a good inch or so in front of his shrunken
belly. But he still stands, beaming a lopsided cranberry grin under the
streetlamps.

Children pry chunks of snow from the base to build mini snowmen
on a nearby wall and throw snowballs at each other and their parents.
We all take pictures with our wintry visitor, sliding hands across the
icy snow and laughing at how our fingers tingle with the cold.

I don't know who those men are, but I am grateful. That single snowman is our White Christmas and Winter Wonderland. He is mittens and mufflers, snowflakes and icicles, red noses and numb toes all rolled into one. And like Christmas itself, we welcome him every year, whether we're wearing rain boots or flip flops to pose beside him.

~Susan Lendroth

Santa Suit

All the world is happy when Santa Claus comes.
~Maud Lindsay

Something magic happens
When you don a Santa suit
You can argue against it
But the point is rather moot

You see, I have firsthand experience
With the phenomenon that happens
It's an eye-opening experience
One of life's biggest transformations

It all started the second
I walked out the door
On the inside, I didn't feel
Any different than before

But all of a sudden
The world instantly changed
Like the molecules around me
Had been magically rearranged

People's faces lit up
The second they saw me
It happened so quickly
It almost seemed eerie

Then my arm started waving
How? I don't even know
And I was ever so startled
When I blurted, "Ho-Ho-Ho!"

The gait of my walk
Changed from a hurried pace
To a nice pleasant stroll
And I found a smile on my face

I started rubbing my pillowed tummy
And stroking my fake beard
I felt a presence well up inside me
The sensation was quite weird

It was the spirit of Santa
It was unlike anything on this earth
You can't put a price upon it
Nothing carries such value or such worth

There is no Santa training necessary
The transformation is complete
The second a child's face lights up
And the feeling can't be beat

So if you don't believe in magic
All that's necessary for you to do
Is don a Santa suit
And you can feel it too

The Spirit of Christmas
Will burst out of you like a beam
And you'll be transported to another world
Like you're living in a dream

At least once in their life
Everyone should put on the Santa gear
It's an experience you won't forget
And one you will always hold dear

~Eric Nanson

Meet Our Contributors

Teresa Ambord is a business writer and editor, working from her home in rural Northern California. What she loves best is writing family stories. Her posse of small dogs serves as her muses. They inspire her writing and decorate her life.

Mary Ellen Angelscribe is a pet columnist and author of *Expect Miracles* and *A Christmas Filled with Miracles*. Her swimming cats were featured on Animal Planet's *Must Love Cats*. Her stories and cat videos can be seen on Facebook under Angel Scribe and Pet Tips 'n' Tales. Learn more at www.AngelScribe.com.

Mary Anglin-Coulter earned her Bachelor of Arts degree, with honors, in Arts from Bellarmine University in 2006. She is an artist, graphic designer, and freelance writer previously published in the *Chicken Soup for the Soul* series, *Small Town Living*, and *The OUTsiders Ally*. She lives with her wife and three daughters in Kentucky.

Joe Atwater lives on a horse ranch in North Carolina with his wife Elizabeth. He tried his hand at writing after quite a bit of encouraging from her. Now they have something in common other than their love of horses and country living.

Katie Bangert lives in Texas with her husband, three children and many family pets. She has appeared in multiple *Chicken Soup for the Soul* books. Somewhere in between watching her kids at Taekwondo and paddling in her kayak, Katie finds inspiration to write in the most unlikely places. Contact her through katiebangert.com.

Glynis Belec, a freelance writer, inspirational speaker and children's author, faces each day with hope and thanksgiving. Counting blessings is getting to be a daily addiction. Glynis loves capturing life in words and can't wait for tomorrow so she can feel inspired all over again. E-mail her at writer@glynisbelec.com.

Jennifer Berger currently resides in Queens, NY with her husband Aaron and their nine-year-old son Josh. A former editor and freelance writer who loves to read and write, Jennifer is now a stay-at-home wife, mother and full-time advocate for her child.

AimeeAnn Blythe retired from the transportation industry. She enjoys gardening and spending time with her three furry children. She is currently working on a book.

Michele Boom has taught elementary school both in the traditional setting as well as online. She has worked as a freelance writer for seven years and is a frequent contributor to the *Chicken Soup for the Soul* series. She lives in Bend, OR with her family, two cats and an aquatic frog named Hopper.

A former newspaper reporter, **Sally Breslin** has been writing a weekly humor column titled "My Life" for five New England newspapers since 1994. She also has authored three novels: *There's a Tick in My Underwear!* (about camping) and two thrillers. She enjoys hiking with her dogs. E-mail her at sillysally@att.net.

Sylvia Bright-Green has written over 1,600 manuscripts in her thirty-one years of writing since 1985 and has been published in ten books and anthologies.

John P. Buentello is the author of many published essays, short stories, nonfiction and poetry. He is currently at work on a mystery novel and can be contacted via e-mail at jakkhakk@yahoo.com.

Jill Burns lives in the mountains of West Virginia with her wonderful family. She's a retired piano teacher and performer. Jill enjoys writing, music, gardening, nature, and spending time with her grandchildren.

Eva Carter is happy to have contributed ten stories to the *Chicken Soup for the Soul* series. Having a background in the entertainment field as well as in the corporate environment, she is now very content to write, travel, take photographs and enjoy life with her husband and cat. E-mail her at evacarter@sbcglobal.net.

Tracy Moeller Cary received a Bachelor of Arts degree from Michigan State University in 1965. She is a native of Saginaw, MI but has resided in Somerset, KY since 1979. She's a wife, mother of three daughters, and grandmother to Katie and Kinser.

Brenda Cathcart-Kloke is a writer who lives in the suburbs of Denver, CO. She is a frequent contributor to the *Chicken Soup for the Soul* series. Besides being an avid Broncos fan, she enjoys reading, writing inspirational stories, and spending time with her family.

Stacie Chambers thanks freelance writer Sheri Zeck of Milan, IL for writing her story. Sheri's work has appeared in numerous *Chicken Soup for the Soul* books, *Guideposts*, *Angels on Earth*, and *Farm & Ranch Living*. Sheri writes about her faith, family and adventures of raising three girls at www.sherizeck.com.

JoAnne Check graduated from Kutztown University and has been a teacher, grant writer, and copywriter. She is the author of six historical fiction books known as the *Heritage Square Series*. When she is not writing books, JoAnne enjoys art, travel, reading, gardening, and camping in the great outdoors.

Kim Childs is a Boston-area life and career coach specializing in Positive Psychology (aka The Science of Happiness), creativity and sacred living. She also publishes a blog, *A Pilgrim on the Path*, and teaches workshops on *The Artist's Way: A Spiritual Path to Higher Creativity*. Please visit her at www.KimChilds.com.

Traci Clayton received a bachelor's degree in advertising from TCU and a master's degree in advertising from The University of Texas at Austin. She now works in (surprise) advertising as a copywriter. She got her love of writing from her Mawmaw, Joan Clayton, who has been published in many *Chicken Soup for the Soul* books.

Tracy Crump enjoys telling stories and is a frequent contributor to the *Chicken Soup for the Soul* series. She encourages others through her Write Life Workshops and webinars and edits a popular writers newsletter, *The Write Life*. Her most important job is Grandma to little Nellie. Visit Tracy at TracyCrump.com or WriteLifeWorkshops.com.

Steph Davenport is a nationally published writer and previous contributor to the *Chicken Soup for the Soul* series. Her stories about food, health, relationships and spirituality have appeared in magazines, collaborative works and newspapers. Steph enjoys life in the Midwest and is passionate about agriculture and creativity.

Michele Ivy Davis and her husband live in the San Diego area. Her stories and articles have appeared in many publications, and her young adult novel, *Evangeline Brown and the Cadillac Motel* (Penguin Group USA), received national and international awards. Learn more at MicheleIvyDavis.com.

John Dorroh taught high school science for thirty years. Currently he works part-time as an educational consultant, writes poetry, short fiction, and business and restaurant reviews. He travels and makes photo notecards for friends... and still writes old-fashioned letters.

Joanna Dylan grew up on a sailboat in California. Surrounded by nature she felt God's presence. She currently calls Boston home, with her author husband Josh, and cat Boss. She enjoys hiking, writing, exploring and petting each animal that crosses her path. She is currently working on a faith-based romantic suspense novel.

Kristine Eckart graduated, with honors, from Columbia College Chicago in 2014. She enjoys reading several books at once and spending time with family and friends. She also ran the Chicago Marathon in 2013. Kristine currently writes for FabFitFun.com, and plans to continue expanding her repertoire in the writing field.

Greg Engle is a published award-winning sportswriter who spent twenty-three years combined active and active reserve military service, much of that in and around the Special Operations community. Greg holds a bachelor's degree in Communications, a master's degree in Psychology and is currently working on a Ph.D. in Psychology.

Kate Erickson lives in Fort Bragg, CA with her husband, playful Catahoula Leopard dog Lucy, and curmudgeon twelve-year-old cat Little Mister. She writes a blog about the quirky aspects of life in a small town on the Mendocino Coast.

Shannon Erickson lives in a cabin on beautiful Kentucky Lake. She enjoys hiking the numerous trails in her area, spending summer afternoons on her boat, collecting primitive antiques and traveling. This is her third published article.

Cinda Findlan earned her Doctorate of Education from Indiana University of Pennsylvania in 2006. She recently retired from her university position to enjoy time with her husband and her two granddaughters. Cinda enjoys acrylic painting and plans to take up writing as her next vocation.

Gloria Hudson Fortner received a bachelor's degree from David Lipscomb College and a master's degree from Nova Southeastern University and earned a National Board for Professional Teaching certification. Her writing has appeared in various educational journals. After thirty years in the classroom, she now spends her time enjoying her family.

Rus Franklin was born in the West, raised in the South, grew up in the jungle and lives in the Arizona desert. Following military service and between several careers, he earned both B.S. and MSL degrees. Rus finally realized his dream of publication as part of the Chicken Soup for the Soul family of authors.

Dusty Grein is a bestselling author, award-winning poet, part-time graphics designer and full-time father/grandfather. He currently resides in Oregon, where he is busy being raised by his youngest daughter, working on his newest novel and trying to avoid becoming trapped in the Facebook authors' groups he moderates.

Chelsea Hall is a world traveler, animal lover, tennis player and professional editor. She graduated from Oregon State University in 2010. She currently resides in Tucson, AZ with her baby girl and husband.

Norma Heffron is a retired teacher who moved to the mountains of western North Carolina, which she refers to as God's Country, soon after her husband retired from Disney in Florida. This year they celebrate fifty years of marriage and have added three great-grandchildren to their family.

David Hull was a preschool teacher for twenty-eight years. Now that he's retired, he spends his time writing, reading and battling weeds in his vegetable gardens — the weeds are winning! He has been published in numerous *Chicken Soup for the Soul* books. E-mail him at Davidhull59@aol.com.

Cindy Hval is the author of *War Bonds: Love Stories from the Greatest Generation,* which tells the stories of thirty-six couples who met/married during WWII. It's available at Amazon.com. Cindy's work is featured in ten volumes of the *Chicken Soup for the Soul* series. Contact her at dchval@juno.com, CindyHval.com or via Twitter @CindyHval.

Rebecca L. Jones is a professional storyteller in and around Seaford, DE. Her husband prevents her from being a "crazy cat lady"; however, her four children have helped sneak a few animals into the house. Rebecca enjoys the arts, bicycling, and crocheting. She is currently writing some fiction and nonfiction works.

Victoria Jones is a recently retired editor for a nonprofit education publication in Chicago. She is the mother of two, and has seven grandchildren and two great-grandchildren. She loves butterflies, and enjoys traveling, writing, and taking pictures of clouds, sunsets, and sunrises. She is currently working on a book.

Vicki L. Julian, a Kansas University graduate, is the author of four inspirational books, various newspaper and magazine articles, a contributor to six anthologies, and the author of a soon-to-be released Christmas-themed children's book. She writes a faith-based blog and is a board member of Kansas Authors Club.

Gregory A. Kompes, MFA, MS Ed., has written *Circuitous Course, Suddenly Psychic, Messages from The Three Sisters, Sky Pirates, The Middle Man, Flash Mob, First Dimension,* the bestselling *50 Fabulous Gay-Friendly Places to Live* and has stories included in over a dozen anthologies. Learn more at Kompes.com.

Jamie Kopf began her writing career during the sixth grade thanks to her teacher pushing her to explore her poetry. She has a huge, amazing, wonderful family that got even more amazing when she married her husband Andrew last year. Christmas is by far her favorite day of the year.

Dani Kuhn is a full-time mother who lives in St. Thomas, Ontario with her husband, five children and two parrots. She is a sarcoidosis warrior and advocate for her exceptional children. She draws on these experiences when sharing her lifelong passion for writing. In her leisure time she enjoys crochet and nature.

Jennifer Land earned her Master of Library and Information Science degree and currently works as a web development manager for her local library system. She also founded and directs Monroe's Mighty Mission, a nonprofit focused on keeping pets and families together through difficult times. She enjoys traveling and writing.

Sharon Landeen is a mother, grandma, great-grandma, and retired elementary teacher. She believes that working with children helps keep her young. She stays busy volunteering at schools, helping the 4-H program, and making blankets for Project Linus. She enjoys traveling, reading, and being an avid University of Arizona basketball fan.

Deborah Lean is a retired nurse, mother of two, and grandmother of seven. She enjoys painting, crochet, and a variety of crafts. Writing is an ongoing interest, with two blogs and a number of ebooks on Amazon.

Although raised in Southern California, **Susan Lendroth** wishes the climate would add a couple of frosty days to the mix at Christmas. A children's author, she's thinking of writing a future story with a snow setting so that she can at least imagine winter! Find Susan at facebook. com/susanlendroth.

Donna Lorrig attended Middle Tennessee State University as an art and animal science major and Pikes Peak Community College where she explored political science. For the past thirty-seven years, she has devoted the majority of her time to supporting her husband and raising their seven children who she homeschooled.

Jim Luke was born and raised in Mississippi, is married to the former Karen Howell and is the father of two daughters, Chanda and Lauren. Jim attended Picayune Memorial High School, Pearl River Junior College, University of Southern Mississippi and is a graduate of the FBI Command College. He is City Manager of Picayune, MS.

Irene Maran is a freelance writer living at the Jersey Shore with her cats and turtles. She writes two biweekly newspaper columns and runs a prompt writing group at the shore. She is a professional storyteller who enjoys sharing her humorous stories with adults and children. E-mail her at maran.irene@gmail.com.

Dave Markwell dreams of… a beach, a beer and a book. His reality… Dad, business owner, writer, thinker, seeker, player of cribbage in bare feet and griller of some pretty good chicken… Life is a funny business and he'll take it….

Katie Martin lives in North Carolina with her husband Paul. A day in Katie Martin's life begins with a vigilant eye and an open mind to the stories that lay behind the daily events of people, places and things. A published author with an appetite for life, Katie brings a warm glow to ordinary things making them extraordinary.

Margaret M. Marty, a lifelong resident of Rock Creek in east-central Minnesota, is a wife, mother, grandmother, and retired certified professional secretary. She is a guest writer for the *Pine City Pioneer* and has had poetry published in *The Talking Stick*, a publication of Jackpine Writers' Bloc of Menahga, MN.

Sara Matson lives with her family in Minnesota, where she writes children's stories as well as the occasional personal essay. This year she and her daughters (now sixteen) will celebrate their seventh Saint Lucia Day with Sylvia. Learn more at www.saramatson.com.

Patrick Matthews is a writer and award-winning game designer living in Central Florida. His first novel is *Dragon Run*, a fast-paced middle grade fantasy adventure. Mr. Matthews also authored the *Mathfinder* series of puzzle books, produces the *Games for Educators* newsletter, and speaks regularly at schools about writing.

Sandra Holmes McGarrity lives and writes in Chesapeake, VA. She is the author of three published novels. Her writing has been published in many books and magazines including three *Chicken Soup for the Soul* books. She enjoys her church, family, puttering in her flower garden, and living life with her husband of forty-three years.

Rosemary McLaughlin lives in retired bliss with her husband Bill in Pittsburgh, PA. She enjoys reading, writing, traveling, volunteering and keeping up with her grandchildren and former students. This is her fourth story published in the *Chicken Soup for the Soul* series. E-mail her at rosemarymclaugh@gmail.com.

Myrna CG Mibus is a freelance writer based in Webster, MN, where she lives with her husband and two teenagers. She enjoys bicycling, baking, traveling, reading and flying. Myrna's essays and articles have been published in a variety of publications, including *Chicken Soup for the Mother of Preschooler's Soul.*

Josephine Montgomery is a British subject and citizen of the world. She has traveled extensively in the Middle East, and for two years she studied written and spoken Arabic at Amman University in the Hashemite Kingdom of Jordan. Josephine is a published writer of three historical novels, travel articles and short stories.

Emily Morgan received her Bachelor of Arts degree, with honors, in English from North Greenville University in 2015. She loves the great outdoors and likes to enjoy it while hiking with her family. She finds inspiration for her writing while she is staring at the mountains. She plans to write books for Christian teens.

Marya Morin is a freelance writer. Her stories and poems have appeared in publications such as *Woman's World* and Hallmark. Marya also penned a weekly humorous column for an online newsletter, and writes custom poetry on request. She lives in the country with her husband. E-mail her at Akushla514@hotmail.com.

Nicole L.V. Mullis is the author of the novel *A Teacher Named Faith*. Her work has appeared in newspapers, magazines and anthologies, including the *Chicken Soup for the Soul* series. Her plays have been produced in New York, California and Michigan. She lives in Michigan with her family and a crawlspace stuffed with Christmas stuff.

Eric Nanson has a B.S. degree from Chico State University. He is a poet, sculptor, designer, photographer, and an artist of multiple disciplines. He writes from many differing perspectives and points of view, and tries to incorporate twists and turns in his poetry.

Irena Nieslony is English, but now lives on the island of Crete, Greece with her husband and their seven dogs and four cats. She has an honors degree in Drama and English from the University of London, and was previously an actress and puppeteer. She loves writing, and has had eight novels published, all murder mysteries.

Katie O'Connell writes from the heart. She believes in the healing power of dark chocolate, a good laugh, and living an authentic and meaningful life. Her essays have been featured in *Reader's Digest*, *Sasee*, *Patheos*, and several *Chicken Soup for the Soul* books. Follow her blog at blog.heartwiredwriting.com.

Karen J. Olson is a writer from Eau Claire, WI. She graduated from UW-Eau Claire with enough knowledge in psychology and sociology to make people watching a job. She loves reading, walking and all things Christmas! She especially enjoys writing humor and inspirational pieces. E-mail her at kjolson@charter.net.

Andrea Arthur Owan is a travel-loving freelance writer. Her work has appeared in other *Chicken Soup for the Soul* books, *Guideposts*, anthologies, magazines and newspapers. Her blog, *Broken Hearts, Redeemed*, helps families recover emotionally, physically, and spiritually from the loss of a child in pregnancy or at birth.

Ava Pennington is a writer, speaker, and Bible teacher. She authored *Daily Reflections on the Names of God*, endorsed by Kay Arthur. Ava has written for magazines such as *Today's Christian Woman* and Focus on the Family's *Clubhouse*, and contributed to twenty-three *Chicken Soup for the Soul* books. Learn more at AvaWrites.com.

Author and Chef **Perry P. Perkins** runs a nonprofit organization called MY KITCHEN Outreach, which teaches nutrition, shopping, and hands-on cooking classes for at risk youth, and he writes regularly for the *Chicken Soup for the Soul* series. Perry's writing can be found at perryperkinsbooks.com.

Connie Kaseweter Pullen lives in rural Sandy, OR near her five children and several grandchildren. She earned her Bachelor of Arts degree at the University of Portland in 2006, with a double major in Psychology and Sociology. Connie enjoys writing, photography and exploring nature. E-mail her at MyGrandmaPullen@aol.com.

Tim Ramsey has been an educator in the public school setting since 1983. He currently teaches fifth grade in Phoenix, AZ. Tim has had four previous stories published in the *Chicken Soup for the Soul* series. In addition, he has been awarded first place three times in the Arizona English Teachers' Teachers as Writers Contest.

Carol McAdoo Rehme fills her historic home with unique traditions, riveting hobbies, and quirky collections. A seasoned editor, writers' coach and ghostwriter, she is the author of seven gift books and is currently penning a whimsical memoir for her grandchildren.

Sauni Rinehart is a writer, speaker, and teacher. She teaches literature and composition online for Liberty University. She has self-published four books, and her work has appeared in several anthologies. She and her husband live in East Tennessee and enjoy hiking, kayaking, and traveling.

Nan Rockey lives in Bloomington, IN with her writer husband and her non-writer dog, Padfoot. She loves playing the ukulele and spending time with her wonderful in-laws.

Donna Van Cleve Schleif received an associate's degree from Kilgore College. She has six grown children, fourteen grandchildren and one great-grandchild on the way. She is married to the love of her life, Rick; they love traveling and she, of course, loves writing.

Edie Schmidt is an internationally published freelance writer. She earned a B.S. degree from University of the Cumberlands in Williamsburg, KY. She enjoys spending time with family and baking cakes by the sea in Daytona Beach, FL.

Donna Faulkner Schulte is the author of *Santa's Search for the Perfect Child* and *The Love Club*. Donna is a lifelong native of Fayetteville, NC. She started her love of books at an early age. Later she started writing poems, then stories. Donna believes with all her heart that love and kindness is the answer and one person can make a difference.

Jay Seate writes everything from humor to the macabre, and is especially keen on transcending genre pigeonholing. He lives in Golden, CO with the dream of enjoying the rest of his life traveling and writing.

Kathie Slief studied Journalism at St. Gregory's College and University of Oklahoma. She put those skills to work at her church where she was Communication Director for twenty-three years. Now retired, she and her husband Greg reminisce about the joys of raising five children who have now doubled their pleasure with ten grandchildren.

David Michael Smith has been published multiple times in the *Chicken Soup for the Soul* series and enjoys the role of "storyteller." He wears many hats, outside of "author," including husband to his wife Geri, father to Rebekah and Matthew, and Deacon in the North American Anglican Church. E-mail him at davidandgeri@hotmail.com.

Laura Snell, her husband Dave, and their dog Gus Gusterson live in Wasaga Beach, Ontario where they operate their web development firm GBSelect.com. Her son Ryan lives in Melbourne, Australia. This is her sixth story published in the *Chicken Soup for the Soul* series. E-mail her at laura@gbselect.com.

Jean Haynie Stewart has been a California resident for forty-four years. Her stories draw heavily from life there with her husband of fifty-six years, twin daughters and their families, as well as from her Georgia upbringing. She is thrilled that this is her eighteenth story published in the *Chicken Soup for the Soul* series. "A New Tradition" ©2009 by Jean Haynie Stewart, was first published in *Christmas Traditions*, ©2009 by F+W Media, Inc. Reprinted with permission. All Rights Reserved.

Mary Stewart-Firth lives in her native North Carolina with her husband Alan, a British citizen who loves calling North Carolina home. She enjoys hiking, traveling, writing and art journaling.

Layla Tavassoli is currently working on her Bachelor of Arts degree in Art History with a focus on the medieval era. In addition to being a scholar, Layla partakes in activities such as writing poetry and creating studio art. She has a strong interest in nature, as well as global affairs.

Nancy Thorne lives just outside of Toronto with her husband, two sons and a yellow Labrador. Her stories have recently appeared in *Canadian Tales of the Mysterious* and *Canadian Tales of the Heart*. She hopes her writing, reflecting the unpredictability of life and new beginnings, inspires others.

Susan Traugh's work has appeared in several *Chicken Soup for the Soul* books, plus local and national magazines. Her young adult novel, *The Edge of Brilliance*, and her special education workbooks can be found on her website at susantraugh.com. She lives with her family in San Diego, CA.

Kristen Velasquez received her Bachelor's of Science degree in Elementary Education and is currently working toward her degree in nursing. She is an advocate for children with cancer and is the creator of Operation GOLD, a program that donates Christmas presents to children with cancer. Learn more at www.operation-gold.com.

Rita Kaye Vetsch resides in central Minnesota with her loving family and her precious fur companions. She has a passion for writing and recently had her first children's book, *The Many Colors of Friendship*, published by Eloquent Publishing. Rita enjoys writing, photography and spending time with family.

Louise Lenahan Wallace has written five novels set in Ohio and Wyoming Territory during and after the Civil War. She has won numerous fiction writing awards and been published in *Grit* magazine, *Chicken Soup for the Single's Soul*, and *Carry the Light* anthologies. She especially enjoys spending time with her granddaughter.

Diana Walters earned her doctorate at Oxford Graduate School in Dayton, TN. She serves as the manager of an assisted living unit in Chattanooga. She and her husband are involved with ministry to people with dementia and their families. E-mail her at dianalwalters@ comcast.net.

Dorann Weber is a freelance photographer for a south New Jersey newspaper where she lives with her family, which includes dogs, cats and chickens. Dorann is a contributor for Getty Images and has a newfound love for writing. She has had verses along with her photos published in Hallmark cards. E-mail her at dorann_weber@yahoo.com.

Maggie Whelan is the mother of eleven and the grandmother of eighteen. She is a retired Special Ed teacher. Maggie has had articles in local newspapers and in *Chicken Soup for the Soul: Answered Prayers*. She gives many different kinds of workshops and has found that writing is the best way to heal.

Mary Z. Whitney is a regular contributor to the *Chicken Soup for the Soul* series. She also writes for inspirational publications like *Guideposts* and *Angels on Earth* magazine. Mary and her husband John reside in Ohio with their little dog Max, enjoying their grandchildren whenever possible.

Whitney Woody works as a developmental editor. She is a proud graduate of Western Carolina University, with a degree in English and concentration in Professional Writing. When work is done, you can find her baking desserts, playing with her cat, or counting the days until fall. Her favorite holiday, of course, is Christmas.

Following a career in Nuclear Medicine, **Melissa Wootan** is joyfully exploring her creative side. She enjoys writing and is a regular guest on *San Antonio Living*, an hour-long lifestyle show on San Antonio's NBC affiliate, where she shares all of her best DIY/decorating tips. Contact her through facebook.com/chicvintique.

Susan Kimmel Wright lives and writes in a 140-year-old Pennsylvania farmhouse, with her husband Dave and a demanding pack of dogs and cats. She writes mystery novels for kids and adults, as well as stories for the *Chicken Soup for the Soul* series. Visit her at susankimmelwright. com or contact her via e-mail at kidsbookwrighter@gmail.com.

Meet Amy Newmark

Amy Newmark is the bestselling author, editor-in-chief, and publisher of the *Chicken Soup for the Soul* book series. Since 2008, she has published 133 new books, most of them national bestsellers in the U.S. and Canada, more than doubling the number of Chicken Soup for the Soul titles in print today. She is also the author of *Simply Happy*, a crash course in Chicken Soup for the Soul advice and wisdom that is filled with easy-to-implement, practical tips for having a better life.

Amy is credited with revitalizing the Chicken Soup for the Soul brand, which has been a publishing industry phenomenon since the first book came out in 1993. By compiling inspirational and aspirational true stories curated from ordinary people who have had extraordinary experiences, Amy has kept the twenty-three-year-old Chicken Soup for the Soul brand fresh and relevant.

Amy graduated *magna cum laude* from Harvard University where she majored in Portuguese and minored in French. She then embarked on a three-decade career as a Wall Street analyst, a hedge fund manager, and a corporate executive in the technology field. She is a Chartered Financial Analyst.

Her return to literary pursuits was inevitable, as her honors thesis in college involved traveling throughout Brazil's impoverished northeast region, collecting stories from regular people. She is delighted to have come full circle in her writing career — from collecting stories "from the people" in Brazil as a twenty-year-old to, three decades later, collecting stories "from the people" for Chicken Soup for the Soul.

When Amy and her husband Bill, the CEO of Chicken Soup for the Soul, are not working, they are visiting their four grown children.

Follow Amy on Twitter @amynewmark. Listen to her free daily podcast, The Chicken Soup for the Soul Podcast, at www.chickensoup. podbean.com, or find it on iTunes, the Podcasts app on iPhone, or on your favorite podcast app on other devices.

Thank You

We are grateful to all our story contributors and fans, who shared thousands of stories about the joy of Christmas in their lives. We loved reading all the submissions and choosing the 101 that would appear in the book. If felt like Christmas in July around here.

We owe special thanks to Barbara LoMonaco and Mary Fisher, who read all the submissions. They narrowed down the list of finalists for D'ette and Amy to make some hard choices. As always, we had way more great stories than would fit in this volume, and many of them will end up appearing in future Chicken Soup for the Soul titles.

Associate Publisher D'ette Corona continued to be Amy's right-hand woman in creating the final manuscript and working with all our wonderful writers. Barbara LoMonaco and Kristiana Pastir, along with outside proofreader Elaine Kimbler, jumped in at the end to proof, proof, proof. And yes, there will always be typos anyway, so feel free to let us know about them at webmaster@chickensoupforthesoul.com.

The whole publishing team deserves a hand, including editor Ronelle Frankel, Senior Director of Production Victor Cataldo, and graphic designer Daniel Zaccari, who turned our manuscript into this beautiful book.

Sharing Happiness,
Inspiration, and Wellness

Real people sharing real stories, every day, all over the world. In 2007, *USA Today* named *Chicken Soup for the Soul* one of the five most memorable books in the last quarter-century. With over 100 million books sold to date in the U.S. and Canada alone, more than 200 titles in print, and translations into more than forty languages, "chicken soup for the soul" is one of the world's best-known phrases.

Today, twenty-three years after we first began sharing happiness, inspiration and wellness through our books, we continue to delight our readers with new titles, but have also evolved beyond the book-store, with super premium pet food, a line of high quality soups, and a variety of licensed products and digital offerings, all inspired by stories. Chicken Soup for the Soul has recently expanded into visual storytelling through movies and television. Chicken Soup for the Soul is "changing the world one story at a time®." Thanks for reading!

Share with Us

We all have had Chicken Soup for the Soul moments in our lives. If you would like to share your story or poem with millions of people around the world, go to chickensoup.com and click on "Submit Your Story." You may be able to help another reader and become a published author at the same time. Some of our past contributors have launched writing and speaking careers from the publication of their stories in our books!

We only accept story submissions via our website. They are no longer accepted via mail or fax.

To contact us regarding other matters, please send us an e-mail through webmaster@chickensoupforthesoul.com, or fax or write us at:

Chicken Soup for the Soul
P.O. Box 700
Cos Cob, CT 06807-0700
Fax: 203-861-7194

One more note from your friends at Chicken Soup for the Soul: Occasionally, we receive an unsolicited book manuscript from one of our readers, and we would like to respectfully inform you that we do not accept unsolicited manuscripts and we must discard the ones that appear.

From the editor-in-chief of the New York Times bestselling series

Chicken Soup for the Soul

Simply Happy

A Crash Course in Chicken Soup for the Soul Advice and Wisdom

Amy Newmark

A fast-paced and funny deep dive into simple ways to create a happy, confident, and positive life. Amy Newmark distills advice and wisdom from her life and more than 20,000 Chicken Soup for the Soul stories into this crash course in how to be happy.

978-1-61159-949-7

Great Holiday Gifts

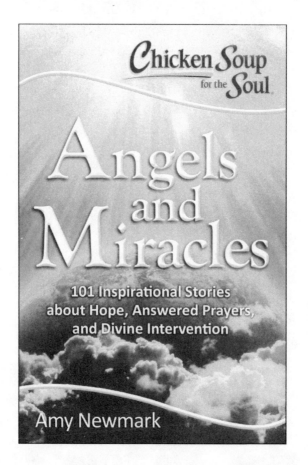

These powerful stories will deepen your faith and give you hope that good things do happen to good people. From guardian angels to divine messengers, from miraculous healing to messages from heaven, from mysterious dreams that come true to divine coincidence, you'll be in awe as you read these 101 stories of true wonder and inspiration.

978-1-61159-964-0

and Inspiration

Chicken Soup for the Soul

Changing the world one story at a time®
www.chickensoup.com